THE SECRET OF EVERLASTING LIFE

The First Translation of
the Ancient Chinese Text
on Immortality

RICHARD BERTSCHINGER

SINGING
DRAGON

London and Philadelphia

First published in Great Britain in 1994 by
Element Books Ltd

This edition published in 2011
by Singing Dragon
an imprint of Jessica Kingsley Publishers
116 Pentonville Road
London N1 9JB, UK
and
400 Market Street, Suite 400
Philadelphia, PA 19106, USA

www.singingdragon.com

Copyright © Richard Bertschinger 1994 and 2011

Library of Congress Cataloging in Publication Data
A CIP catalog record for this book is available from the Library of Congress

British Library Cataloguing in Publication Data
A CIP catalogue record for this book is available from the British Library

ISBN 978 1 84819 048 1

Printed and bound in Great Britain by
MPG Books Group

To my mother

The idea of everlasting life has nothing to do with hankering after life. The truth is that actually there is no death.

How can there be no death? Because actually there is only one single energy, one all-encompassing motivating force which lies at the root of our life's activity, not two. The Great Void which is the common ground of all life is there already, with life continuously being born within it. So what need is there for life and death?

It is because our desire for things assumes undue importance that we go astray and begin the separation of life and death. If we view them from this space of quiet and tranquillity we can see there has never been any life or any death. Evidently there is only this one single energy flowing and circulating about.

From the Preface to
Can Tong Qi Shuliu, 1564

PREFACE
TO PERENNIAL EDITION

Welcome! The book you hold in your hand is the granddaddy of all qigong classics. These writings on internal alchemy have spawned countless commentaries and editions – presented here, for the first time, in English translation, along with the voices of its Chinese commentators.

> *Nourish yourself thus within*
> *tranquil and still in the void,*
> *while at source concealing the brilliance*
> *which illuminates up your whole body.*
> *shut and close up the mouth,*
> *repressing within the spiritual trunk,*
> *the senses all swallowed up*
> *to gently support that pearl so young.*
> *observe it there, the unobvious –*
> *so close by and easy to seek.*

Welcome again! to a timely reprinting of this translation, which first saw the light of day some twenty years ago. Since then it has appeared in German, Portuguese and Dutch editions – to spread its elegant calling across the globe, available to us all.

> *The ear, eye and mouth – these three jewels,*
> *block and stop them up, do not let them gape.*
> *the truth in man lies at the very depths,*
> *he roams wide yet guards a proper compass within.*
>
> *these three are the crux of the affair –*
> *to be in a relaxed body, resting in an empty room,*
> *abandon the will and go back to the void,*
> *and thus beyond thought find constancy.*

Welcome, thrice welcome! to the catalogue of events which led to Wei Boyang and his followers – including the dog – all of whom gave their lives that the message in this book might be complete, and sent on to you. Even the Yellow Emperor himself is one of our tribe…this from the speech made by the great sage Guang Cheng, proficient in the art of fostering life:

> *In essence, it is profound and shrouded in mystery –*
> *dark it is and hushed in quiet –*
> *let your soul be at peace and the body rights itself!*

The above few lines, from the legendary instruction of the Yellow Emperor, come from the Zhuangzi book. There is another tale in the Zhuangzi about the boy who captures a pearl from the dragon of the deeps, who nestles a pearl under his chin…the headman of his village demands the pearl be destroyed! Who knows what calamities it might bring?

Here, at least, is a single pearl which survived! Give thanks.

Richard Bertschinger
September 2010

CONTENTS

ADDENDUM

LIST OF ILLUSTRATIONS

魏伯陽

Fig. 1 Wei Boyang with his cauldron and dog

INTRODUCTION

The current Western fascination with Chinese philosophy and ideas is evident from the widespread interest in areas as diverse as Taoism, Feng Shui, acupuncture, Chinese herbal medicine, Tai Chi, Qi Gong, etc. This book will be of interest to students of all these as it takes the reader on an extensive journey through the minds and wisdom of the Immortals (the great sages), including such influential figures as Confucius and Laozi (Lao Tsu), who laid the foundation of Chinese thought.

The Secret of Everlasting Life is in the tradition of such well-known Chinese texts as the *Daode Jing* (*Tao Te Ching*) and *Yi Jing* (*I Ching*). The first translation of the classic Taoist text of the *Can Tong Qi*, it provides the Western reader with invaluable and hitherto unpublished insights into Taoist thought and practice.

Central to the above are themes which most readers will recognize – the Dao (Tao), the Yin and Yang, the sixty-four hexagrams, etc. – but this text expands greatly on the relationships between them. For example, an introduction to the process by which the One divides into the Yin and Yang occurs in both Chapters 1 and 2, and 19 and 20: these chapters should be read first by anyone initially picking up the book. For the reciprocal ebb and flow of the Yin and Yang lines within the trigrams and hexagrams, see Chapters 4 and 5; for an account of the formation of the hexagrams, see Chapters 21 and 22; for an explanation of the ever-fluid relationship between the Yin and Yang, see Chapter 8. These sections will guide the reader's understanding and progressively direct it towards the very roots of Daoist inner practice and philosophy.

The poetic imagery of the *Can Tong Qi* takes the reader on a journey into the heart of traditional Chinese symbolism: the dragon and tiger (Chapter 28), the Great Yang Pearl (Chapter 14), and the Inner Cauldron (Chapter 35), are all mentioned. As the commentators explain, however, all of these are only aspects of the One (Chapter 25).

Students of Chinese medicine will find Chapters 15 and 25 of particular interest as they explain the symbolic relationship between the organs of the human body and the five elements, as well as illustrating the healing power of meditation – that is, the creation of a Golden Elixir through harmonizing the flow of one's inner energies.

Amongst many other things, the text is a meditation manual. Not only does it give valuable practical information for would-be meditators (Chapter 11), but also includes the all-important attitude required to attain that which one seeks – the attitude of *wu-wei*, meaning active inaction or effortless effort (see Chapters 8 and 10).

All these chapters provide a succinct but convincing explanation of the 'alchemy' which initiates an inner transformation within the self. There is a certain in-built resistance to things alchemical within the modern Western psyche – a resistance that comes from misunderstanding and ignorance rather than anything else. An immersion in 'things Chinese' and baptism by 'alchemic fire' may well provide an inestimable service in breaking down some of this prejudice.

Wei Boyang's *Can Tong Qi*, or *Akinness of the Three*, is an early and important alchemical classic, which stands supreme in the Daoist canon of books. It is dated around AD 142 during the Eastern Han period (AD 25–220), a time of the greatest activity in the early chemical sciences. Primarily a work of 'internal' alchemy (*neidan*, as opposed to *waidan*, or 'external' chemical alchemy) it ranks alongside Heshang's commentary on the *Daode Jing* or *Tao Te Ching* (*The Way and its Power*), the *Huanding Jing* (*Book of the Yellow Courtyard*) scripture, and the Song dynasty *Wu Zhen Bian* (*Book on Awakening to the Reality*), as one of the four great classics of Daoist internal science. These books form the basis of study for any Daoist, outlining as they do the 'gateway to the Dark Female' of Laozi (Lao Tsu) – the door to the unconscious realm within and the origin of all human activity and life.

What is so unique about this early text is the extent to which later scholarship understood it as being uniquely concerned with *neidan*. This form of yogic meditation was directly opposed to the more common *waidan* of the earlier Chinese alchemists: they were trying either to fashion gold or else to concoct an actual chemical elixir, which when drunk would confer immortality. Some have even wondered if this was actually Wei Boyang's intent, but a careful reading of the text leaves no doubt that the inner world was his main concern.

The *Can Tong Qi* explicitly advocates the contemplative life as a means of achieving immortality. Wei Boyang writes in the rich style of his period, using images and metaphors, one piled upon another, in order to help us understand the significance of his work. Along with the thought of the *Book of Change*, he combines ideas from the Chinese almanac, observations of the sun, moon, and stars, observations of the weather, the response of plants and animals to the seasons, and deductions from natural science. The agglomeration of liquids, the echoing of sounds, the formation of glues and dyes, the dispersion of fluids by heat, the subduing of fire by water, the mating of animals, the natural affection between the sexes, the physiological and psychological effects of Daoist yoga (sense-withdrawal) and more, all find their place in this extra-ordinary work.

In addition, numerology is used to illustrate the reciprocal balance which exists between all elements of the natural world.

And yet all these ideas and terms are only seeking to explain one thing: how to knit together our various parts – our energies, essences, souls, body, mind, whatever – into a single whole; and at the same time, to realize this wholeness which we possess along with all processes of life.

The quotation with which I preface this book best explains the philosophical stance of the work. There is everlasting life, because there is no death; but if there is no death, there can be no life either! There is only one all-pervading and suffusing energy, which gives birth to and eventually consumes all things.

It is the realization of this truth which is the gift passed on from generation to generation among the inner schools of Chinese alchemy, and is now presented for the first time in translation. As the text makes clear, the matter is described in terms of Yin and Yang, the male and female counterparts of the Dao (Way, or Path, or Method), the set of eight trigrams (eight-line figures), and the sixty-four hexagrams which are made up of alternating solid (Yang) and broken (Yin) lines. It is the consolidation and dissolution of these figures which form the alchemical process whereby the fashioning of an elixir of everlasting life and its ultimate truth, are realized.

The Text of the Can Tong Qi

The *Can Tong Qi*, or *Akinness of the Three* is an outlier of the great alchemical tradition which flourished in China around the turn of the millennium (the second century BC to the second

century AD), was perpetuated well into the Qing dynasty and sur-
vives to this day. The earliest work to survive on alchemical
theory, it has had an overwhelming impact upon the development
of alchemy throughout the world. Its influence spread through the
Arabs, into Byzantium and medieval Europe, to jostle against the
burgeoning ideas of the Renaissance. It is well known that even
Isaac Newton, in his rooms in Cambridge, performed the alchemical 'transmutation of metals' whilst conceiving his universal
theory of gravitation.

As to the enigmatic title of the book, I have left it untranslated in
the main, rendering it in the Chinese – *Can Tong Qi*. There is no
consensus as to what the Chinese words mean, for they can be
taken in different ways.

Two views are represented by our two main commentators,
the seventh Patriarch of the Northern School of Daoism, Master
Shangyang (the Master who 'honours the Yang'), and the young
Yuan author Yuyan.

Master Shangyang explains (Chapter 33):

> The three sections of the *Can Tong Qi* [which can translate as 'com-
> bining similars together'] are all essentially practical and not meant to
> be confusing. The method may be somewhat mystical in nature, but it
> is nevertheless unnecessary for it to be prolonged. *Can* ('combining')
> refers to the process of combining along with the essential creative
> power of heaven and earth; *tong* ('similars') refers to depending on the
> practicality of similar things interacting together; and *qi* ('together')
> refers to the joining together in the work of this creative power and this
> interaction of similars.

And Yuyan, commenting on Chapter 16 says:

> *Can Tong Qi* can translate as 'the Threefold as One'. Firstly comes
> change, as it is displayed in the ancient book, the *Zhou Yi* (Changes of
> Zhou) – which gives the idea for the material ingredients for the Elixir;
> second is the 'quietist and non-active' Daoist tradition of nourishing
> one's inner nature, which yields the idea of the inner 'furnace' and
> 'cauldron'; last is the alchemic tradition of firing metals, which com-
> pletes the process, bringing in the idea of the firing-times for the Elixir.
>
> Out of these three, the *Zhou Yi*, Daoism and alchemy are all brought
> together in the book as three paths which yet emerge from a single
> gate. Thus they are the 'Threefold' as 'One'.

Master Shangyang's commentary (*c.* AD 1330) and that by the
younger Yuyan (AD 1284) have been my favoured texts. I have

used perhaps a third of Master Shangyang's writings, but not even a tenth of Yuyan's. Both are prolific, not to say profligate writers!

The Reputed Author – Wei Boyang

When we ask who the author of the Can Tong Qi was, we encounter a dilemma. The usual answer is that it was the Eastern Han alchemist Wei Boyang. This was the view accepted, for example, by Wu and Davis in their well-meant but misguided chemical translation in Isis in 1932. (How they used Yuyan's 'internal' commentaries but never realized that they were dealing with internal alchemy is beyond comprehension!) However later scholarship has cast doubt on Wei Boyang's sole authorship.

Generally Yuyan's explanation of the text is the easiest to follow. He states that Wei Boyang, the probable author, takes the philosophy of the Yi Jing or I Ching (especially that of the Great Appendix) and mixes it along with the thought of 'Huang-Lao' Daoism[1] then in vogue, to form the theoretical basis for a description of the practice of internal alchemy.

Wei Boyang was a Daoist alchemist and philosopher of the second century AD. According to tradition, in AD 121 he was summoned to court but declined as he had no taste for officialdom. He describes himself and the writing of the Can Tong Qi well in Chapter 18:

> In the state of Kuai, a common man,
> Alone in a valley barely existing,
> Clasps to his bosom rough simplicity,
> And pleasures in neither circumstance nor honour.
>
> In rude habit he spends his time,
> Careless of either fame or profit,
> Grasping onto the quiet and solitude,
> Those rare times, so tranquil and still.
>
> So there, dwelling in idleness and ease,
> Then I composed this work,
> To sing of the order of Great Change,
> The Three Sages' forgotten words ...
> I looked at their obvious meaning,
> And saw one thread connecting the whole.

The 'Complete Biography of the Immortals' (Lie Xian Quan Zhuan) has a fanciful report concerning Wei Boyang. He was one of those 'who entered into the hills to make an efficacious medicine.

> With him went three disciples, two of whom he thought lacked complete faith in the work.
>
> When the medicine was complete, he tested them by saying, 'The Golden Medicine is made but it ought first to be tested upon the dog. If no harm comes to the dog, we may try it ourselves. But if the dog dies, we should not attempt it.'
>
> The medicine was fed to the dog and it instantly died. Then Wei Boyang said, 'The medicine is not yet finished. The dog has died of it. Does this not show clearly that we have failed. If we try it ourselves we shall go the same way as the dog. What shall we do?' The disciples said, 'What would you do Sir?' He replied, 'I have abandoned the ways of the world and forsaken all company to come here. I would be shunned if I returned without reaching the heights of immortality, so to live without the medicine would be just the same as to die through taking the medicine.' And at once he put the medicine into his mouth and collapsed.
>
> On seeing this, one of the disciples said, 'Our teacher was no common man. Although he took the medicine and fell down, he must have had a special reason why he did this.' And he took the medicine and also collapsed upon the ground. Then the other two disciples said to each other: 'The purpose of making an Elixir is to attempt to attain longevity. Now taking this medicine has caused them to die. We would be better off not taking it, and so be able to live a few years longer!' So they left the hills together without taking the medicine, intending to get suitable supplies for burying their teacher and their friend.
>
> After their departure, Wei Boyang revived. He administered a drug to the disciple and the dog and in a few moments they both came to. He took the disciple, whose name was Yu, and the dog, and went the way of the Immortals. Through a wood-cutter in the forest whom they met, they sent a letter of thanks to the other two disciples who were later filled with remorse when they read it.

This popular account of Wei Boyang's life shows the folklore surrounding the chemical alchemists of the Han. Increasingly, as more and more fatalities occurred due to Elixial poisoning, the outer chemistry of the early Daoists yielded to an 'inner alchemy' – which was concerned both with salvation and longevity in this world.

The Early History of Chinese Alchemy

The texts of Chinese alchemy are initially baffling. Why are there so many terms? What do they all mean? Where does one begin?

A historical approach is probably the best to begin with. This allows us to see alchemy in a human perspective. As we tackle its terms and central concepts, we should always remember that 'as we get the images, we can forget the words' and that 'if the writing does not come alive for us there is just confusion'. This is the view of one of the best of the later Song teachers, Xiao Tingjin (*fl.*1250). I can only hope to go some way towards reaching this goal!

The history of breathing exercises is relatively easy to trace. There is an inscription on a piece of jade, at least 2500 years old, which may have formed the knob to a staff. It runs as follows:

> Hold the breath and it collects,
> When collected it expands,
> When expanded it goes down,
> When it goes down it becomes quiet,
> When it becomes quiet it solidifies,
> Solidified it begins to sprout forth,
> After it has sprouted forth it will grow,
> As it grows it will be pulled back again above,
> Pulled back above it will reach the crown of the head.
> Above it presses up against,
> Below it presses downwards,
> Whoever follows this will live,
> Whoever acts against this will die.[2]

The roots of this art were certainly planted deep in the soil of Bronze-Age China, and established long before the country was unified in 221 BC. The oldest medical classic in China, the *Huangdi Neijing* (*Yellow Emperor's Book of Medicine*), an amalgam of various medical schools which flourished probably from the first century BC onwards, represents the culmination of these ideas.

In its opening chapter, 'Upon our Natural Endowment in Ancient Times', the Yellow Emperor asks his sage-physician Qi Bo:

> In the olden days people lived to be over a hundred years of age and yet remained active and did not decline as they grew old. But nowadays at only half that age already they are failing ... Why is this?

And Qi Bo replies:

> If you can be quiet and remain indifferent to things, and completely humble and empty – then the true breath will follow. When the mental powers are guarded within, how can disease arrive? Breathing the essence of life, one stands alone, guarding the spirit, flesh and sinews as one.[3]

One can appreciate the inner repose which was fundamental to the civilized Chinese. This paragraph encapsulates the protective, preventive and rehabilative attitude common in Chinese medicine. The Daoist chemists were certainly widely involved in forming both outer and inner Elixirs, and attempting to take control of the immensities of the processes of nature with a view to delaying old age and our inevitable decline. As Yuyan says:

> I would say that man as he exists in the universe is merely a thing in that universe. Yet because his spirituality is greater than that of other creatures, he is given the special name of 'man'. How, then, can he stand co-equal with Heaven and Earth? If he seize for himself the secret forces of Heaven and Earth, in order thereby to compound for himself the great Elixir of the golden fluid, he will then exist coeval with Heaven and Earth from beginning to end. Such a one is called the True Man ... Each time that Heaven unites itself with Earth, seize for yourself the secret springs of the creative activities of the Yin and Yang.

This view was essentially modern in character. The great contemporary philosopher Fung Yu-lan comments thus:

> Here we are urged to 'seize for ourselves the secret forces of Heaven and Earth' and the 'secret springs of the creative activities of the Yin and Yang', in order thus to 'put all things to our service'. In other words, we are to obtain our end through gaining control over the forces of nature. The stress here upon power is essentially scientific in spirit.[4]

Other suggestions of early 'yogic' patterns occur in the fourth-century BC Daoist writer Zhuangzi (Chuang Tsu), who recounts many legends which suggest meditation and the training of the spirit. In his chapter 'Letting Things Alone', he describes an interview with none other than the Yellow Emperor himself.

> The Yellow Emperor had ruled over the throne for nineteen years and his command was established throughout the land when he heard that a certain Master Guangcheng, proficient in the ultimate method of 'Fostering Life', was living not far away on Mount Gong Dong – the 'Peak of Emptiness and Identity'. He decided to pay him a visit.
>
> I have heard, said the Emperor, that you have mastered the ultimately perfect method itself, may I know its details? I would then be able to further help the people and ensure their continued prosperity.
>
> Master Guangcheng answers: What you say you want to learn is the true essence of things. But what you want to control is the disintegration of them!

Ever since you have been on the throne, the rain has fallen without waiting for the clouds, the leaves of the trees have dropped without waiting to turn yellow, the sun and moon have shadowed ... shallow indeed! Yours is the speech of a charlatan and a trickster! What good would it do to tell you of the ultimately perfect Method!

Upon this the Emperor withdrew. He gave up his throne. He built a solitary hut and lay down in it on a bed of straw. For three months he remained alone, seeking and speaking to no-one.

Then he went once more to speak to Master Guang.

Master Guang was lying down, looking towards the south. The Emperor crept up to him on his knees, his head bowed in an attitude of extreme submission.

Sir, he began, I have heard that you possess the perfect Method itself. May I be allowed to ask how I may preserve myself and my energies?

At this, Master Guang leapt up with a start. A good question, a good question! he cried out. Now listen and I will inform you about this perfect Method of Great Ultimacy –

In essence, it is profound and darkly shrouded –

Mysterious it is and hushed in silence –

Let your soul be at peace and the body will right itself.[5]

The Zhuanz book and its predecessor the Laozi (or *Daode Jing*, probably fourth century BC) were written in a world which knew well the techniques hinted at above – and likely as not their authors were well-versed in their practice. During the cultivation advocated in the Can Tong Qi the mind is stilled and turned inward, the breath tempered and made gentle and long. Zhuangzi referred to such things as 'guarding the One', 'sitting and forgetting', and 'the fasting of the heart' – all practices which were later taken on by certain schools, and ridiculed by later more philosophically minded alchemists! Yet the famous 'Song on Smashing Superstition' goes as follows:

To 'circulate the breath' is not the Way!
The body's fluids are not a magical water.
To 'guard the thoughts' is not the Way!
How can you eat a picture of a cake!
Sexual practices are not the Way!
When the seed has gone, life passes.

The newly born foetus is not the Way!
What is unclean has nothing to do with the true Energy.
To stop eating salted foods is not the Way!
Your food then lacks stimulating flavours.

> A vegetarian diet is not the Way!
> Going hungry only injures the stomach and spleen.
> Abstaining from sex is not the Way!
> Yin and Yang then lose their honoured positions.

The perverted practices which later inner alchemists railed against had perhaps not yet become corrupt in Zhuangzi's times (although he is well known for his sarcasm concerning the 'puffing and panting, hailing and sipping, spitting out the old breath and drawing in the new, practising bear-hangings and bird-stretchings' adopted by his contemporaries.)

Here is Zhuangzi's method of 'sitting and forgetting':

> Yan Hui: I can sit down and forget everything!
> Confucius (much startled): What do you mean, sit down and forget everything?
> Yan Hui: I smash up my limbs and body, drive out perception and intellect, cast off form, do away with understanding and make myself identical with the Grand Thoroughfare. This is what I mean by sitting down and forgetting everything.[6]

And again:

> Your will must be one! Do not listen with your ears but with your heart. Do not listen with your heart but with your vital energy. Let listening stop with the ears, let the workings of the heart stop with themselves. Then your vital energy will be empty, receptive to all things. The Way itself abides in emptiness. Emptiness is the fasting of the heart.[7]

Here is the last section of the Inner Chapters of his book, and it carries a moral:

> The ruler of the Southern Seas was called Light. The ruler of the Northern Seas was called Darkness. And the ruler of the Middle Kingdom was Primal Chaos. From time to time, Light and Darkness met on Primal Chaos's territory and he made them welcome. Light and Darkness wanted to repay him for his kindness and they said: 'All men have seven openings through which they see, hear, eat and breath, but Primal Chaos has none.'
>   So every day they bored one hole – and on the seventh day Primal Chaos died.[8]

The ruining of Primal Chaos implies the downfall of sensory experience; it suggests that the root of decay lies here in the world.

Herein lies our fall from grace. The thread of quietism was in China long before the influx of Buddhism. It can be seen throughout the *Can Tong Qi* – 'the ear, the eye, the mouth, these three jewels, block and stop them up, do not let them gape' (Chapter 25), as well as in both the commentaries of Master Shangyang, where it assumes a rather puritan aspect, and those of Yuyan, who is more physiological.

Indeed the quieting of the senses is the sole way to cultivate the Golden Elixir of everlasting life. It was obvious to the practically minded Chinese that anything, any mechanism, would last longer if cared for. Thus many believed that preserving our mental and physical health through quiet would lead to a longer and more active life. There was a general tendency among several Daoist schools to avoid excesses ('a high wind does not last all morning, nor a thunderstorm all day ... standing on tiptoe one is not steady, striding one cannot keep up the pace'),[9] and to seek inner sobriety, a settled mind within a calm body.

In all these affairs the Chinese were undoubtedly pioneers. Many skills have been handed down by word of mouth for thousands of years – and only now are being recognized in the West. The modern practice of Qigong or Chi Kung (Breathing Therapy) and the well-known Taiji Quan or Tai Chi Chuan are only the best known outside China. In the last few years there has been the discovery of some forty or so marvellous drawings on silk from the Han tombs at Mawangdui (dated 168 BC). These are coloured drawings of men and women, young and old, each occupied in exercises still practised today. In addition, there is a long history of the sexual arts, with a written history stretching back thousands of years.[10] The aim of these techniques was to ensure maximum health for both partners (rather than maximum pleasure), and to check any decline in vitality. They emphasized delaying orgasm for the male (although not unduly) and also increasing satisfaction for the female.

Other Daoist 'arts' involved exposing the body to the rays of the sun and moon, the consumption of various herbs, minerals and animal substances, and dietary restrictions, notably the abstinence from cereals and cereal products[11] as well as the many skills of mind control, bordering on meditation, self-hypnosis and trance.

This evidence must alert us to the fact that something was going on at this borderline 'twixt sleep and wake', which led to peace of mind and equilibrium of purpose – and perhaps also to longer life.

The Idea of the Elixir Of Everlasting Life

The alchemical tradition of the Golden Elixir arose from the coming together of three main threads: the avid search made by the early Chinese for health-giving plants, minerals, drugs and elixirs; the metallurgical discoveries of the means of making or faking gold ('aurifaction' and 'aurifiction'); and the wide-spread habit of using inorganic substances as therapy, which all existed early on in China.[12] These practices were widespread by the third century BC, well before the active Jin and Han times, and they reached a unified form by the end of the first century AD before the *Can Tong Qi* was written. Joseph Needham expresses it clearly:

> After the beginning of the fourth century BC the conviction everywhere spread that there were technical means whereby men could enlarge their length of days so much as to be virtually immortal, not some-where else out of this world, nor in the underworld of the Yellow Springs, but among the mountains and forests here and for ever. Something happened at this time to strengthen greatly this belief, perhaps a message from Babylonia, Persia or India about a drug-plant, herb or medicine of immortality, even perhaps slightly misunderstood so as to interlock with Chinese world-views. The result was a great wave of activity concerned with what is sometimes called the cult of the *hsien* (immortal, fairy), a distinctively material immortality in which the body was still needed, preserved in however etherealised or 'lightened' a form, whether the deathless being remained among the scenic beauties of earth or ascended as perfected immortal to the ranks of the Administration on high ...[13]

One can read about this in Chapter 11 of the *Can Tong Qi*:

> Nourish yourself thus within,
> Tranquil and still in the void,
> While at source concealing the brilliance
> Which illuminates within your whole body.
> Shut and close up the mouth,
> Repressing within the spiritual trunk,
> The senses all swallowed up
> To gently support that pearl so young.
> Observe it there, the unobvious –
> So close by and easy to seek.
>
> Diligently practised then,
> Day and night unceasing,
> A subdued appetite over three years

Develops lightness and far you roam –
Pass through fire without getting burnt,
Enter water without getting soaked,
Able to choose either care or neglect,
And to grow in happiness without being sad.

The path comes to an end, the power is attained,
And secretly subdued, you await the hour
When Great Oneness himself summons you
To reside upon the Solitary Isle;
Then your work realized you rise above,
Borne upon the List of Immortals.

It just so happened that from the fourth to the first century BC the conditions in China were ripe for the development of the elixial idea. An association of ideas between the consumption of health-giving substances (elixirs) and the making of gold happened for the first time. It is important to realize the uniqueness of this occurrence in China. Elixirs giving permanent life and medicines of immortality had never been a serious element in Hellenistic proto-chemistry, which concerned itself more with the making and faking of gold.
    Needham says:

It can hardly be too much emphasised that in China proto-chemistry was elixir alchemy from the very beginning (as it was not in other civilisations of equal antiquity), and by the same token alchemists were very often physicians too (much more so than they tended to be in other civilisations). ... The basic elixir notion was a pharmaceutical and therapeutic one ...[14]

During this period there was no 'ethical polarization' within Chinese thought like that which attached itself to the contemporary Judaic, Indo-Iranian and European civilizations. Thus eternal life, here on earth, was quite believable. There was no need to invent some other 'paradisal' world. Uniquely Chinese alchemy contained, as a fundamental part of its quest, the search for the health-giving medicine of life – a concept which first appeared in the West only in twelfth-century texts by way of translations from the Arabic.
    Alchemy in China has always been special in possessing this dual character, at once both chemical and spiritual. This is not to say that certain alchemists did not eschew one or other of the paths, but the two strands ran close together for more than a thousand years.

Another point needs emphasizing here. Alchemy was spiritual in China only to the extent that it could bring the self into equilibrium and union. For the Chinese the path could never be purely psychological; indeed sometimes it was emphatically physiological (the inborn 'enchymoma' and 'macrobiogens' of Joseph Needham), and often discreetly philosophical.

Alchemy was never primarily conceptual for the Chinese. Their ideographic language was simply not suited to abstract thought. Nor were the Chinese searching for some kind of 'individuation' (the term used by C. G. Jung for the personal path for each individual). Their work was more physical, more akin to the actual brewing of an inner medicine within the body (the 'enchymoma'). Whether this is described as an elixir or the continued adjustment of our autonomic nervous system, the regulation of the production of the neurotransmitters which affect mood, and the learning of a technique of relaxation, is unimportant.

The outcome was a practice which could at once manipulate the body's biochemistry, deal with philosophical issues of meaning and paradox, and at the same time encourage and develop peace of mind. As it resolved issues it could also revitalize tissues – and perhaps also promote a longer life.

However it is crucial for a complete understanding of what follows that we attempt to 'get under the skin' of the Chinese language. The great alchemist Xiao Tingjin puts it succinctly:

> Once one can get an image, one can forget the words.
> If the writing does not come alive there is just confusion –
> For those who understand, it all happens easily,
> For those who go wrong, there are difficulties.[15]

The alchemists were actually aiming at a little more than just living longer and we should always keep the proverbial 'grain of salt' in our pocket when we read their rhymes. Yuyan describes the 'ultimate medicine' (Chapter 1):

> Some would call it the 'deep intercourse of the dragon and tiger', or else the 'metal and wood jointed together'; or else the 'tortoise and snake encoiled', or the 'red and black pitched in together'; or else 'heaven and earth peacefully entwined', or the 'variegated dark and yellow'; or else the 'infused metals and earth', or the 'metals and the mercury at one in the cauldron'; or else the 'metals and the fire at one in the furnace', or the 'mixed up red and white'; or else the 'sun and moon in one palace', or the 'crow and rabbit in a single burrow'; or else the 'happy union of husband and wife' or the 'ox-herd and

spinning-maiden keeping tryst'; or else the 'male and female tailing each other', the 'hun-soul and po-soul cast together', or the 'water and soil on the same territory'. Yet whatever you call it, it is no more than the mind [*xin*] and the breath being together as one. It is simply the Yin and the Yang influenced internally with their spirit and energy enjoined.

What is meant here may well become clear later.

The Philosophical Background to the Text and Commentaries

The whole of chemistry finds its roots in the 'aurifactive dream' of the alchemists and their pondering of the transformations of matter. However from the very earliest times, the Chinese saw the refining of gold out of base metal as akin to the developing of an inner strength within the individual and it is in this truly unique sense that the *Can Tong Qi* was understood throughout most of its history.

The alchemic idea of personal salvation involved the plucking of the secret of the heavens – the eternal brightness of the sun and moon – in order to irradiate and strengthen the inner self. It encompassed a meditation upon and careful pondering of the cycles of the moon (the month) and the sun (the year) in order to understand how Yin and Yang themselves (as 'dragon and tiger', 'lead and mercury', breath-energy and vitality) merge, emerge and re-emerge, engage and disengage, within the world and within the body. More particularly it involved the condensing of a mystical Elixir within the body:

> Before the night-time airs are over and passed, you need only focus the mind and gather together the inner energies, sitting upright for a short while. Then, in a little while, the mind's energies will return to their roots; so that within nothing, will be born something – gradually condensing, gradually gathering and building, until it consolidates into a single seed of Golden Grain.

Thus Yuyan comments on Chapter 5 of the *Can Tong Qi*. But before we get in too deeply let us carefully examine where we are going.

The illustrations included within the text form a good introduction to its background philosophy. They are mostly taken from Yuyan's critical commentary and redrawn for this publication. The 1284 preface to Yuyan's work begins: 'The method of our spiritual Immortal's restored Elixir is "very simple and very easy". It lies simply in this ○ and nowhere else besides.'

The constant occurrence of the circle (a 'cycle') in Yuyan's diagrams is clear. The circle stands for the 'supreme pole', the 'One', before it divides up into Yin and Yang. It stands for the single undifferentiated energy which makes up the inner world, the world literally 'before heaven' (*xiantian*), that is before the existence of the world as we know it. It is this inner world which concerns those who tread the path of the Elixir of everlasting life. That this path divides is tantamount to saying that the Path, the Dao, the Method, the single energy, the circle, divides up into Yin and Yang, movement and stillness and thus all myriad things. Thus is the outer world (*houtian*) created.

These ideas were fundamental to the Neo-Confucian philosophy embraced by every later commentator on the *Can Tong Qi*. In addition they formed the 'orthodox' view for all the earlier Han texts which were sorted out and formulated during the Song – to be later memorized by every aspiring scholar. Other examples are the reordering of the Confucian canon under Zhu Xi (1130–1200), the medical classics recompiled by Lin Yi (between 1068 and 1077), and the popular and well-known Chan (Zen) compilations, the *Blue Cliff Record* (eleventh to twelfth century) and *Gateless Gate* (1229). The retrospective vision directed onto Han texts by the Song and their adoption of much of Buddhist metaphysic, gave a softness to their culture, which is epitomized in Neo-Confucian philosophy.

The diagram of the 'supreme pole' (*taiji*), and 'no pole' (*wuji*) (see Figures 2 and 3) is worth pondering carefully.

Yuyan's Preface explains it thus:

> The 'supreme pole' stirs itself and gives birth to the Yang. As the movement travels to its utmost it becomes still ... it is still and gives birth to Yin. As the stillness reaches its utmost point it stirs again. Stirring and stilling are linked together at the root and herein lies the marvel of all creation, which forms the self-actualizing and natural character of the Dao.

He is quoting the text which accompanies the 'supreme pole' diagram, attributed to the philosopher Zhou Dunyi (1017–73).

This 'self-actualizing and natural character of the Dao' (*ziran*) is all that is actually described in this book.

Master Shangyang also comments (Chapter 3):

> When the supreme pole (*taiji*) splits apart, there come into being the prenatal inner and postnatal outer worlds.
> What is meant by the prenatal? It is all that 'precedes form' – which

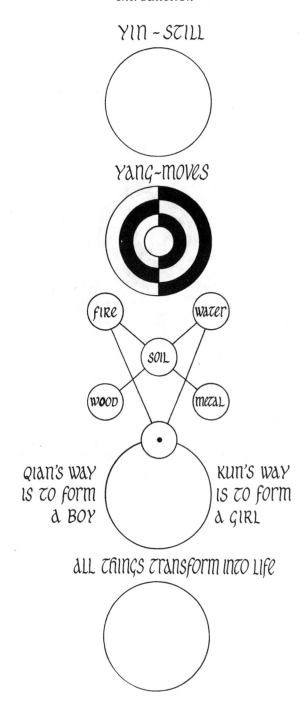

Fig. 2 The diagram of the supreme pole

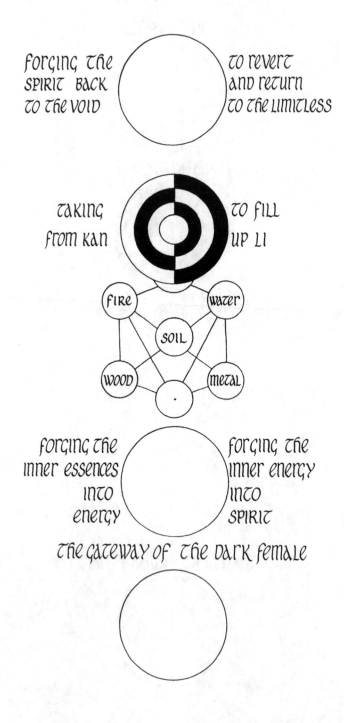

forging the
SPIRIT BACK
to the VOID

to revert
and return
to the limitless

taking
from kan

to fill
up li

FIRE

water

SOIL

WOOD

metal

forging the
inner essences
into
energy

forging the
inner energy
into
SPIRIT

The gateway of the Dark female

Fig. 3 The diagram of the limitless (no pole)

means the Dao, the Path, the Method; which is being entering into nothingness. What is meant by the postnatal? It is all that 'succeeds form' – which means an apparatus, a capacity, or an ability; which is nothingness entering into being.

Laozi said: The nameless is the beginning of heaven and earth, the named is the mother of the myriad things. (*Dao de Jing*, Chapter 1)

There is another saying: Entering into being from nothingness, they all do this! Entering into nothingness from being, how many of them do this?

If people conclude with the work of the ebb and flow of Kan and Li, then their work is all in the outer world and postnatal, meaning it involves the 'apparatus', the 'form', the dregs of matter; which is never far apart from the ebb and flow. This is by no means as important as the inner world and the prenatal. Therein lies the method of everlasting life through which you are able to attain to the foothills of the lands of the sages!

Before closing we should also acknowledge the rich Mahayana Buddhist influence on both Shangyang and Yuyan's commentaries. Buried and surviving within their texts are the *dharmakaya* or 'body of the dharma', the 'instantaneous' grasp of enlightenment (as we take hold of the Elixir), and the Buddhist idea of *tathata* or 'suchness', the merging of object and subject as a direct perception of self-nature. So then where did Chan Buddhism go after the Yuan? Not only, as is commonly thought, to Japan but also into the Golden Elixir alchemy of China.

The Actual Alchemy

The trigrams and hexagrams of the *Yi Jing* (*Book of Change*) are used as illustrators in the alchemic process and we must understand clearly these 'markers' or 'tokens of change' if we are properly to understand alchemical change. Qian (heaven, father), Kun (earth, mother), Kan (water) and Li (fire) are used in the main. Qian and Kun become, as it were, the furnace and cauldron within which the water and fire (Kan and Li) concoct together the medicine of the Elixir.

In addition, Qian and Kun also decide general location – above and below, north and south, as they might perhaps refer to localities either within the human body or in space.

Kan and Li then describe the passage of the energy, or fire, during its transformations as it arrives and departs, rises and falls,

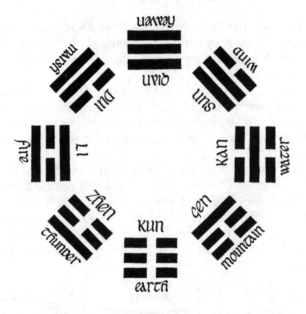

Fig. 4 *The eight trigrams of the inner world*

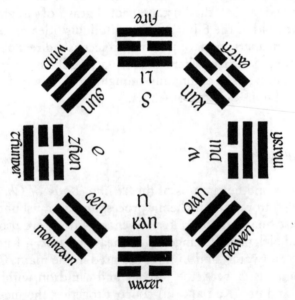

Fig. 5 *The eight trigrams of the outer world*

exits and enters, either sensed or in the world. Kan and Li are also
spoken of as the sun and moon and their action 'between heaven
and earth' describes these transformations in detail.

The other four trigrams are Zhen (thunder, eldest son), Sun

(wind, eldest daughter), Dui (marsh) and Gen (mountain). These act as markers in the processes of growth and decline. They depict the passage of heat – 'the firing-times' – within the world: the cycle of the moon, the passing of the months. They also reflect the firing of an Elixir within the body. The body is the cauldron within which a medicine is formed through repeated cycles of heating.

One particular characteristic of alchemical texts which allows them to work upon many levels at the same time is the use of various 'courtesy names' – names which all point towards the same thing. This is partly metaphor, partly Chinese poetic licence and partly a technique for communicating something beyond words. After all, 'the Way which can be told is not the eternal Way'.[16]

Qian and Kun (heaven and earth) may be seen as heaven and earth, but also Yang and Yin, male and female, Hun-soul and Po-soul, ruler and minister, host and guest, papa and mama, husband and wife, son and daughter, and so on; each term adding a little more.

Thus the ingredients in this marvellous chemistry are variously described as Kan and Li, water and fire, sun and moon, the firm and yielding, black and white, odd and even, tiger and dragon, crow and rabbit, our inner nature and feelings, the little child and the mild-mannered maiden, the unstable pearl and the Golden Flower, and so on. Again these terms mean different things in different contexts. None of them is a direct or exact equivalent, for the Elixial method itself is an art which keeps changing its terms of reference. Any description of it is more akin to a painting, a poem or a myth, and never an exact and dry scientific record.

In fact whether the text talks about hours of the day, phases in the waxing and waning of the moon, spring, summer, autumn or winter, or their noticeable effects on nature, it is basically describing one and the same thing – the timing of the production of an inner medicinal Elixir.

The whole of the *Can Tong Qi* is concerned with identifying the exact moment when life restores itself through the Yang Elixir – either within our own bodies or in the world. That this moment can be detected and deliberately fostered through an observation of minutely changing qualities and quantities was the unique discovery of the alchemists. The 'lead' and the 'mercury', the Yin and the Yang, Qian the father, Kun the mother and Zhen the son, depict the resolution of differences through love. They inform us that however far apart we are, or however split inside, we are yet

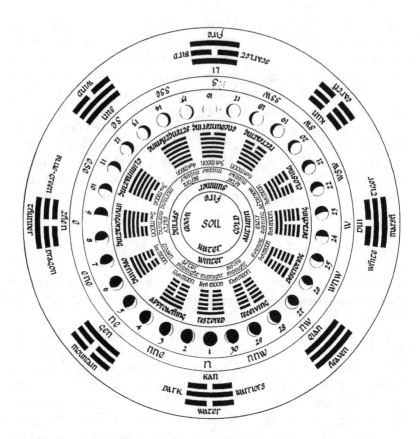

Fig. 6 The bright mirror revealing the method of the elixir

bound close together – through our very opposition. This expresses the fundamentally philosophical idea of the One, which underpins the thought of the early Han Chinese. It also depicts the common sense and sanity which lies at the heart of their traditional culture. It is basically the law of Yin and Yang, as they are at once antagonistic and dependent upon each other.

To borrow a phrase from C. G. Jung and R. Wilhelm,[17] I hope this translation may go some way towards reheating the 'roots of consciousness' – that the reader may experience the primal source of 'inner-world' reality, and through the guidance of a teacher revalidate his or her own thinking.

Do we still not understand what is meant by the Golden Elixir? Then let Yuyan (Chapter 17) have the last word:

> It is just the same as when the cicada falls silent in cold weather or the
> rhinoceros gazes at the bright stars, or as the old oyster which holds

inside itself a moon-lit pearl, or the mere block of stone which contains jade. It is just the same as the butterfly straightening and bending its wings, or the glow-worm brightening and dulling its light, or the closing and opening of the cat's eyes. It is just the same as the turning one way and then another of the deer's tail, or the taken-in breath of the tortoise in hibernation, or the spat-out sand of the sand-turtle. It is just the same as the windsock blowing in the wind, or the drip-tile on a roof dripping water, or the lodestone pulling at a needle, or amber attracting small particles. It is just the same as the turning well-sweep which brings up water, or the sweet flag in the rice-fields which collects the dew, or the snake entering into hibernation, or the fish resting in still water, or the dung-beetle rolling his ball, or the solitary wasp driving out its young, or the baby chick contained in the egg, or the young rabbit harboured in the womb. It is just the same as the ox having a yellow hide, or the dragon harbouring a pearl, as plums and walnuts having kernels, or the sweet melon shedding its skin. It is just the same as the banana tree woken by spring breezes, the parasol tree hanging with autumn drizzle, the evening moon seen over the blue lake, or the morning mists shrouding the green hills. All these are revelations of the Golden Elixir.

These images deeply involve our feelings – they also engage us in projecting outwardly our unresolved parts and thus gradually achieving wholeness through the interplay of text and brain. This gradual yet graduated path, referred to clearly in the text, leads us to greater certainty and energy, both so urgently needed in a troubled world. May the translation contribute to the arts of peace, so much more necessary than the arts of war!

Notes

1. 'Huang-Lao' is the name given to the Daoist religion which evolved during the later Han, based upon legends of the Yellow Emperor and Laozi, author of the *Daode Jing*.
2. J. Needham, *Science and Civilisation in China*, Vol.II, p.143, translation adapted. Compare also the closing lines with the end of Chapter 10.
3. Author's translation.
4. Fung Yu-lan, *A History of Chinese Philosophy*, Vol.II, p.432.
5. The *Zhuangzi*, Chapter 11.
6. From 'The Great and Venerable Teacher', Chapter 6 translated from *Chuang Tzu* by B. Watson.
7. From 'In the World of Men', Chapter 4 translated by B. Watson.

8. From 'Fit for Emperors and Kings', Chapter 7, author's translation from Chuang Tzu adapted from Gia-fu Feng and Giles.
9. *Daode Jing*, Chapter 23.
10. See Needham, Vol.II, pp.146ff.
11. Mentioned throughout Ge Hong's *Bao Puzi* ('Book of the Master who Preserves Solidity', *c.* AD 300).
12. Needham, *Science and Civilization in China* Vol.V:2, p.14.
13. ibid., p.81.
14. ibid., p.xxx.
15. From his poem 'On Reading the *Can Tong Qi*', contained in his *Jin Dan Da Cheng* ('Great Compilation on the Golden Elixir').
16. *Daode Jing*, Chapter 1.
17. R. Wilhelm, *The Secret of the Golden Flower*, p.96.

WEI BOYANG'S TEXT

1

THE YIN AND YANG, INNER
VITALITY AND ENERGY

This first chapter describes the method of the Golden Elixir as involving the 'embrace of the hexagrams Qian and Kun'. Qian provides the inner vitality or necessary seed, whilst Kun provides the energy. It outlines the 'dazzling lights' of Kan and Li, hexagrams or trigrams which represent the moon and sun; and the use of the remaining sixty hexagrams as markers in the process of firing an Elixir. Finally it stresses the mix of the dark inner and bright outer worlds, so crucial to a successful outcome.

> Qian is firm and Kun is yielding,
> They are fitted to embrace each other,
> As Yang endows, then Yin receives,
> The cock and hen depend on each other,
> Depend on each other in order to create,
> And send their inner vitality and energy abroad.

In order to speak about the idea of change in the world, the *Zhou Yi* or *Chou I* (Changes of Zhou) adopts the idea of the eight trigrams, Qian ☰ and Kun ☷, Zhen ☳ and Sun ☴, Kan ☵ and Li ☲, and Gen ☶ and Dui ☱; they describe respectively the natural phenomena of heaven and earth, thunder and the wind, water and fire, and the mountain and the marsh. These images describe the interplay of the two powers, Yin and Yang, and form the origin of all the myriad material things in the universe.

In the *Can Tong Qi*, Wei Boyang is influenced by three main topics: the idea of Yin and Yang, and the eight trigrams; the contemporary tradition of second-century 'quietest and non-active' (*qingjing wuwei*) Daoism; and the methods and terminology of the outer chemical alchemists. With these he establishes his subjects – the inner cultivation and development of an Elixir of everlasting life.

Qian	heaven	father	☰
Kun	earth	mother	☷
Zhen	thunder	eldest son	☳
Sun	wind, wood	eldest daughter	☴
Kan	water, moon	middle son	☵
Li	fire, sun	middle daughter	☲
Gen	mountain	youngest son	☶
Dui	marsh, lake	youngest daughter	☱

Fig. 7 The eight trigrams

This chapter explains how the hexagrams, six-line figures (or trigrams, three-line figures) Qian and Kun, Kan and Li, which derive from the *Book of Change*, are the key to the inner development of an Elixir. It points out how Qian's nature is firm and forceful, while Kun's is yielding and gentle. As the firm and yielding benefit each other, Qian and Kun join together in strength. The trigram Qian is Yang and thus in command of bestowal; the trigram Kun is Yin and thus in command of receiving nourishment. It is just as in the later section: 'As cocky Yang sows upon the dark bestowing earth, so henny Yin transforms it through her yellow covering' (Chapter 21).

The Yang cannot be without the Yin, and the Yin cannot be without the Yang; only through their mutual accord can the act of creation take place, and their inner vitality (*jing*) and energy (*qi*) be sent abroad. It is the same in the tempering of the inner Elixir.

Master Shangyang says: Confucius [in the Great Appendix II.6 to the Zhou Yi] states: Qian represents all Yang things; Kun represents all Yin things. Yin and Yang join together their strengths and the firm and yielding find substance. Thereby we take as substance the principle of heaven and earth; and can understand the strength of the divine light (shenming).

So as Qian becomes strong, firmness is built up 'correctly within', pure as unadulterated vitality; whilst as Kun becomes strong, so the yielding tenderness of 'favourable devotion' arises and thus 'the true individual (chunzi) takes action' [cf. Hexagram 2, Receptive, in the Zhou Yi]. This fitting together of Qian and Kun is the true method of the Golden Elixir.

He continues: One who can be fully set within the 'firm and yielding', is one who grasps the true method of the Golden Elixir. Thence the strength of the Qian-Yang lies in its command of endowment and donation; while the strength of the Kun-Yin lies in its special ability to take and receive within itself. So then, the cock and hen depend on each other to form an 'inner vitality and energy'; and for this vitality and energy to be sent abroad it demands there be a cock and hen.

Yuyan comments: It is a great matter indeed that man has his breath!

There is a saying: As you breathe, so the firm and yielding rub against each other, so they form the very image of Qian and Kun, opening and closing.

He continues: Before man is born, he dwells in his mother's belly, following his mother's own breathing, seeing nothing, aware of nothing with only the one single breath protected there within. And then he is born, cut off and cast out, away from his umbilical cord so that then the single point of true energy gathers there beneath his navel.

One day passes, and then another; the spirit emerges forth and the energy passes on. Consequently he can never hold on again to that one single breath which was his within the womb.

Now the method of inner development which produces a divine Immortal uses man's ability to 'reflect back his brightness to light up within [huguang neizhao]'. His outbreath and inbreath merge together into a stage of supreme peace.

And it follows then that immediately, by 'turning back to the source and travelling back to his original nature [fanben huanyuan]', he can restore again his own life and receive back its very first energy.

As the old saying goes: I join with the true vapours within and retain the breath, so that quite naturally created there I see a little child's face.

Again the *Supremely Spoken Spiritual-Source Song* says:

One thousand books, 10,000 essays, all discussing the abstruse! But the stalk of life has its origin actually in the true breath! Beyond the true breath, there exist only false views and distractions. They will never guide me onto the true self-actualizing path!

Now when Wei Boyang says 'Qian is firm and Kun is yielding, they are fitted to embrace each other', he means the moment you create the Elixir, the Qian-Yang joins itself on beneath the Kun-Yin, causing the outbreath and inbreath to merge together; and the firm and yielding match each other, both fitting together just as husband and wife. If you succeed in this for just a short space of time, your spiritual energies revert to their root, your life rolls up into one and the ultimate medicine is born!

Some would call it the 'deep intercourse of the dragon and tiger', or else the 'metal and wood jointed together'; or else the 'tortoise and snake encoiled', or the 'red and black pitched in together'; or else 'heaven and earth peacefully entwined', or the 'variegated dark and yellow'; or else the 'infused metals and earth', or the 'metals and the mercury at one in the cauldron'; or else the 'metals and the fire at one in the furnace', or the 'mixed up red and white'; or else the 'sun and moon in one palace', or the 'crow and rabbit in a single burrow'; or else the 'happy union of husband and wife' or the 'ox-herd and spinning-maiden keeping tryst'; or else the 'male and female tailing each other', the 'Hun-soul and Po-soul cast together', or the 'water and soil on the same territory'.

In the end whatever you call it, it is no more than the mind [xin] and the breath being together as one. It is simply the Yin and the Yang influenced internally with their spirit and energy entwined.

He concludes: In general, the method of the Elixir involves both the dissimilar prenatal inner and postnatal outer worlds, both non-action and action. Within the inner world you focus the mental energies and enter them into the Kun-belly to generate a medicine; when you arrive at the outer world you shift these energies so that they enter into the Qian-crown at the top of the head and finally complete the formation of the Elixir.

The prenatal inner world then is non-active; the postnatal world is active. It is not possible that there can be one exact rule for them both.

> As Kan and Li, they come out excelling,
> As dazzling lights they are diffused;
> Darkened, unseen, and difficult to fathom,
> And so impossible to define.

As Qian and Kun join in accord, they produce the trigrams Kan and Li. In the heavens, Kan and Li are displayed dazzlingly above as the sun and moon; they govern all the myriad creatures on the earth. In the human body, Kan and Li form the 'lead' and 'mercury' – the quintessence of our very selves, which can be fashioned and formed into an inner Elixir. However these are deep and profound truths, which do not easily adapt to explanation.

Master Shangyang says: What is meant by 'as Kan and Li, they come out excelling'? Qian ☰ is firm and it joins with Kun ☷; Qian ☰ then becomes empty within and forms into Li ☲. Kun ☷ is yielding and it receives Qian ☰; Kun ☷ then becomes solid inside and forms into Kan ☵. Therefore Kan and Li follow from Qian and Kun but excel them, through coming forward out of the mixing of Yin and Yang.

Moreover as the proper positioning of the firm and yielding is attained, the sun's light within Li and the shining moon within Kan diffuse down to illuminate the world below.

Darkened, mysterious, dull and unseen, this process is difficult to fathom and understand, as it cannot be clearly defined. It is only the sages who are able to 'guess at an approximation' to it, and 'decide upon an order as a foundation' [see below].

> The sages guessed at an approximation,
> Decided upon an order as a foundation;
> These four in makeshift chaos
> Directly enter back on into the void.
>
> While the sixty hexagrams are about them
> Spread out, expanded like a carriage:
> Being yoked up with mare and dragon,
> The enlightened ruler manages the times.
>
> When at peace, he follows ahead
> Travelling a level path without turning,
> But if he strays off course he is gone,
> Overturning the family and state!

It is because these truths are so fundamentally difficult to fathom that the ancient sages resorted to allegory. They used the imagery of the *Zhou Yi* in order to elucidate this study.

Qian and Kun form the 'cauldron and furnace' within; Kan and Li are the medicinal substances from which the Elixir is made. The rest of the sixty hexagrams consequently make up the 'firing times' – through which the Elixir is taken. The analogy is with driving a carriage: as the carriage-driver sits within the carriage, his hands on the reins, so the ruler governs his state,and so the alchemic practitioner develops his inner Elixir (cf. Chapter 19).

Master Shangyang comments: The enlightened ruler in government is as one travelling a long road, he is untiring in his concern for the people. At peace with his inner spirit he follows each happening as it occurs and responds accordingly.

He continues: The true-hearted person strives to create a kingdom, only fearing that its authority is not present in the ruler; small people consider themselves first, only fearing that the power of the kingdom does not rest in themselves.

The true-hearted person and the small person belong to every place and time. The true-hearted should endure and put up with those inferior. It is right that those small accompany and follow the true-hearted. Then the kingdom's authority will not be over-turned and the whole world will be at peace.

Thus, also, in your inner development, the creation of peace comes first. When there is peace, any matter will follow the dictates of the heart and accord with it.

The Wings [to the *Zhou Yi*] say: Good fortune through peaceful joy. In your actions there is nothing doubtful [the 'small image' to Hexagram 58:1].

Thus once your affairs are finally at peace you should correct the heart, find sincerity in your purpose and protect yourself against anxiety. Then there are no obstructions and no harm is done to the production of the inner Elixir. But it can be missed by a hair's breadth! Can you not be careful?

Yuyan comments: The 'foundation' is the very root of it all. The book Awakening to Reality says: If you want to find the Valley Spirit which grows and never dies, lean upon the Dark Female and set her up as foundation ['Four-line Stanzas'].

Generally the subduing of the 'lead' and controlling of the 'mercury' wholly rests in the 'dark female'. For this reason the 'dark female' forms the very root of it all in smelting the restored Elixir.

He continues: These 'four' are the Qian and Kun, the Kan and Li. Join them together and they form one. The text refers to their 'makeshift chaos'.

The book *Pointing into the Dark* says: *Like shooting sprouts, or a dangling hem, like floss or down, north, south, east and west are all joined into one.*

This refers to the Qian and Kun, the Kan and Li joined together to form one. When they are joined together to form one, the mind and the inner energies revert to their root, passing across to enter into the void, into an obscurity and darkness, where none will ever find them!

He continues: An old saying goes: I take my spirit as a carriage while my inner strength acts as the horses.

To the end of my days I guide them on and on without ever tiring. Being never tired, they act 'as floss silk, which can barely be seen, but which in use is never failing' [*Daode Jing*, Chapter 5]. As they never fail, they also are never forgotten, yet are never aided. It is as if they are there and yet as if they are not. Thus I never find a time when I am oppressed with weariness.

When Master Guangcheng explained this to the Yellow Emperor, it was said perfectly – 'Guard the One, and thereby dwell in peace. Thus I have cultivated myself over some 1200 years and my body has never decayed [cf. *Zhuangzi*, Chapter 11].'

The body is like a kingdom, the mind is like a ruler. If the mind is settled, then the spirit is focused and the inner energy at peace.

He concludes: For the main part, the energy and blood which dwell within the human body should never really be disturbed. This work of the inner development of an Elixir is actually 'very simple and very easy'; it involves no more than protecting the original energy within and 'guarding the One'. You open out yourself inside until you soften up and become like a little child or newborn babe.

Therefore the occasion of fashioning an inner Elixir involves no other techniques but emptying the mind and stilling it to a single point. You focus the mind until it enters into the 'burrow of the energy', whilst you follow after its progress, continuously, without hurrying, and without a single interruption.

After a long while, then the mind itself comes into focus and the breathing itself settles.

As the breathing settles, so the inner energy gathers itself together; and, as the inner energy gathers itself together, so the inner Elixir is formed. Again this does not make any use of any rubbing, or massage, or the tiring practice of any breath-technique or manipulation of thought.

2

THE PERSON OF TRUE VIRTUE
WHO FULLY UNDERSTANDS

From the very beginning, guard against the severe troubles which can arise from a failure to refine the Elixir properly. These troubles are described in detail below. The hexagrams, which depict the cycle of the moon phases, are used in this task, along with the cycling five elements, wood, fire, earth, metal or gold, and water, the basis of Chinese science.

'When the person of true virtue who fully understands
Comes out with words of goodness,
One thousand miles and beyond there is a response':
As it is said . . .

'Even the Lord of ten thousand chariots
Who takes his seat 'tween heaven's realms,
Calls an order yet obeys
The regulation of Yin and Yang.'
So store up your ability, and await the time,
Not to disobey the hexagrams of the moon.

Sprouting Forth is used midnight and afternoon,
Innocence applies early dawn and late e'en,
The remainder of the sixty hexagrams
Each has its own day;
Merely extend these two images,
You cannot scrutinize them all fully.

Standing by righteousness devise penalties,
Acting through human-heartedness bestow powers,
Rebel against them – then misfortune,
Yield to them – then good fortune.

This section uses the metaphor of a ruler governing his kingdom. The first three lines are from the Great Appendix (I.8) to the *Zhou Yi*. The idea here is not to lose the opportunity of timing the firing of the inner Elixir. The idea of the sixty hexagrams of the moon which govern the firing is a theme carried over from the first chapter. When the opportunity has not yet come one should wait in stillness; when the opportunity arrives one should act swiftly!

As stillness reaches its extreme point, it turns to movement. The Sprouting Forth hexagram ䷂ depicts the active sprouting of young plants. The inner body of this hexagram takes in the time of 'midnight', and the outer body the time of 'afternoon'. This is the same as in Chapter 19, where it states, 'Spring and summer receive substance within, from midnight reaching to late morn.'

Movement turns ultimately to stillness. The Innocence hexagram ䷘ depicts a time of retreat and withdrawal. The inner body of this hexagram takes in the time of 'early dawn', and the outer body the time of 'late e'en'. This is the same as in Chapter 19, where it states, 'Autumn and winter match their use outside, from midday to late evening' (see Figure 6).

These two hexagrams only serve as an example; the others cannot be rigidly applied to every case. The idea here is the same as in Chapter 19, where it states, 'Reward and punishment echo spring and autumn, confusion and understanding come as heat and cold, righteousness and human-heartedness are spoken of in the lines, joy and anger arise with the times.'

If you follow this one rule, your inner development is fulfilled. If you do not it must lead to corruption and decay.

Master Shangyang comments: In the Great Appendix [I.8] to the *Yi Jing* it states: When the person of true virtue who fully understands comes out with words of goodness, one thousand miles and beyond there is a response. How much more so will this happen within yourself!

It also states: Words and deeds are the hinge and lynch-pin of the true-hearted person. The action of the hinge and lynch-pin determines success or disgrace. His words and deeds influence heaven and earth. Can he then not be careful!

It also states: Consider and then say it; think carefully and then act. Considering and thinking carefully you will be successful in effecting transformation.

He continues: The method is ultimately wordless. But if there are no words, then how can it be revealed? What is meant by 'word-less' only implies that the words of a virtuous scholar should be well chosen. How much more so then should the actions and methods of one who is developing the Elixir!

Laozi said: Those who know, do not speak: those who speak, do not know [*Daode Jing*, Chapter 56].

Yuyan comments: The scholar who practises the inner develop-ment of the Elixir contains his light until it reaches a single point; he 'reflects back his brightness to light up within [*huiguang neizhao*]'. In this 'utter emptiness' and with a 'deep sense of peace', the very breath itself of heaven and earth arrives, and is restored [cf. *Daode Jing*, Chapter 16].

How does this come about? 'When "here" is touched, then "there" responds.' This is the principle behind spontaneous and natural development.

He carries on: The plan when refining the Elixir is first to know the moment it is coming. Whilst waiting for this moment, and before it has arrived, just contain your light until it reaches the one single point, taking a humble attitude and awaiting it. This is all you can do. You cannot make it come any earlier.

He continues: Midnight, afternoon, early dawn and late e'en simply stand for midnight, midday, dawn and dusk, or spring, summer, autumn and winter, or tortoise and snake, dragon and tiger. They are all simply speaking in allegory [see Figure 6].

Now when you use the sixty hexagrams to observe these changes, they begin in Sprouting Forth [Hexagram 3] and Inno-cence [Hexagram 4], and end in Already Over [Hexagram 63] and Not Yet Over [Hexagram 64]. In between there occur the Yin lines and Yang lines, all interweaved together. And yet although each hexagram is dissimilar, through each following on as an inversion of the other, each can be united with the other.

Really all these hexagrams are exactly the same. What Wei Boyang means when he says 'merely extend these two images, you cannot scrutinize them all fully', is that those who want to under-stand must closely observe the images of the two hexagrams Sprouting Forth and Innocence. From these two, you can get a general idea which can be developed. Then you can identify the meaning of the rest of the hexagrams.

In general a hexagram has six lines. Two hexagrams then have twelve lines, which corresponds to the twelve double-hours in a

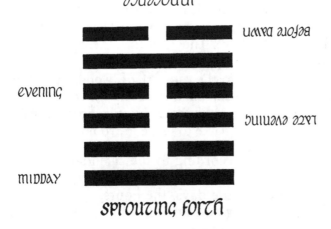

Fig. 8 Sprouting Forth and Innocence

day. Sixty hexagrams have three hundred and sixty lines, which correspond to the three hundred and sixty double-hours in a single month.

Wei Boyang's original idea is simply to borrow these hexagrams in order to talk about the unions and disunions, openings and closings within the timing of the firing of an Elixir within his own body. And this is everything. It is just the same when moving on to the hexagrams Waiting [Hexagram 5], and Lawsuit [Hexagram 6] where one would say: 'Waiting uses midnight and afternoon, Lawsuit makes use of early dawn and midday.' And then shifting on to the Army [Hexagram 7] and Relating [Hexagram 8] and saying: 'The Army uses the latter part of the night [yin chou], Relating uses the early part of the afternoon [wei shen].' The other hexagrams would follow similarly. Thus the text says, 'Merely extend these two images, you cannot scrutinize them all fully.' [See Figure 23].

He continues: The western direction signifies righteousness; the eastern direction signifies human-heartedness. Penalties command killing and subduing; powers command the giving and bringing of life.

Now the text says 'standing by righteousness devise penalties' which means to work with the 'lead' of the western direction. 'Acting through human-heartedness bestow powers' signifies refining the 'mercury' of the eastern direction.

Lead belongs to the category of 'metals'. It is by nature extremely firm and unyielding, and it lies stored up within the trigram Kan ☵. If it is not fiercely heated and worked hard, it cannot sublimate and fly upwards above. Thus you use a fierce flame to compel it upwards. Do not apply just a mild heat.

Mercury belongs to the category of 'wood'. It is naturally extremely soft and yielding, and it lies hidden within the trigram Li ☲. If it once meets with the true lead it is spontaneously arrested. Thus you use a mild flame to refine it. Do not apply a fierce heat.

> Press on according to the calendar,
> With total sincerity and accuracy,
> Watching the days, the hours,
> The ebbing and flowing of time.
> The minutest errors
> Bring the plunder of remorse.
>
> When the solstices are out of true,
> Crooked and no longer in line,
> In deep winter it brings great heat,
> And in high summer frost and snow;
> Once the two equinoxes disagree
> And cut across one another,
> Deluge and drought fell each other
> And tempests and storms go unchecked,
> Locusts burst out and boil over,
> Flocks of sheep run this way and that,
> In the sky strange sights are seen,
> Mountains collapse and the earth rips open!
>
> Once the dutiful son sets his mind,
> He affects the ridgepole of the sky.
> And what comes out from his own mouth
> Spreads afar to unfamiliar lands,
> Perhaps it causes calamity,
> Or else it brings happiness,
> Sometimes an Age of Great Peace,
> Or else war and revolution.
> All of these happen entirely
> Because of his own felt convictions.

This section is entirely based upon images taken from the natural world. To 'press on according to the calendar' means to develop an inner sincerity of purpose founded upon the natural rhythms of the heavens; the pattern of the solstices and equinoxes show the prevalence of the natural law.

Deluge, drought, calamity, war or revolution; these all follow a breakdown in this law. It is only in stillness and quiet that the elixial crystal can be formed. Only as one's thoughts are corrected are the conditions ripe for its inward creation.

Master Shangyang says: Generally, the method of the Elixir does not uniquely derive from oneself: it also derives from nature. If nature is interfered with, one must use one's own property, one's treasure, one's own pure sincerity, in order to influence it. It is not permitted to turn against the natural law. If you can follow, and go along with it, then the Golden Elixir is made!

Therefore the hexagram People At One [Hexagram 13:5] says, 'People at one first howl and wail, later they laugh.'

The 'Wings' [Great Appendix I:8] comment by saying: The ways of a person of true virtue bring him sometimes into the world, whilst sometimes they keep him at home; sometimes he is silent, sometimes he speaks out. If two people are at one in their hearts, their words can cut through and sever metal, while the speech of their single heart sounds out as sweet as orchids.

The hexagram of People At One ☰ signifies people together, who are at one in their hearts. In this hexagram there is one Yin line and five Yang. When the Yin are more and the Yang less, the Yang exerts an influence; when the Yang are more and the Yin less, the Yin exerts an influence. The hexagram People At One uses a solitary Yin line which exists along with the old Yang lines. Hence if you want to acquire the heart of People At One you must cut it through and sever it.

Therefore the person of true virtue, who fears the secret wrongs and misdoings of others, has no truck with false speech but upholds words of distinction. As there are troubles in completing the method of the Elixir, you must always believe in yielding to the natural law and upholding it.

Yuyan says: Heaven and earth have their night and day, their dawn and dusk; man's body also has its night and day, its dawn and dusk. Heaven and earth have their new moon and full moon; man's body also has its new moon and full moon. Between these two, cold and heat arrive, passing backwards and forwards; and Yin and Yang successively face away.

Examine then how we are altogether similar to heaven and

earth. In the method of the Elixir you take the sky as the cauldron and the earth as the furnace. You take the moon as the functional medicine and, to pluck it out, you must keep a watch on its waxing and waning; you take the sun as the method of timing its firing and, wherever you are, you must observe daily its rising and setting. From beginning to end, every instant, you must be united with these mysteries of the universe.

> Movement and quiet follow a regular pattern,
> So receive with both hands their dark reins.
> Then as the four seasons yield as they should,
> Their energies adapt to each other –
> Hardening then softening, softer then harder,
> Without interference, the one from the other.
> The cycling five guarded at the boundary
> In order wax and wane;
> Changing, they assist in the flow,
> Bending, stretching and returning.

The idea of the 'dark reins' occurs again in Chapter 19 – they are dark because they lead into darkness. This section continues on the theme of timing the firing of the Elixir. The ways of heaven and earth tie in closely with the ways of man, and so, only by following on closely the natural law can we reach a final conclusion.

Spring and summer, autumn and winter, hardening and softening, brightening and darkening, these all depict the varying degrees of intensity of the fire which smelts the Elixir. As the cycling five, the 'wood, fire, gold (metal), earth and water', are brought together as one, in their progression they form the key to the formation of the Elixir.

Yuyan comments: In general when the cycling five are scattered they circulate the body as an inner energy; as they are gathered together they form a precious jewel at the dantian [lower belly]. Now through them being guarded and focused at the dantian, you are not thrown out by their wax and wane. So then their form is fused together and transformed into a single energy, which distils into the true Golden Fluid.

He goes on: Change is no more than the sun and moon. The sun and moon travel the path of the ecliptic and the nights and days come and go, turning about without cease.

Fig. 9 Yin and Yang, Po-soul and Hun-soul

During the first half of the month, the Yang is extending and the Yin contracting, the Hun-soul growing and the Po-soul ebbing; during the second half of the month, the Yin is extending and the Yang contracting, the Hun-soul ebbing and the Po-soul growing. These two circulate around, turning about and returning, without ever ending.

In man's body his head occupies the position of Qian while the belly occupies the position of Kun; which is just the same as in heaven and earth. Their two inner energies rise above and fall below, just as they do in heaven and earth.

He continues: The key here lies in the two vessels, the Governing [*du*] and Supporting [*ren*] vessels of the body. For the most part the Governing and Supporting vessels stand for the whole Yin and Yang of the body, they are the true source of the inner energies of the five main organs (heart, liver, spleen, lungs and kidneys). Here is how they work jointly together.

The Supporting vessel rises from the very lowest central point of the body and travels up across the border of the pubic hair, following inside the body to arrive at the 'gate primal' [the acupuncture point Ren 4]. It finally arrives at the throat and is entrusted with the task of being the sea of all Yin vessels. The Governor vessel rises from the actual lowest point of the body and travels up within the spine to the 'palace of the winds' the [acupuncture point Du 16]. There it enters into the brain and rises up to the crown, following the forehead down to the bridge of the nose. It is entrusted with being the sea of all the Yang vessels.

He concludes: The Immortals' manuals of longevity have a saying which proceeds as follows: Standing, walking, sitting, lying, turn round Kan to meet up with Li.

And again they say: Quietly, and in your own time, will you learn the method of longlife. Then day and night, without a sound, turn around the wheel of prayer.

3

SECRETLY HIDDEN AWAY AND
FORGOTTEN

Now the work of Kan and Li (the moon and the sun) as Yin and
Yang, is depicted. For all the myriad things of this world depend
on them as they, in turn, depend on the Wu- and Ji-soils which are
positioned at the Central Palace.

> Secretly hidden away and forgotten,
> Change is happening in their midst;
> Completely enwrapped, all manner of things
> Form the guiding thread to the method.

This section describes the method of the energies of Yin and Yang,
as they lie secretly hidden away and engulfed in the body. They lie
'forgotten' in the depths of each person, or else they generate
change in the midst of all manner of material things, or else they
energetically set about their task of promoting living and killing.
In all these ways they form the 'guiding thread' to the Elixial path.

Master Shangyang comments: If these were not the functions of
Qian and Kun, and the guiding thread to the mysterious path, then
we might expect the path to cease!

Yuyan comments: In general the mother of the Golden Elixir is
no more than the one single energy of the prenatal inner world
[*xiantian yi qi*]. This is all it is. Split it apart and it becomes two.
Divide it up further and it becomes three. Scatter it apart and it
turns into the ten thousand myriad things. But every possible thing
derives from out of this one single energy.

   Thus the text says, 'Completely enwrapped, all manner of things
form the guiding thread to the method.' This signifies the method
of the Golden Elixir.

> Taking nothingness to create being,
> The apparatus works through its emptiness.
> Thus concluding with an ebb and flow,
> Where Kan and Li never lose out.
>
> These words I have not carelessly written,
> Their discussion not vainly begun,
> Guided by experience, I have seen obvious results
> Comparable to the divine light;
> I have argued by analogy, with characters
> Drawn from real life as proof:

This section continues to explore the subtle function of the trigrams Kan ☵ and Li ☲. The author emphasizes that this work draws on his own practical experience.

The lines of trigrams Kan and Li are not fixed in position in the manner of the lines of the other trigrams: yet neither are they without any role to play at all. They take control over each of the other trigrams – Zhen, Dui, Qian, Sun, Gen, Kun – this is what is meant by using 'nothingness' to create 'being'. In this whole wide world it is only 'nothingness' which is of practical use – in generating the 'ebb and flow'. 'Being' means materiality, whose functioning exists through virtue of emptiness and openness.

Master Shangyang says: 'Taking nothingness to create being, the apparatus works through its emptiness' – nothingness and being are paired together here. Why is this so?

When the supreme pole [*taiji*] splits apart, there come into being the prenatal inner and postnatal outer worlds.

What is meant by the prenatal? It is all that 'precedes form' – which means the Dao, the Path, the Method; which is being entering into nothingness. What is meant by the postnatal? It is all that 'succeeds form' – which means an apparatus, a capacity, or an ability; which is nothingness entering into being. [The origin of these ideas of 'preceding form' and 'succeeding form' is in the Great Appendix I.12.]

Laozi said: The nameless is the beginning of heaven and earth, the named is the mother of the myriad things [*Daode Jing*, Chapter 1]. There is also another saying: Entering into being from nothingness, they all do this! Entering into nothingness from being, how many of them do this?

If people conclude with the work of the ebb and flow of Kan

and Li, then their work is all in the outer world and postnatal, meaning it involves the 'apparatus', the 'form', the dregs of matter; which is never far apart from the ebb and flow. This is by no means as important as the inner world and the prenatal. Therein you have the method of everlasting life and are able to attain to the foothills of the lands of the sages!

He continues: The men of the world give themselves over to walking the path of the postnatal. Thus they have a single life, a single death and the wheel of life and death turns on without cease.

The sages were good at turning back [*ni*] to make use of the path of the prenatal. Thus they reached a knowledge of all things. They corrected their hearts and developed their inner souls, and their ideas were preserved a long time without fading.

Our destiny proceeds away from us and we are given over to it. To know how it arrives within us is to turn it back upon itself. Thus the true method of mastering change lies in turning back our destiny [Cf. the 'Shuogua' appendix to the *Zhou Yi*, Chapter 3].

He continues: What is meant by 'arguing by analogy, with characters drawn from real life as proof'? It is, for instance, the Elixir being born from out of the idea of the moon phases; or else water being used to represent the trigram Kan, or else the sun and moon which take the lead in forming the model of change. These are all the 'characters'.

'Drawing from real life as proof' means Yin moving to an extreme and then becoming Yang, or Yang moving to an extreme and then turning to Yin. To go and proceed along with Yin and Yang is to enable the birth of man and all material things; to turn back the applicability of Yin and Yang is to complete the Golden Elixir. This is real life!

Yuyan comments: The *Daode Jing* [Chapter 11] says: Thirty spokes share a single hub but it is space within which makes the carriage useful. Turn clay to make a pot and it is the space within which makes it useful. Cut doors and windows to make a house and it is the space within which makes them useful. Thus any benefit comes from what is there – any usefulness comes from what is not there.

He continues: These three [*a carriage, a pot, a house*] are all metaphors for the usefulness of emptiness. Thus the verse says: Any benefit comes from what is there; any usefulness comes from what is not there.

A carriage, a pot, and a house are all really of benefit; but the usefulness of a carriage, a pot, or a house comes from them having space and emptiness within. Now this is what Wei Boyang signifies by 'taking nothingness to create being, the apparatus works through its emptiness'. Actually this is exactly the same idea as Laozi's.

Now the method of the Elixir takes the Great Void as its cauldron and furnace, whilst within this Void we have the subtle practice of natural law at work. Something so rare indeed!

There is an old saying which goes: A cloth shaken in empty space creates a breeze, blowing out onto something solid creates droplets of water.

The implication is that if you know how something shaken in empty space can create a breeze, then blowing with your own inner bellows you will create a subtle energy; and if you know how blowing out onto something solid can create droplets of water, then the subtle energy of your own holy spiritual foetus will be able to transform your inner seed.

Anyone who misunderstands this, and seeks something other as cauldron and vessel, is not following the path which proceeds out the Great Void. This is all there is to say.

He continues: 'Flowing' means the time of advancing the firing – the three lines of Kun all change into Qian; 'ebbing' means the time the token retreats – the three lines of Qian all change into Kun.

Now from the moment of the new moon, when Zhen ☳ takes up the work, you pass through Dui ☱ to reach Qian ☰. After the full moon has ended, and Sun ☴ has taken up the work, you pass through Gen ☶ to reach Kun ☷. The lines of Kan and Li are not seen in this sequence [see Chapter 4].

> The Kan and Wu-soil are the moon's essence,
> The Li and Ji-soil form the light of the sun.
> As the sun and moon together form Change
> The firm and yielding fit as they ought.
>
> With the earth ruling over the four seasons
> Connecting them from beginning to end,
> Green, red, white and black,
> Each find their own station;
> All endowed from the Central Palace
> With the work of Wu and Ji.

This final section advances the idea of Kan and Li matched together in the Central Palace of the element 'soil' (earth).

Kan ☵ is the moon, and it receives centrally within Wu-soil; the Wu-soil finds its source in Qian ☰, the Yang line stored within the Yin lines, like a fine essence protected within. Li ☲ is the sun, and it receives centrally Ji-soil; the Ji-soil finds its source in Kun ☷, the Yin line attached to the Yang lines, while a bright light is displayed outside.

When the sun's light and the moon's fine essence merge together in the Central Palace, they are as Yin and Yang which make a perfect match.

Spring, summer, autumn and winter all have their time. In the cycling five elements, 'wood (spring), fire (summer), metal (autumn) and water (winter)', each one governs its own season — but only through its dependence upon the central element of 'soil'. Herein lies the main factor in the practical work of developing an Elixir.

The easterly direction and green dragon belong to 'wood'; the westerly direction and white tiger belong to 'metal'; the southerly direction and scarlet bird belong to 'fire', and the northerly direction and 'dark warrior' (tortoise and snake entwined) belong to 'water' (see Figure 6).

Metal and wood conquer each other; fire and water also conquer each other. Whilst developing an Elixir you should resolve their differences to enable the four images and five elements to get along together. Then you will have success. But this all comes about through the adaptation of each element to the other, which is brought about by the true 'soil' of the Central Palace.

Master Shangyang comments: Kan, the Wu-soil, the moon and its fine essence are properly established due north as Kan ☵. Central to their shape lies the true 'soil', which is the Yang-soil. This 'secretly hidden away' Yang essence is the Wu-soil which is the central 'gateway', the hub of the moon wherein lies concealed the 'hornless rabbit'; it is white within and black without. It is the Yang within the Yin, being female without and male within.

Li, the Ji-soil, the sun and its light are properly established due south as Li ☲. Central to their shape lies the true 'soil', which is the Yin-soil. This 'forgotten' Yin light is the Ji-soil which is the central 'door', the wheel of the sun wherein lies concealed the 'three-legged crow'; it is black within and white without. It is the Yin within the Yang, being male without and female within.

He concludes: Firstly these lines speak of each separate Yin and Yang as 'fitting together' in position; then they mention 'each finding its own station'. All other views misrepresent our Immortal's true intended meaning.

Yuyan comments: Now if you do not come into harmony with the 'true soil', Yin and Yang are mislaid and set apart, the firm and the yielding split apart and you cannot form the Elixir. Alas indeed!

Wei Boyang wrote this book in order to elucidate the secrets of the Elixial method. He always had the idea of being 'guided by experience', of seeing what were the obvious results of his work and of observing what actually worked.

Later fearing that his views would not be emphatic enough to convince those coming after him, he also took, as comparison, the divine light of the sun and moon and used them as his model.

Zhu Yuanyu comments: In general, Kan and Li form two different things; but these two things are never apart from the true 'soil', and so these three (Kan, Li and the 'soil') form the 'three families' [see Chapter 14].

If you mention the 'two families', it is the four images which appear; if you mention the 'three families', it is the cycling five

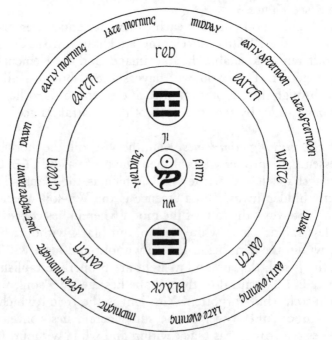

Fig. 10 Kan the moon and Li the sun

which appear. Now the medicinal substances and the timing of the firing both appear! The great function of Qian and Kun is exhausted in the Kan and Li, whilst the mysterious application of the Kan and Li is encompassed totally through the Wu- and Ji-soils. Herein lies the key to understanding this book, the *Can Tong Qi*.

4

THE MATCHING OF THE MOON-PHASES

This chapter illustrates the refining of the Elixir by relating it to the moon-phases taken throughout a complete month; this is named the 'lesser circuit of the sky'. The sexual union of Yin and Yang, depicted in the joint union of the sun and moon at the new moon, begins the work. The Yang lines, or 'nines', depict the proceedings; they rise and sink, resembling the 'ancestry of change'.

> At the interval of the new moon,
> As the match arrives, something occurs within –
> Chaotically, through a teeming void,
> As male and female tail one another
> Excitedly, their juices shimmering,
> Produce a transformation throughout –
> The divine light of heaven and earth
> Cannot be truly calculated,
> It is best to practise quietening the self,
> And conceal away the body:

This important section describes the coming into union of Kan (the moon) and Li (the sun), and the birth of the medicine, which is all echoed in the successive moon-phases of a single month. They are what are known as the 'firing times of the lesser circuit of the sky'.

At the time of the new moon, the sun and moon are united together, male and female follow one another, and Yin and Yang are linked as one. This depicts, in the human body, the actual time Kan and Li intertwine, the 'living midnight' when the medicinal substance of the Elixir is created. This transformation, which involves the 'divine light of heaven and earth', is something totally mysterious, it cannot be 'truly calculated'. [See Figure 11]

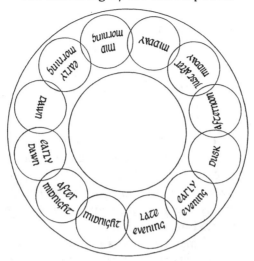

Fig. 11 The hours

Once the medicine has been formed and before it is made use of, it should be stored away carefully until the moment it can be consumed. Thus it is best to practise 'quietening and concealing away' the self.

Master Shangyang says: This chapter uses as an illustration the phases of the moon. Thus it relates them to the action of the lines as they match.

He continues: The method and nature of this Golden Elixir is subtle and mysterious. Though it is of 'heaven and earth', it cannot be fathomed; and although it gives a 'divine light', it 'cannot be calculated'. So then what is it? It is the refined energy of the prenatal inner world.

The sages' goodness lay in their joining together of their virtue with heaven and earth; they turned back the forces of creation in order to generate a refined energy. The sages' ability lay in the joining together of their light with the sun and moon; they inverted the sun and moon's function in order to circulate around this refined energy. The sages' craft lay in them joining in step with the order of the four seasons; they made use of this refined energy and thus cold and heat did not detain each other. The sages' latent strength lay in their joining together in fortune with the ghosts and spirits; they succeeded in this refined energy and the ghosts and spirits were given visible form.

Therefore again the divine light of heaven and earth 'cannot be calculated'. It is only the sages that are capable of discerning it.

Yuyan comments: 'Chaotically, through a teeming void' describes the one single energy before it has split apart; 'male and female tail one another' as Yin and Yang run together in its midst, before they are yet distinguishable.

At the point of time when they are distinguishable, the mind is focused, the inner energies gathered together and fused into one single mass. Inside you are without awareness of yourself; whilst outside you are without knowledge of the world. Along with the Dao, all your plans are obscured and merged into one – and altogether abandoned into the infinite.

This is not something which it is possible to name. If I had to name it I would call it 'Great Oneness holding to himself the true energy', or else it could be called 'the one single energy of the prenatal inner-world.'

He continues: Now to develop oneself within a divine Immortal is like nothing else in its skilful accomplishment. It is simply to capture and get hold of the one single energy of the prenatal inner world, which can then be taken as the mother of the Golden Elixir.

He continues: Yet this 'capturing' is a capturing through not capturing; and this 'getting hold of' means getting hold of through not getting hold of. The process consists in being silent and still within and not moving, so that it is possible for it to happen.

The old saying goes: It does not rest in the weariness of the world nor in the hills, it must directly be sought in obscurity and sober skills.

How is it that anyone can doubt this? The people of the present-day world do not understand the ancestry of the Great Method. Either they point to the 'true lead', or the 'single oneness of heaven generating water', or the 'single point of energy which shines betwixt the two kidneys', or the 'space beneath the navel', or the 'tip of the nose', or the 'shine in the eyes', or the 'inner circulation of the breath' as the prenatal.

But these are all partial views which search among the branches or pluck away at the dried stalks of knowledge. They are nothing to do with the prenatal energies of the Great Method.

He continues: The poem goes: A thousand miles, from the dark depths, the springtime breezes join – from the nine-layered heavens, the penetrating dew on the flower condenses.

This is mysterious indeed! Yet it gives a true picture of the moment of intercourse between Yin and Yang. The pure clear consciousness (*shen*) flows through and about, reaching every small corner – above it borders on the sky, below it coils around the earth. It obscures everything, like mists around the hills; soaking through everything, like fogs enveloping the waters; whiting out and freezing, like snow slowly settling; sinking and setting, like jumbled thick soup slowly clearing . . .

These are the enshrouding mists of heaven and earth, the mingling embrace of man and woman, which happens within your own body!

He concludes: 'Believe me indeed! Only when you forget form and lose all sense of anything at all happening here, will you see what is meant! If you should retain any thought, idea, or calculation in your mind, it is not what is meant by the divine!

At the new moon, the sun and moon are remade, together in the northern realms; their light and brightness is hidden away and unseen.

The Elixial Method takes this moment – when one day changes to another. In the middle of the night, join them together in intercourse in the belly of Kun. Coil up your legs and sit up straight, solid as a rock fixed and unmoving upon the mountainside. Your mouth sealed, closed off with your tongue and breath – just like a snake curled up in its winter hibernation.

This is the practice of 'quietening the self and concealing away the body'.

> Beginning in the north-east,
> The constellation Sagittarius
> Turns to the right, the wheel spins,
> And out it shoots from the very depths,
> A shape seen – appearing,
> Scattering a fine light:
>
> And far above in the Pleiades –
> Here comes Zhen! ☳ The first crack
> Of Yang energy strung on a string.
> 'The first nine, the submerged dragon'.
>
> Yang takes three to get going,
> Yin takes eight to move freely,
> On the third day Zhen ☳ stirs,

On the eighth day Dui ☱ acts.
'The second nine, the dragon seen'.

Good-tempered, brightening,
On the fifteenth day its power is complete,
And Qian's ☰ body fully formed.
'The third nine, in the evening apprehension'
At the failing of the magic charm.
Fullness and decline gradually turn,
In the end reverting again to the beginning.

After the medicine is formed, it is further brewed in order to form it into an elixir. The timing of this firing of the medicine is crucial.

The first ten lines here describe the single Yang line of Gen ☶ turning about to become Zhen ☳. The 'downturned bow' of the moon belongs to Gen and the north-east (see Figure 6). The lines beginning 'Yang takes three to get going' describe the advancement of the Yang. Three is the number of the younger Yang and of Zhen (wood), the youngest son; eight is the number of the older Yin and Dui (metal), the eldest daughter (see Figure 7).

Fig. 12 The Lesser Circuit of the Sky

When the power of the Yang is complete, at the time of the full moon in Qian ☰ then, as the Yang moves to its extreme, so the Yin is born. This is the cause of the apprehension. Very gradually, Qian ☰ turns to Sun ☴ (see below); finally, the whole cycle reverts back again to its beginning.

> Sun ☴ comes forward to continue the lead,
> Determined to maintain support.
> 'The fourth nine, perhaps kicking forward'
> And slipping back on its perilous path.
> Gen ☶ is halting the advance
> And we cannot avoid its hour,
> On the twenty-third day its special charge
> Is the final quarter of the moon.
> 'The fifth nine, the flying dragon'
> Seated in the sky, good fortune for all!
>
> On the thirtieth day Kun ☷ takes a hold,
> Bound in her arms are the past, present and future,
> Her children are kept close and fed,
> For to this world she is mother-in-kind.
> 'The topmost nine, the arrogant dragons'
> Fighting for power in the open wild.
>
> The use of the dragon-nines flying to and fro
> Are as square and compasses to the path,
> The fate of the Yang lines once settled,
> Returning, they will arise again:
> Extending sympathies, joining in their natures,
> Turning – each giving to the other,
> As driven by jade gears on pearl bearings,
> Rising – then sinking down below
> To circulate throughout all six lines.
> They are difficult to observe
> And without regular position:
> The ancestry of change.

Sun ☴, Gen ☶ and Kun ☷ describe the retreat of the Yang. The Yang energies are gradually condensing within the cauldron and gathering together.

Qian is the father and Kun is the mother, the eldest son and daughter are Zhen and Sun, the middle son and daughter are Kan

and Li, whilst the youngest son and daughter are Gen and Dui (see
Figure 7). All six children depend upon their parents; if one parent
was lacking they could not survive. They depend upon their Qian-
father to begin with and on their Kun-mother to carry them
through to the end.

In the cultivation of the medicine of the Golden Elixir it is the
same. The Qian trigram is pure Yang, and as the Yang reaches its
final end it turns into a flock of 'arrogant dragons'. The arrogant
dragons and the pure Yin fight together, producing the 'dark skies'
which cover over the 'yellow earth' (cf. *Book of Change*, text to
the top line in Hexagram 2, the Receptive); whilst within their
struggle is born again the Yang essence, once more forming the
body of Zhen and the new moon.

The use of the dragon-nines, flying to and fro, illustrates the
double function of Kan and Li, which follows around inexhaustibly.

This whole process describes the fashioning of a Golden Elixir.
It begins at the new moon, with Kan repressing Li, which lays the
groundwork for the Elixir. Then we pass through Zhen, Dui,
Qian, Sun, Gen and Kun; three Yin and three Yang rise and fall;
the sun advances and the moon retreats, and then the moon
advances and the sun retreats.

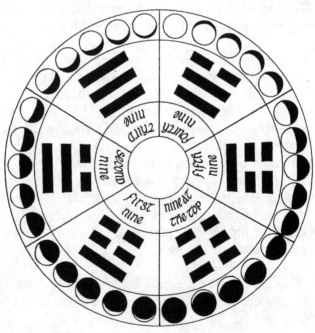

Fig. 13 Moon-phases, trigrams and nines

Note that in this process, Kan and Li do not appear directly, but everything draws its motion from their function.

Yuyan says: In this section, use is made of the six trigrams which derive from the prenatal inner-world diagram [Figure 4]; the six lines [nines] of the Qian hexagram act as an image of the waxing and waning of the moon's body.

At the same time some use is made of the passage of the moon through the stars. But it is all metaphor. Those who try to learn without properly understanding the meaning behind this rhyme will find great trouble in reading it. But then it is not unusual to find people whose hearts and eyes are completely dulled over.

The inner development of the Elixir and the 'timing of its firing' are no different at all from the ebbing and flowing of the phases of the moon.

He continues: Wei Boyang uses the six trigrams to illustrate the 'firing times' of the Elixir, but he also matches them with the six lines of the hexagram Qian. Why does he do this?

Because the Elixir is the most precious treasure of the purest Yang, and Qian is the hexagram of the purest Yang.

He concludes: The number nine is the number of the Yang. The Book of Change says that 'three is assigned to heaven and two to earth, and from these come the other numbers' [from the 'Shuogua', the Eighth Wing].

Now when using the five elements' 'generated' numbers, heaven is one, heaven is three and heaven is five. The three heavenly numbers accord with each other to form nine ($1+3+5=9$). Earth is two, and earth is four and both earthly numbers accord with each other to form six ($2+4=6$). This explains the use of the sixes in Kun and the use of the nines in Qian.

The Elixial method mentions the 'use of the dragon-nines' to split up the 'firing times'. In general they are modelled on Qian.

5

THE FUNCTION OF THE SHIFTING LINES

This important chapter complements Chapter 4. It describes the
work involved in the production of the Elixir and compares it to
the passage of the twelve months of the year, or the 'firing times of
the greater circuit of the sky'. It stresses the primacy of both Yin
and Yang, and how although 'separate they are yet joined
together'. Indeed, it is through this dark intimacy – a 'closeness
without disrespect' – that the seed of new life represented by the
Yang Elixir is born.

At the new-moon's light lies the hexagram Restored ☰☰,

And the Yang energy first begins to come through,
'Entering in and leaving without injury',
Standing outside, minute yet strong.
The Yellow Goblet stands there at midwinter,
And millions stir at its shadow.
It stimulates the weak and slack,
Until the masses find constancy.

At Approach ☰☰ the furnace is adjusted,

Starting the path to bring forth the light,
A light dazzling, gradually increasing,
Daily growing in strength,
At after-midnight's palace
Built beneath the Pleiades.

Thus now to complete Flourishing ☰☰,

With the firm and yielding prospering together,
Yin and Yang joined together as friends,
The small depart and the great arrive,
And the wheel spins on to early dawn,
Turning to keep up with the time.

Gradually comes the season of Great Vigour ䷡,
Boldly standing at the Gate to Dawn,
The elm-seeds fall down
Returning back to their roots,
And penalties and powers turn their backs
As night and day draw apart.

At Breakthrough ䷪ the Yin lines retreat,
For the Yang lines rise before them,
Flapping their feathers free
And clear of overnight dust.

The Creative ䷀ vigorous, is bold and bright,
It broadly suffers those from any direction,
The Yang reaches its end just before midday,
At the midway point of the heavenly stems.

This whole chapter illustrates how the intertwining of Qian and Kun, and the formation of an Elixir, echoes the six Yin and six Yang sections of the year. These are what are described as 'the firing times of the greater circuit of the sky'. The twelve hexagrams illustrate the shifting passage of these times (see Figure 14).

Midwinter (*zi*) can also stand for midnight, or the time of the new moon. As the 'yellow goblet (the moon) stands there at midwinter' it describes the single Yang stirring and about to be restored, which lays the foundation for forming the Elixir. As Kan (the moon) and Li (the sun) join together, they generate the medicinal materials.

When the medicine is first born, it must be worked upon. But during this time it is extremely small, and it needs stimulation in order to endure. The Yang fire is built up beneath it; whilst within the cauldron, it is gently supported until very gradually it inclines itself towards growth.

At the time of Flourishing (Hexagram 11), the number of Yin and Yang lines is equal. But it is still the time to turn up the flame – so 'the wheel spins on', increasingly rapidly. When the 'elm-seeds return back to their roots', as they do in the early spring, it is the image of 'penalties occurring within powers'.

At the spring equinox, night and day are equal in length – but thereafter they draw apart. Then the Yang lines emerge freely in Breakthrough (Hexagram 43), advancing forward; and soon the six Yang lines are fully formed into the Creative (Hexagram 1), the Yang reaches its peak, and its light is shed on all quarters.

It reaches its ultimate point just before midday, because at the peak it can only decline.

Master Shangyang comments: The last chapter spoke of the moon-phases as an idea of exploring the completion of a refined Elixir. This chapter takes the idea of the active work carried out during the twelve months of the year.

The very starting point in this work of producing an Elixir is represented by the Restored hexagram [Hexagram 24]. In Restored a single Yang line crouches under five Yin lines. The saints and sages undertook this work and acted so that they might transcend and rise above the common things of life in order to enter into sagehood.

He continues: Confucius said that the idea of 'being restored' formed the very core of heaven and earth ['Tuan' commentary to Hexagram 24]. The common people of this world do not understand this core. Laozi named it the 'dark female' [*Daode Jing*, Chapter 6], while in Buddhism it is referred to as 'the gateway to life and door to death'.

He continues: 'At the new-moon's light lies the hexagram Restored, and the Yang energy first begins to come through.' This signifies what lies at the heart of the sages attaining the One. In the hexagram Restored, the Yang energy is first subdued so it can then be restored. The beginning Yang energies 'enter in and leave' as one, and suffer 'no harm'.

'Standing outside, minute yet strong' means that as the energy of Qian stirs, it comes out directly.

He continues: 'It stimulates the weak and slack, until the masses find constancy.' Herein lies the actual mystery involved in creating the Elixir, which may be summed up as 'closeness without disrespect'.

The 'masses' refer to the multitude. As you restore the single Yang energies to those weak and slack, they all may be returned to the constant path.

Yuyan comments: Restored [Hexagram 24] is the hexagram of the single Yang. During the day it stands for midnight, the halfway point of the night; in the month it stands for the interval from the first day until halfway through the third day; during the year it describes when the handle of the Dipper constellation sets up the first month of the year (midwinter). This is the time.

At this moment the Yang energies first appear. This illustrates the first stirring of the Yang-fire within the body.

Approach [Hexagram 19] is the hexagram of the two Yang. During the day it stands for the time the cock crows – just before the day; in the month it stands for the interval from halfway through the third day until the fifth day; during the year it describes when the handle of the Dipper sets up the second month of the year. This is the time.

During this period the Yang energies gradually move forward. This illustrates the Yang-fire gradually clearing within the body.

Flourishing [Hexagram 11] is the hexagram of the three Yang. During the day it stands for the moment of dawn; in the month it stands for the interval from the sixth day until halfway through the eighth day; during the year it describes when the handle of the Dipper sets up the third month of the year. This is the time.

At this moment the Yang energies are leaving the earth [the initiation of spring]. This illustrates the Yang-fire rising up within the body – gradually, gradually it rises and turns upwards. Quickly you should set up the 'chain water-pump', circulating it around and around, restoring the energy within the cauldron.

Great Vigour [Hexagram 34] is the hexagram of the four Yang. During the day it stands for when the sun rises up at dawn; in the month it stands for the interval from halfway through the eighth day until the tenth day; during the year it describes when the handle of the Dipper sets up the fourth month of the year. This is the time.

At this moment the Yin energies are subordinate to the Yang and all creatures assemble and appear. This illustrates the Yang-fire just halfway on within the body, with its energy well blended.

Breakthrough [Hexagram 43] is the hexagram of the five Yang. During the day it stands for early morning, the hour of the first meal; in the month it stands for the interval from the eleventh day until halfway through the thirteenth day; during the year it describes when the handle of the Dipper sets up the fifth month of the year. This is the time.

At this moment the Yang energies are already full and they draw near the borders of the sky. This illustrates how the Yang-fire within the body has climbed up above.

The Creative [Hexagram 1] is the hexagram of all six Yang. During the day it stands for nearing midday, the latter part of the morning; in the month it stands for the interval from halfway through the thirteenth day until the fifteenth day; during the year it describes when the handle of the Dipper sets up the sixth month of the year. This is the time.

During this period the Yang energies are at their peak and they spread throughout the whole world. This illustrates how the Yang-fire is rounded and full within the body, and the Elixir's light shines forth.

Yuyan concludes: The Yang reaches its end as it nears midday. At 'the midpoint of the heavenly stems' the Yang-fire's fate is ending, so then the Yin-shadow [yin fu] takes up the work.

> Encounter ䷫ begins the next sequence,
>
> 'Treading on frost . . .' at the very first,
> As at the well-bottom the spring chills,
> And midday finds a visitor in lush vegetation –
> It is a submissive and shadowy guest,
> With the Yin becoming the host.
>
> Withdrawing ䷠ their position in this world
>
> They gather in the harvest to sort out the seed,
> Cherishing their power to await the time,
> And slowing down, in dark confusion.
>
> And so Decline ䷋ clogs up and stagnates,
>
> And no new shoots are produced,
> The Yin extended, the Yang is bent up,
> Its clear name sunken and gone.
>
> Observing ䷓ weigh your strength and survey
>
> The conditions at the second month of autumn,
> Then lay by the young grain,
> That the withered may yet return to life,
>
> Shepherd's purse and wheat both shoot,
> For as they prosper so they stay alive.
>
> Tearing Apart ䷖ the body is broken,
>
> Dismembered and its form destroyed,
> The transforming energy is exhausted
> And loses the ultimate magic . . .
>
> If the path trails off then turn back again,
> Returning to the true Receptive ䷁,

To the perennial openness of the earth's features,
Retrieving the cloth of heaven's display.

There is a dark secret, remote and slight,
That separate they are yet joined together,
They respond in measure, bearing a seed –
The primacy of Yin and Yang.
In the boundless emptiness it appears in flurried confusion,
And no-one knows its beginning:
'At first deceived and losing the track
Latterly you come out in front as leader.'

Now the single Yin begins to form – for as the Yang reaches its
ultimate position the Yin is born and the trigram Sun ☴ is made.
This shows as a dark fluid within the cauldron, it shows as the
water at the bottom of the wells again beginning to chill during the
days of summer. 'Treading on frost' leads on to the idea of solid
ice, as in the text to the hexagram Receptive (Hexagram 2) in the
Book of Change.

The Yang lines now withdraw and yield to the Yin, and by Decline
(Hexagram 12) the number of Yin and Yang lines is equal. But the
Yang lines are returning to the sky and the Yin lines to the earth, so
they untwine, the situation stalls, and 'no new shoots are produced'.

Now you 'lay by the young grain, that the withered may yet return
to life'. The shepherd's purse and wheat both sprout in the autumn –
which is an image of 'powers occurring within penalties'.

At Tearing Apart (Hexagram 23) the Yang is dismembered and
nearly gone, and all of nature withered up and shrivelled. How
then can the situation ever be remedied? 'If the path trails off then
turn back again' to when heaven and earth were first closed in and
confined together. When the original spiritual soul is sunken and
obscured deep within, silent, still and unmoving, this is when the
great medicine is first born.

Just at the time of midwinter, when all things are quietly hidden
away in hibernation, the heavenly energies have fallen deep within
the earth. Then the earthly energies, with their 'perennial openness', copy this pattern and begin themselves very gradually to
'retrieve the cloth of heaven's display'.

It is a 'dark secret, remote and slight' that from heaven's high
vault to earth's dark realms, whatever it is that comes about deals
with the light of the sun and the fine essence of the moon. These
two are so similar, and deeply related – like a lodestone attracting
iron it just happens to be so.

This is 'the primacy of Yin and Yang', which bring about creation. No-one knows their beginning – but never is there even the slightest obstacle standing between them.

Master Shangyang says: 'There is a dark secret, remote and slight, that separate they are yet joined together.' In just these two lines is the most perfect and complete summary of what is meant here. The 'dark secret, remote and slight' concerns the two objects Yin and Yang. Totally hidden and secret, they can never be grasped; totally remote and slight, they can never be conceived – although in their creative capacity, they double up as heaven and earth.

'Separate they are yet joined together' meaning that the two objects Yin and Yang are 10,000 miles apart in their activity – but if they gain the 'old yellow dame' to act as match-maker, although far from each other, they come very close together. And then the two materials respond in due measure, bearing as a seed 'the primacy of Yin and Yang'.

The sages worked in this fashion and practised the Elixial method. 'In the boundless emptiness it appears in flurried confusion' and can never be grasped – which means it never has measurable shape or form. The sages inferred from this the practice of 'reversion' [ni] and turning back.

'At first deceived and losing the track, and then latterly coming out in front as leader' means softly yielding to the path and 'favouring devotion'. When the true-hearted person takes action first he is deceived and loses the Path; then he yields and achieves constancy. This is all the text from the commentary to the *Book of Change* [Receptive Hexagram 2].

Yuyan comments: Encounter [Hexagram 44] is the hexagram of the single Yin. During the day it stands for noon, the hour of midday; in the month it stands for the interval from the sixteenth day until halfway through the eighteenth day; during the year it describes when the handle of the Dipper sets up the seventh month of the year. This is the time.

At this moment the Yin energies are just born. This illustrates how the Yin-shadow starts to connect up within the body. For just as the Elixir is popped into the mouth – within a minute there bubbles back up a chilling spring within the body. You should gradually mark out its path, and help it run back down to the 'Elixial field' [*dantian*, or lower belly]. Do not panic at this or become flustered.

Withdrawal [Hexagram 33] is the hexagram of the two Yin. During the day it stands for the sun beginning to decline, after midday; in the month it stands for the interval from halfway through the eighteenth day until the twentieth day; during the year it describes when the handle of the Dipper sets up the eighth month of the year. This is the time.

During this period the Yin energies gradually lengthen. This illustrates how the Yin-shadow pulls away and apart from its central position within the body and, through contracting in, draws on downwards.

Decline [Hexagram 12] is the hexagram of the three Yin. During the day it stands for the latter part of the afternoon; in the month it stands for the interval from the twenty-first day until halfway through the twenty-third day; during the year it describes when the handle of the Dipper sets up the ninth month of the year. This is the time.

During this period the Yang energies are gradually failing. This illustrates how the Yin increasingly sweeps its shadow over and down in the body – just like the stern and forbidding air of autumn.

Observing [Hexagram 20] is the hexagram of the four Yin. During the day it stands for the time the sun sets in the west; in the month it stands for the interval from halfway through the twenty-third day until the twenty-fifth day; during the year it is when the handle of the Dipper sets up the tenth month of the year. This is the time.

During this period the Yin energies subordinate the effort of the Yang, and all creatures curl up and reduce in size. Thus it illustrates how the Yin casts its shadow more than halfway down within the body and it enters into the 'Elixial field' [lower belly].

Tearing Apart [Hexagram 23] is the hexagram of the five Yin. During the day it stands for nightfall and the late evening; in the month it stands for the interval from the twenty-sixth day until halfway through the twenty-eighth day; during the year it describes when the handle of the Dipper sets up the eleventh month of the year. This is the time.

At this moment the Yang energies have gone over and passed away, the fruit lies over-ripe and burst open on the ends of the branches, it falls and splits apart on the ground. Within the body this illustrates the Yin nearly attaining full shadow – and the ultimate magic of the Yang has practically gone.

He continues: These small and unimportant side-paths, these lesser techniques, those who practise them only know the 'One', they do not know the 'two'. So, in the end, what can they achieve?

He concludes: The Receptive [Hexagram 2] is the hexagram of the six Yin. During the day it stands for when man settles himself down, during the first half of the night; in the month it stands for the interval from halfway through the twenty-eighth day until the thirtieth day; during the year it describes when the handle of the Dipper sets up the twelfth month of the year. This is the time.

During this period the purest Yin is taking up the work and all creatures, at this time, return to their roots to recapture their destiny. This illustrates how, within the body, the Yin-shadow is at its most extreme point and silent without moving. It has returned to its origin and is again still. Thus the text says, 'If the path trails off then turn back again, returning to the true Receptive.'

Yuyan comments on the whole section: In general heaven and earth, the sun and the moon are all one and alike. The moon receives the sun's rays and the sun never fails, but the moon's light is the light of the sun. The energies of the heavens fall down upon the earth, and from within the earth are born all material things – yet these are all formed from the heavens.

Man's body is modelled on this image of heaven and earth. Within his body Yin and Yang move each other to join – which is no different from what happens in heaven and earth.

He continues: Before the night-time airs are over and passed, you need only focus the mind and gather together the inner energies, sitting upright for a short while. Then, in a little while, the mind's energies will return to their roots; so that within nothing will be born something – gradually condensing, gradually gathering and building, until it consolidates into a single seed of Golden Grain.

He continues: The single Yang is not born in the hexagram Restored [Hexagram 24], but in the hexagram Receptive [Hexagram 2]. Although the Receptive hexagram is ultimately Yin, within the Yin is born the Yang. Truly this is the actual source of the production of the medicine.

He concludes: 'In this chapter, Wei Boyang reveals his thoughts about the actual source of the production of the medicine. He also reaches the limit of the mystery of 'care' and 'neglect', of 'being' and 'nothingness', 'host' and 'guest', and 'former' and 'latter'. In this way he details them all exhaustively – without adding one word which is superfluous.

The old saying goes: 'Standing on the misty shore, you may only scoop the moon from the water. You may think you understand this but it is only phantasms in a mirror! If you do not delve into the Elixial method itself, you will never acquire any knowledge of it!

'Nothing level does not slope . . .'
This is the natural course of the path,
Change, change and change again,
Ebb and flow the cause of each other.

In the end the Receptive retrieves the beginning,
Just like the following-on links of a chain,
Thus the Emperor manages to preserve his rule
Throughout 10,000 autumns!

In the natural law of heaven and earth, Yin and Yang support, oppose, balance and counterbalance each other. They link together, ebb and flow; there is never anything preserved or cared for which is not then lost, or anything lost which does not come again and return. The six Yang and six Yin hexagrams come and go, movement turning to stillness and stillness turning to movement; the Yang fills and the Yin empties, the Yin fills and the Yang empties. And on the darkest day, or at the moment of the new moon, it is the Receptive hexagram Kun ䷁ which 'retrieves the beginning' – bringing forth her eldest son Zhen ☳ in the hexagram Restored ䷗. This motion circles round and round, turning and returning, never ending.

The mysterious functioning of the firing times for the Elixial method complies above with the movements of heaven and earth, whilst below it exists within the human body.

Inside it is able to conquer the mind, outside it conquers the world. Thus as the Emperor manages to preserve this rule, he retains his command of the people for a long time.

Yuyan says: 'Nothing level does not slope, nothing leaving does not return' [From the *Book of Change* text for Flourishing, Hexagram 11] This is the natural course of the Path.

The method of the Elixir is such that when stillness reaches its utmost point it moves, and when movement reaches its utmost

point it becomes still. Movement and stillness are linked together
at their root; they appear quite naturally, just as the sun and moon
turn about, producing cold and warmth. The warmth departs and
the cold arrives, the cold departs and the warmth arrives. There is
nothing here which is not simply the course of nature.

The firing of the Golden Elixir describes the passage of change
within the body. As change becomes exhausted, so it alters; as it
alters so it moves on. Fullness and decline resign themselves to
each other, ebb and flow are the cause of each other. In general if
something is not finally finished, it will not alter; or it will alter,
but not move on.

The Yang begins in the hexagram Restored [Hexagram 24];
the Yin comes to an end in the Receptive [Hexagram 2]; the end
and beginning are joined up to each other, 'the tail thrust into
the mouth at the head'. Thus the text says, 'In the end the Receptive retrieves the beginning, just like the following-on links of a
chain.'

Zhu Yuanyu comments: This chapter carefully outlines the firing
times for the greater circuit of the sky and complements the description given in an earlier chapter.

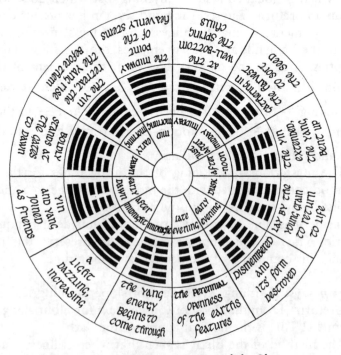

Fig. 14 The Greater Circuit of the Sky

In general, once Kan and Li join together they generate the medicine; once this great medicine is produced, it can be captured; once it is captured it can be put into the furnace and so smelted and refined. The earlier chapter described the timing of its capture; this chapter now describes the timing of its smelting process.

For its capture you must comprehend the application of the moment of the 'living midnight' [*huo zi*]. You must directly await the new moon, when both 'bows' of the moon merge and it appears in the west; then the 'gold is born within the water', in a total 'flurry of confusion', from out of a 'dark obscurity'.

Afterwards you may hunt for the original pearl within these deceptive images and apply the true fire through gentle non-action within. Thence you ultimately arrive at the moon's full disc and the Elixir is formed, and termed the Golden Elixir.

As for its smelting and refining, you must comprehend the application of the moment of the 'true midnight' [*zheng zi*]. You must directly await the moment 'just before midnight', when the single Yang begins to stir. The 'fire arises from out the water' and from then on you use the method of shutting the Supporting [*ren*] Vessel and opening up the Governing [*du*] Vessel of the body, blowing with the wind of the trigram Sun and rousing it with the bellows and tubes.

Take advantage of the fire's power, as it strengthens, to engage the 'chain water-pump' filled with precious fluid. Then convey it back up from the great original passes of the body below to the fissures of the sky far, far above.

The moment this fluid arrives, all the pulses come in tune; their blood penetrates through the joints of the body, the precious seed-essences reach the crown of the head and their silvery waters dash against the sky! This vista can never be quite described ...

Following on from this magnificent moment, when the Yang has reached its extreme point and the Yin is born, you are fully occupied with reopening the passes to withdraw back again the fire. Slowly, slowly, it falls back down; and, during this time, one should properly 'protect against mishap and take thought of danger'.

Clear the mind of troublesome thoughts in order to convey the medicine directly back into the earthenware pot, where it remains. This is what is meant by 'Directly Qian and Kun stop having intercourse, immediately pop them back into the Yellow Court!'

Once the Elixir has been put into the cauldron, you should follow the firing times of the circulating sky, dawn and dusk, etc.

Then the Elixir is able to condense and the 'holy babe' will form. Again this infant must be 'gently supported' and cared for, and also let suckle at the breast until he becomes fully formed and well shaped. Then the little child moves his house across to the 'upper field'; and the prenatal original spirit of the inner world is volatilized. It emerges and quite spontaneously body and spirit come together mysteriously as one, merging into the infinite Dao. This is the true meaning of the nine-times-cycled, golden-fluid restored Elixir.

However we are concerned with two sorts of activity here, one esoteric and the other exoteric – which are as far apart from each other as the sky and the depths of the sea!

From ancient sages and teachers these ideas have been transmitted by word of mouth and never committed to writing. Furthermore Wei Boyang never dared reveal completely the dark workings of the natural world. Instead he tentatively took the moon-phases to briefly represent the intricacies of fashioning a Golden Elixir and the six Yang and Yin hexagrams of the single year in order to reveal the task of the nine-times-cycled and fully refined and restored Elixir.

He contained within these images his secret true and proper – it described how he timed the Elixir's firing. This was so that any students of the alchemic method who had met their own teacher might understand the significance of these images and then forget them as images.

6

THE RULER AND MINISTER IN MANAGING GOVERNMENT

In this chapter, the last of those which form the first part of Wei Boyang's writings, the problems which arise in cultivating an Elixir are illustrated through samples of those difficulties which occur in government. 'Renewal' and 'recasting the old' suggest the time the 'single Yang' or inner vitality of the body returns. When the will of the people is gained, the nation is at peace; while when the whole heart is set on the task, the method of the Elixir is complete.

> At the foremost in beginning government
> Is renewal and recasting the old.
> Take control of the most intimate
> And open out what is most precious,
> The real way to the power of the throne
> Is to rule through the linking feature of Change.
>
> As the lines and images move within
> So good fortune and bad arise without:
> When the five planets obey in turn
> So they echo the effect of the times,
> But when the stars in the sky turn cruel
> They separate away from the Path's to-and-fro.
> The stars over the Dipper record the whole
> And the stars under the Dipper give their support,
> All palaces have their presiding official
> Each in charge of a particular region.

This chapter uses the analogy of governing a state. It emphasizes that the basis of good government is the same as that which lies at the heart of a careful mastery of the process of firing an Elixir. The 'most intimate' and 'most precious' aspects of Change are those which lead to a settled state.

The ruler is seen as standing in the position of the Pole Star, while the handle of the Dipper is seen as governing the whole sky and taking command over all the myriad creatures on the earth. Its progress through the skies depicts the passage of the year. The five planets Venus, Jupiter, Mercury, Mars and Saturn echo the elements metal, wood, water, fire and earth respectively. The movements of the stars and planets in the heavens are intimately linked to what happens here below on earth.

Master Shangyang comments: Our revered Immortal here speaks of difficulties in the inner development of the Elixir. An analogy is drawn with affairs of state. If you know how confusion among the people is difficult to control, then, when cultivating an Elixir, you know how errant and sudden ideas are difficult to tie down.

The old, the worn, the rough and dirty, are united together and cast anew. This is the foremost task in beginning any government.

He continues: When you 'Open out what is most precious', you find a way outside to gain the people's joyful hearts; whilst you find what is most precious within the self to be the true inner breath-energy [*qi*]. This is the 'real way to the power of the throne'.

If you rapidly open out the 'most precious' you are ruling through the 'linking feature of change'. This 'linking feature' is central to any grasp of the Elixial method. If you further perfect this rule, there is no bitter taste left at all in the application of your method.

Yuyan comments: The very first moment the single Yang stirs and creates an Elixir is likened to the very first steps taken by a ruler in government.

He continues: To 'take control of the most intimate' is for the eyes to contain their light, the ears to condense their sweetness of sound, the nose to regulate its breath and the tongue to seal up the voice. Coil your legs up under you and sit up straight. Pull your attention back into yourself and guard it within. You should not let one chink of the mind be employed outside.

Then, once the eyes are not seeing, the Hun-soul returns of itself to the liver; once the ears are not hearing, the vital secretions return of themselves back to the kidneys; once the tongue is not sounding, the attention returns of itself back to the heart; once the nose is not sensing the Po-soul returns of itself back to the lungs; and once the four limbs are not moving, the will returns of itself back to the spleen.

Then the Hun-soul rests in the liver and does not leak out from the eyes, the Po-soul rests in the lungs and does not leak out from the nose, the attention rests in the heart and does not leak out from the mouth, the vital secretions rest in the kidneys and do not leak out from the ears, and the will rests in the spleen and does not leak out openly into the four limbs.

Once these five are entirely kept from leaking out, the vital secretions, the attention, the Hun-soul and the Po-soul merge together along with the will, which carries them into action. They are fused together and destroyed until they form a single energy, which gathers in the 'Elixial field' [lower belly].

When the single breath is recovered at the nose, your own small heart is dismembered! Then the dragon and tiger storm the gate, which rolls back, showing the true path . . . a great stream flowing and winding out, full to the brim with sweet nectar wine!

He concludes: The sky has the multitude of stars spread across it, which divide up into their separate constellations; in the case of the Elixir there are the multitude of hexagrams marked out as tokens of the firing.

'All palaces have their presiding official, each in charge of a particular region.' This explains how, just as in each year the twenty-four solar periods (two to each month) are arranged across the whole of the twenty-eight constellations, so the firing times of the cauldron and furnace can also be neatly inserted in and settled.

From what is said here it is clear that the majesty of all the myriad things in heaven lies truly within your own self.

> From start to finish, a thread
> Connects care continuously to neglect.
> If the ruler wrongly proud of himself
> And full of schemes, abandons the path,
> Or a minister corrupt and persuasive
> Acts without following the track,
> Then the moon's crescent, changing,
> Obstinantly turns to blame and misfortune.
> So uphold the law on ridicule,

> And keep out errors to hand down the rule –
> As the Pole Star dwells in rectitude
> It unhurriedly bears with those below;
> From the clear-lit court extend your government,
> And the country will suffer no ruin.

This section continues the parallelism of the microcosm and macrocosm – the idea that each individual human mimics the universe. It emphasizes that the key to accuracy in timing the firing of the Elixir lies wholly within your own heart. Just as arrogance in a ruler is insulting and treachery in a minister is divisive, so the darkening of the moon's disc will obscure the true path and all will be lost.

Only hold to the centre and the state may be preserved.

Yuyan comments: The 'start' refers to the new moon; the 'finish' refers to the old moon. The thread 'connecting care to neglect' signifies the interval of the new moon. As the Yin is about to be finally extinguished, but not quite extinguished, so the Yang is about to be born, but not quite born.

However all this talk about the old and the new moon is only by way of analogy. It does not really mean that the finish of the firing should be on the twenty-eighth day of the moon or that its start on the very first day of the moon.

He continues: The ruler stands for the quiet attention of the mind [*shen*]; the minister stands for the breath. When you are fashioning an Elixir, the 'lead' and 'mercury' are returned to the 'earthenware pot'. The body and mind are settled, still and unmoving. If the body moves, then the breath scatters; if the mind moves, then the attention scatters. You must draw in the attention and gather in the breath so that mind and breath follow one another. Afterwards the 'magical foetus' can be formed.

If you do not do this then 'the moon's crescent, changing, obstinately turns to blame and misfortune' within your own body!

He concludes: There is an old saying: At the Eastern Palace, the dragon and tiger sojourn in my heart. The heart here is the same as the 'clear-lit court'.

Master Zhuxi comments drily: Here everything is written in metaphor. Yet there is also within it much which one should take great care in evaluating.

7

FOSTERING YOUR INBORN NATURE AND SECURING YOUR LIFE

Beginning in this chapter, and through to Chapter 11, Wei Boyang describes the primary importance of fostering our natural endowment of life. These five chapters form the 'core' of Wei's writings. To guard our vitality or seed within enables us to generate an energy without. Whilst considering the ultimate origins of human life, the idea of alchemy is first broached and its material ingredients outlined – you need water, fire and gold. In vivid imagery the creation of an Elixir is depicted as the generation of a foetus within the womb.

If you would foster your inborn nature,
Lengthen your years and turn back time,
Consider the final outcome of all things,
And ponder that which comes before –
Man is endowed with a solid body
Which fundamentally is pure and empty:
The original vital seed showers out as a cloud,
Depending on an energy to surround it at the beginning.
As the Yin and Yang become the measure
They come to rest as souls, the Hun and the Po.

The Yang spirit of the sun is the Hun,
The Yin spirit of the moon is the Po;
The Hun and Po join together
And link in accord to set up home.

Our inborn nature acts as host within,
Sets up its position as the citadel,

> Our feelings are in command outside,
> Ranging unbroken as the city wall.
> The city and its wall once complete
> All people and things are secure.

This section examines our inborn nature (*xing*) and our life (*ming*). Our solid body is, in reality, purely empty; our structure is mostly space. Our inborn nature acts as a spirit within, our gift from the heavenly inner world; our material energy is as a substance outside, our place in the physical outer world. As our inner energy is built up strongly so our place in the world is secure.

The ultimate principle in the development of an inner Elixir involves the same stages as the outer extension of our physical life. The original vital seed is Yang in nature but the original energy is Yin, so as Yin and Yang join they complete a man. In the postnatal outer world there are the Hun- and Po-souls, also shown as Kan and Li. The Hun is the Yang, the trigram Li and the sun; the Po is the Yin, the trigram Kan and the moon. At all times during our life these two interrelate and involve each other, they can never be set apart.

The Hun acts as the spirit of our inborn nature, as a ruler setting up his palace within; the Po acts as our life and our feelings, as a minister setting a guard on the city wall to protect us outside. As they go about their duty, Kan and Li intertwine, laying the foundation for the inner Elixir.

Master Shangyang comments: This chapter describes the importance of fostering our inborn natural endowment – that we may then cultivate an active life.

What is meant by our inborn nature? It is something belonging to Qian. If man can foster this, then the Qian-Yang will not waste away. With his vital seed guarded within and an energy generated outside, he will be able to smelt an Elixir and enter into the holy life.

The people of this world do not understand that their inborn nature [*xing*] and life [*ming*] are one, so what is it they work with? They either guess that their inborn nature involves some kind of clever state of knowledge or awareness, or else take their nature to be the dull and stupid, fleshy mass which makes up the heart.

Some acknowledge their 'thinking' and 'mental processes' to be their nature; some point to the 'ungraspable' as their nature, or to sitting 'dull and vacant'; or else they take the 'here and now' as their life.

But how can they understand something so vague and unclear to be their life? How can they understand a profession which includes so many births and changes to be anything to do with life? They are only wildly guessing and getting involved in dreams and fantasies. How can this ever be a way into the holy life?

The *Yin-Shadow* scripture says: The heavenly nature is born in man. The heart is the crux. The true-hearted person discovers it and works away solidly at it. The small person discovers it and fritters away his life.

Confucius said: Work tirelessly at principle, wholly acting according to your inborn nature. Thus you arrive at life's destiny.

Mencius said: Protect the heart and foster the inborn nature. Then you wait for heaven's life-mandate to arrive.

Whether we live a long life or die an early death, it is all the same. We develop ourselves and await our destiny. By this means we secure our life. The path of the sages which was transmitted to Mencius is absolutely clear.

The Yi Jing ['Shuogua', Eighth Wing] *says*: In ancient times when the sages created the *Book of Change*, they intended that it should in principle conform with our inborn nature and life. Therefore they drew up the Dao of heaven, and called it Yin and Yang; they drew up the Dao of earth and called it the firm and yielding; and they drew up the Dao of mankind and called it human-heartedness and righteousness.

Now our honoured Immortal speaks about developing our inborn nature, not about developing our life. How can we enter into the holy way of life? To develop a life we must first develop an inborn nature. From this position we can then enter into cultivating a particular path of development.

The received opinion is that the Buddhists cultivate their 'nature'; and the Daoists cultivate their 'lives'. But how can there be two separate paths in this world? In no way can this be comparable to Mencius's idea of 'protecting the heart and fostering the inborn nature', and the path of 'developing the self' and 'securing our life'.

In general if you wish to secure your life you should primarily foster your inborn nature. If you are not aware of your inborn nature, how can you understand your life!

Thus the Unvarying Mean [a Confucian text] *says* 'our inborn nature is the life-mandate of heaven', and 'to follow to the end this inborn nature is what is meant by the Dao'. For this reason the sages would never allow duplicity. This is implied when the text says, 'If you would foster your inborn nature, lengthen your years and turn back time . . .'

He continues: Just hold fast loyally to the mean within. This is to 'foster your inborn nature'. Man and woman mingle their seed, and a myriad creatures are born and transformed. This is what is known as 'securing your life'. To accumulate vital seed and build up energy. This is to 'foster your inborn nature'. Flowing through the Wu-soil and on to the Ji-soil. This is to 'secure your life'.

He continues: You should think, 'Where is it that my body and self come from?' The reply may be, 'It is the inner energy of Yin and Yang, from my mother and father, who gave me life.' So then it is the inner energy of Yin and Yang which can lengthen your years and actually form you into an Immortal or a Buddha.

Therefore the inner development of the supreme Elixir begins with the body first receiving its motivating energy. It receives it in one mass – without there being any distinctions – except those that exist between going along with or turning against [ni] *the flow*.

He continues: To go along with the flow of this energy is to produce living creatures, such as man himself; to turn against it is to produce an Elixir and to enter into the holy life. This is what is meant by 'his original vital seed showers out as a cloud, depending on an energy to surround it at the beginning'.

He concludes: The Hun and Po 'link together in setting up home'. So then both Yin and Yang are joined and relate to each other. Our inborn nature acts the host by solidifying our vitality within, setting up its position 'as a citadel'; whilst our feelings are in command and subduing our energy outside, which range along the outside of the body 'as a city wall'.

What is this 'wall'? It is as a wrapping to a flower. Where is this 'city'? It is the space in which the alchemy can take place.

> Then, at this moment, we are one,
> In close contact with Qian and Kun.
> Qian moves out directly,
> The energy spreads out and the seed flows through,
> Kun is settled in and contracted,
> The place for lodging the furnace.
> 'Firmness is applied and then withdrawn,
> Softness transformed through stimulation,
> The nine is restored, the seven recycled,
> The eight returned, the six remains.'

The boy goes white, the girl turns red!
The gold and the fire seize one another.
Then water is used to settle the flame,
That the 'cycling five' may begin.

Here we enter into the prenatal inner world: the postnatal turns back to the prenatal. The 'four images' and 'five elements' are jumbled up all together as one energy, until they form into an Elixir.

The positions of Kan and Li in the outer-world diagram are identical to those of Qian and Kun in the inner-world diagram (see Figures 4 and 5).

Qian is firm and active, Kun is yielding and quiet. As the firm and yielding overcome each other's deficiences, activity and quietness unite, Yin and Yang find union and Kan and Li mingle their seed.

In the River Diagram (Figure 15), first suggested in the Great Appendix to the *Book of Change*, the 'generated' and 'completed' numbers of the elements are described. Heaven, being Yang, depicts the odd numbers; earth, being Yin, depicts the even.

Heaven is one and generates water; earth is six, and completes it. Earth is two and generates fire; heaven is seven, and completes

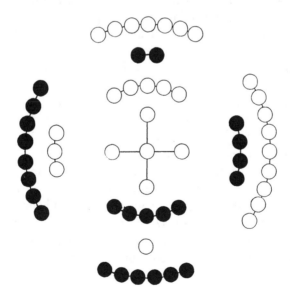

Fig. 15 The River Diagram

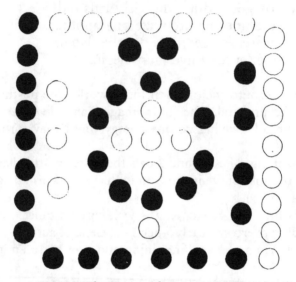

Fig. 16 The Great Gloss on Numeracy

it. Heaven is three and generates wood; earth is eight, and completes it. Earth is four and generates gold (metal); heaven is nine, and completes it. Water, fire, wood and gold (metal) are the 'four images'; and, along with the soil, they form the five elements, or what are termed the cycling five.

Water, fire, wood and gold also correspond to north, south, east and west. However none of these 'four images' or 'five elements' lies beyond the scope of Kan and Li, of water and fire.

Master Shangyang comments: At this very instant it is in Qian's nature to move – and it acts directly. So then the vital seed and the inner energy merge. Kun's inclination is to be settled in and contracted, to form the place for lodging the furnace. The firm Qian then straightens out, acts once and then pulls back. The softness of the Kun is transformed; she becomes fertilized through being stimulated and the Elixir born within the cauldron. It is restored and recycled through the task of completion [see Figure 15].

What is meant by the 'nine restored'? When the earth is four it generates metal [gold]; heaven is nine which completes it as silver. The dragon and tiger combine together, restoring the inner energy of the gold and silver in the cauldron. Thus the 'nine' is restored.

What about the 'seven recycled'? The earth is two which generates fire; heaven is seven which completes it as sand. The Hun- and

Po-souls dote on one another, and the fine essences of sand and
fire are recycled back to blaze in the cauldron. Thus the 'seven' is
recycled.

What about the 'eight returned'? Heaven is three which generates wood; earth is eight which completes it as mercury. The Wu-
and Ji-soils join together, and the true wood and mercury are
returned to be smelted within the cauldron. Thus the 'eight' is
returned.

What about the 'six remains'? Heaven is one and it generates
water; earth is six which completes it as lead. As our feelings and
our inborn nature affect one another, so the mysterious 'lead' and
'mercury' retreat back to dwell in the cauldron. Thus the 'six'
remains.

The boy belongs to the wood of the green dragon. He receives
the inner energy of the Dui-gold, smelts it, and turns it back to
pure white. The girl belongs to the gold of the white tigress. She
takes the vital seed of the Li-fire, smelts it, and restores it back to
red.

He continues: Water is used to settle the flame just as in the finest
and most dignified religious services.

If medicines are to be properly employed then it is always
necessary to add a certain amount of water. In short this determines the quality of heat involved in the boiling and smelting process. Now we are present at the actual first moment of the creative
cycling of the five elements!

Yuyan comments: Convey the vitality and inner energy to return
to the 'primal sea', and they form into the residence of the Dao.
Very generally, as you are protected with Qian so you move; you
move, the energy spreads out, and the vital seed flows through
you. As you are protected with Kun so you are still; you are still,
the energy gathers in, and the vital seed condenses within.

He continues: 'Firmness is applied and then withdrawn – softness
transformed through stimulation.' The Qian is the Yang below,
overcome by the Kun. The Kun softens, yields and complies with it
and as a result the medicine is born. Once it has passed through
the fire, and been heated and changed, so its firmness has been
applied and is then withdrawn. The Yin is soft and circulates
above, transforming into sweet-tasting spring-water which moistens the whole body through.

'Six', 'seven', 'eight' and 'nine' stand for water, fire, wood and gold [metal]; as trigrams, they are Kan, Li, Zhen and Dui; as directions, they are east and west, south and north; as images, they are the tortoise and snake, the dragon and tiger; as the seasons, they are spring, summer, autumn and winter; as hours of the day, they are midnight, midday, dawn and dusk. They are all these things [Figures 16 and 6].

Now the text says the nine is 'restored', the seven 'recycled', and the eight 'returned', and they all have the same meaning. But the six alone 'remains'. This is because it represents the northerly direction and the position of Kan. It is the original neighbourhood where the true 'lead' dwells. It is the true 'lead' which dwells here. And so the nine-gold, the eight-wood, and the seven-fire, the true energies of these three directions, like the spokes of a wheel or as rivers returning to the sea, also all gather here.

Zhu Yuanyu says: Now the mysteries of the creation of the post-natal outer world lie only in the single Kan and Li. All 10,000 changes and transformations differ only in name.

According to the terms of Kan and Li's original positions, they are 'water' and 'fire'; in terms of the two 'bows' of living energy [the upturned and downturned 'bows' of the moon-phases], they are 'gold' and 'water'; in terms of the practicality of east and west, they are 'gold' and 'wood'; in terms of the forging process, they are 'gold' and 'fire'.

As to their 'inverted and intertwined' use, this cannot be finally

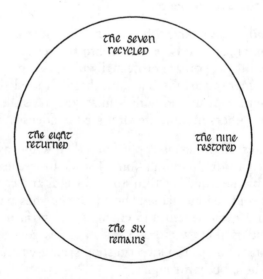

Fig. 17 Six, seven, eight, nine (1)

determined. There are, in the last analysis, only two materials – water and fire. But although, as postnatal water and fire, they occur as two separate things they are, in the last analysis, only the one single energy of the prenatal inner world.

Once Kan and Li have been returned back to become Qian and Kun, they are the 'nine restored, the seven recycled, the eight returned and the six remaining', which create the one single energy of the prenatal inner world.

> The highest good is like water,
> Clear-running without a stain;
> The form of its method resembles
> True Oneness – it is difficult to describe;
> If broken up, each droplet scatters
> Yet each is settled by itself.
> It is something like a chicken's egg
> In which white and black mutually tally.
>
> One inch wide across
> When first it begins.
> Four limbs and five organs,
> Tendons and bones all fully formed,
> Complete at ten moons,
> It slips from out of the womb,
> Its bones soft and curled
> Its flesh smooth as putty . . .

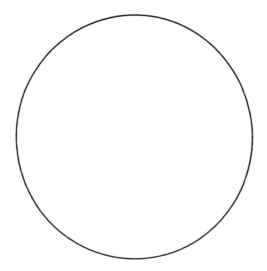

Fig. 18 'The very image of the Dao itself'

This section reveals the form of the inner Elixir. It is Laozi (*Daode Jing*, Chapter 8) who said: 'The highest good is like water, water gives life to all the myriad creatures and does not strive. It flows in places men reject and, in this way, is close to the Dao.'

Water is clear-running, it is pure in quality, and even when broken into droplets it forms itself into perfect shining spheres. It is the very image of the Dao itself.

White and black mutually tally as Yin and Yang. The chicken's egg and the foetus in the womb both depict the formation of the Elixir as they form the very stuff of life.

Master Shangyang comments: Being 'one inch wide across' resembles the first formation of the appearance of the Elixir. It is like a single small grain of rice.

8

HOW THE SON AND DAUGHTER
NEED EACH OTHER

In this chapter the utter dependence of Yin and Yang upon each other is illustrated through the images of their related trigrams, Kan (water) and Li (fire). These represent the son and daughter, the sun and moon, the cock and hen, the Po- and Hun-souls. The significance of their linkage, which is overtly sexual, is that each can check the extravagances of the other – and thus both together come into harmony.

> Kan, the son, is the moon,
> Li, the daughter, is the sun;
> The sun then bestows his virtue,
> And the moon spreads out her light.
> The moon receives the sun's influence,
> Although her body is never injured.
>
> But as the Yang slips its bonds,
> So the Yin encroaches on its brightness.
> As the old moon erodes the new,
> Shutting off its brilliance, so it collapses.
> As the shape of the Yang melts away
> So the Yin passes over and disaster is born.

This section describes how, if the intimate connection between the sun and the moon is lost, it leads to mishap and misfortune. This loss is comparable to Kan and Li losing their connection – in which case the Elixir cannot be formed.

Only if Kan and Li are in proper proportion can an Elixir be made. If this is not the case, the true 'fire' cannot sink into and warm the centre of the 'water', nor can the true 'water' be absorbed within the 'fire'. In each case the Elixir goes unformed.

The ideas in this chapter are comparable with those of Chapter 33 – 'The practice of this art of the cycling five is comparatively concise, and not uncomplicated.'

Master Shangyang comments: Kan is water, it is the moon; it is the middle son. Li is fire, it is the sun; it is the middle daughter.

Kan ☵ has the Yin outside with the Yang inside. It contains the Wu-soil, which stores up the 'gold and water'. It nourishes the Yin Po-soul, which contains our feelings and forms the way into a sense of morality and right. It stands for the white within the black.

Li ☲ has the Yang outside with the Yin inside. It contains the Ji-soil, which manages the 'sand and mercury'. It takes command over the Yang Hun-soul, which acts in the fulfilment of our nature and forms the essence of human kindness in action. It stands for the black within the white.

Yuyan comments: 'The central line of Qian ☰ lies with Kun ☷ to complete Kan ☵. Thus Kan is the middle son. The central line of Kun ☷ lies with Qian ☰ to complete Li. Thus Li is the middle daughter.

So it follows that Li originally had Qian's body, while its central line was drawn from Kun; which is the Yin within the Yang. Thus it forms the image of the sun. Kan had originally Kun's body, while its central line is drawn from Qian; which is the Yang within the Yin. Thus it forms the image of the moon.

The book *Awakening to Reality* says:

> The sun dwells in Li's position contrariwise as a woman,
> Kan's toad sits in his palace – but is male.
> If you cannot understand within them the idea of 'inversion',
> Cease your tunnel vision and highflown chatter!

Now here Yin and Yang are turned head over heels within the body and inverted. You scholars, truly you must never indulge in tunnel vision. The sun 'bestows its virtue', which is the way of the husband; while the moon 'spreads out its light', which is the way of the wife. Here the moon [Kan] is the middle son so the wife is seen as the son; and the sun [Li] is the middle daughter so the husband is seen as the daughter. Herein lies the idea of 'inversion'.

He continues: Now Wei Boyang takes the sun and moon as an example of the Elixial method and concentrates on their alternation, their ebbing and eroding away. The whole meaning of the text lies entirely in this. You scholars, why can you not 'reflect back your brightness to light up within [huiguang neizhao]?' Search within yourselves for the sun and moon, and the interval of the new moon!

There is an old saying: From watching the Dipper's handle turning round the sky, I suddenly awoke to the mysteries of the divine Immortals!

> The son and daughter assist one another,
> Cherished, rejected, through excitement.
> The cock and hen mess around together,
> Each kind seeking the other out.
>
> As gold transforms it becomes as water,
> Water by nature is uneasy and hasty.
> When fire transforms it becomes dry soil,
> So the water then cannot overflow.
>
> As the son outside applies his strength,
> The daughter is still within, concealed.
> If he overflows he goes unchecked,
> So she acts the lady to restrain him.
>
> Thus the Po stamps the Hun,
> With neither extravagance nor waste.
> Neither frigid nor too heated,
> They both move forward and back with the times,
> Each finding harmony; as evidence
> Witness their complete tallying.

This last section continues the idea that an 'intimate connection' enables the link-up necessary for success in the forming of the Elixir. Its ideas should be compared with those of Chapters 32 and 33.

The son and daughter, the cock and hen, water and fire, the Hun- and Po-souls, cold and heat, they can all be classified as Yin and Yang. Yin and Yang are interdependent. Each forms the foundation for the other – through the Yin being contained within the Yang and the Yang within the Yin. There is cherishing, then rejection; there is rejection, then cherishing. These two complementary forms stimulate each other's growth; which is the constant rule throughout the world.

After Kan and Li have been joined, the goal within the inner development of the Elixir is to generate a supreme medicine; to 'extract the lead to eke out the mercury' in order to forge completely a purely Yang, unspoilt, inner Elixir. If there is any Yin still remaining within the Yang, how can you reach your goal?

The 'lead' stands for the central line in Kan, while the 'mercury' is presented in the trigram Li. Although the 'lead' may be able to control the 'mercury', it must not be present in too great a measure. Otherwise, as you advance the firing, the true 'mercury' is not continuously eked out and the true 'lead' is gradually scattered; the lead is finally used up and the mercury gone.

The book *Awakening to Reality* says:

> In using lead you are not to use it as common lead,
> Once the true lead is used, it is squandered and destroyed!
> This is the true secret to do with using lead.
> 'Using lead is not to use it', this is the most honest truth!

Thus, according to this verse, the use of the 'lead' (the central Yang line of the trigram Kan) can truly only be accomplished through 'not using it' – through the action of non-action. The 'lead' must be from the prenatal inner world. Only as cold and heat are carefully balanced in the firing process and used in accordance with the time, can you complete the production of an Elixir. The idea of 'mutual tallying' is central to the *Can Tong Qi*.

Master Shangyang comments: The great significance of this chapter lies in the words 'uneasy and hasty' and 'overflows'. As 'extravagance and waste' go unchecked, so 'the Yin passes over and disaster is born'. It is like having great warmth in midwinter or excessive cold in midsummer – the son acts but the daughter does not follow, the Yang is fiercely active and the Yin cannot find her way close to him. Then Yin and Yang attack and blunder into each other; it is all because he is 'uneasy and hasty', 'extravagant' and 'wasteful'.

The inner development of the Golden Elixir is not easy. It wholly rests in 'closeness without disrespect'.

Yuyan comments: Son and daughter, cock and hen, they all describe the Yin and Yang within one's own body. As the two creatures' energies are of the kind and belong together, they sometimes quite naturally cherish or reject each other. Eventually they join and knot together, to form a little babe.

The old saying goes: In my own body there exists both husband and wife. But tell this to your friends and they will burst out laughing! [Cf. Daode Jing, Chapter 41]

This is the method for certain! Students of this method should use 'quietness and non-action' [*qingjing wuwei*] in order to seek it out. They should not use unorthodox opinions or any other instruction.

He concludes: When you capture the medicine and bring harmony to the firing, you move neither swiftly nor slowly. You simply desire an evenness between both and allow them to mingle together.

The book *Returning Back to Life* says: Firmness and gentleness meet together, their breath just evenly balanced. The mystery lies in injuring neither Dui ☱, nor Zhen ☳.

Thus the real importance of this technique lies in prizing a peaceful attitude.

9

A LUCKY MATCH FOR OUR GOOD PRINCE

This chapter continues the familiar theme: in order to create life we must combine together similar substances which match, that is, one Yin and one Yang, one male and one female, and so on. It begins with the famous opening lines to the ancient *Book of Songs* and uses analogies to argue – against the prevailing views of the chemical alchemists – that substances will never combine if they are dissimilar.

> 'Guan! guan! go the water-birds
> Together on the island in the river:
> Shy and modest, the true young maiden
> Is a lucky match for our good prince.'
> The cock cannot settle alone,
> The hen cannot remain single,
> Dark warriors both, as the tortoise and snake
> Tangle together in conspiracy, they bond together.
> Therefore understand that male and female
> Are only really suited to each other:

This chapter uses the idea of the necessary pairing of Yin and Yang to illustrate the inner development of the Elixir. Its whole gist can be summed up in the two lines 'the cock cannot settle alone, the hen cannot remain single'.

The first four lines come from the opening of the *Book of Songs*, a collection of Chinese folksongs, ballads and court odes from ancient times, traditionally said to have been compiled by Confucius. The mating behaviour of the water-birds is seen as illustrating the origin of natural human relationships; just as, in nature, every living creature is drawn to procreate so, in human life, the desire for reproduction is natural and inevitable.

In Chinese mythology the tortoise and the snake together represent the element 'water' and the direction north. They are eternally coiled and encircling each other and thus named the 'dark warriors'.

Yuyan comments: The supreme method of the Golden Elixir concerns one Yin and one Yang, and that really is all! They combine together the affairs of mankind and the principle of all living things, without anything being excluded.

Now Wei Boyang takes this idea of the mating water-birds and the prince and his maiden, as analogous to the male and female elements pairing up within the body.

> Supposing you allow two girls in one home
> Whose charm and prettiness is beyond question,
> Then even with Su Qin's influence,
> Or Zhang Yi acting as go-between,
> There would be argument, sharp words,
> Rousing fine phrases,
> Forcing their hearts
> To try and agree as husband and wife –
> Yet when their hair was gone, their teeth rotted,
> Still they would not know one another!

The illustration is of two young girls living together. But however this is tried, they will never relate and prosper together as husband and wife. Here, only the solitary Yin (two young girls) is mentioned, but the same would apply to the solitary Yang.

> If medicinal substances
> Are of the wrong kinds,
> And names and sorts are dissimilar,
> Then their weights combine imperfectly,
> For you have let slip the guiding thread.

> Even with the Yellow Emperor to build the furnace
> And Great Oneness himself to attend the firing,
> The Eight Lords to pound down material
> And Huai Nan to stir them together;
> If you set up a High Altar
> Under cover, with white jade steps,
> And unicorn and phoenix meats offered up,
> With a list of lengthy prostrations,

> Prayers to the earth-spirits,
> Wailing pleas to the ghosts and sprites,
> If you bathe, fast and abstain,
> Hoping for that so long hoped for;
> Even then, like mixed glue to repair a pot,
> Or sal ammoniac daubed on a sore,
> Adding ice to get rid of cold,
> Or using hot water to do away with heat,
> A flying tortoise or dancing snake
> Would be equally unreasonable!

The imagery comes from the activities of the outer alchemists. If the original medicinal substances are of the wrong kinds, they cannot be forced together – there has to be a spontaneous reaction. This is a central idea in the *Can Tong Qi*.

The implication is that outer elixirs formed on the chemistry bench or herbal medicines can only perpetuate our life – they cannot bring the true bliss of immortality. Only through using the true 'lead' from within Kan and the true 'mercury' from within Li, which occur within the body, and immersing them in the 'earthenware pot' of Kun, can the Elixir be formed.

Zhang Boduan states in the opening verse to his 'Four-Hundred Character' poem:

> True earth clutches onto true lead,
> True lead governs true mercury.
> The lead and mercury revert to the true earth
> And the mind becomes still and unmoved!

Master Shangyang comments: Our Immortal here points to the necessity of using similar kinds of things as medicinal ingredients when creating a Golden Elixir. The single Yin and the single Yang necessarily rely on the intercourse between themselves. A single male and a single female can then create life.

Supposing you have only one of them, how then can you find the catch which works the transformation? If there are many hens without a cock, is this the method for creating life?

If you wish to forge the restored Elixir you must search out the single energy of the prenatal inner world [*xiantian yi qi*] in order to achieve success. The verses of this chapter are truly revealing and I cannot explain them any further.

Our Immortal wrote this text to disclose the catch to the creative powers of heaven and earth. Their power lies in the sudden impulse for Qian and Kun to bear fruit; their pattern is as brilliantly clear as the sun and moon joining their lights; their effect is actively to reverse the slipping away from us of Yin and the Yang.

He continues: The prenatal inner world is the real world – yet it is no distance from the postnatal outer world. Moreover you are entrusted with the timing of the real world and it is no distance from you. In fact it lies in every man!

Those who command this method are the sages; those who practise it become holy men.

Yuyan comments: This is just the same as the daughter Dui and son Gen, above and below, responding to and influencing each other, as in the hexagram Stimulation [Hexagram 31].

In the trigrams Li and Dui you have two girls who live together, but whose minds travel on opposite tracks, as in the hexagram Opposition [Hexagram 38]. This explains how the real value of Yin and Yang lies in them agreeing together. One or the other of them should never be fixed and determined.

Therefore if you are at the furnace and involved in the firing of the Elixir, you should also emphasize Yin and Yang in just proportion. If the substances you are using belong to the wrong categories then, whichever way you combine them, you let slip the guiding thread to their method.

10

UNDERSTANDING THE DOUBLE-
ENTRANCED CAVE OF
KNOWLEDGE

This lengthy chapter describes that which is essential to the alchemical process – the law of the 'double-entranced cave' or cavity. It identifies the fundamental need for the 'water', its relationship with the 'gold' and the necessity for the 'true lead' and 'true mercury'. It also describes the maze which appears to be built up around the process during its initial stages. The 'gateway to life' is revealed as the 'door to death' – one and the other, they are two sides of the same coin.

> The most powerful is non-action
> For nothing is then sought;
> The least powerful is action
> For its use is never-ending.
>
> The most obstructive is called 'being',
> The least obstructive termed 'nothingness';
> For nothingness raises one on high,
> On high where spiritual values dwell.
> This is the law of the 'double-entranced cave',
> Where the gold and inner energies assist each other.

The most powerful path is the highest path, it involves 'nothingness' and non-action; the least powerful path is the lowest path, it involves 'being' and action. Yet these two arrive always together, so their knowledge lies further entangled at the opening to this 'double-entranced cave', the 'inner energies and gold' showing the two paths which lead in.

The 'inner energies' are the energies of the true 'lead'; they are the 'sunken silver' which lies 'under the surface of the White-Jade pond of water' (a phrase from the book *Awakening to Reality*).

Master Shangyang comments: The 'most powerful' reveals a man whose body is whole and powerful. This is the scholar 'who leaves nothing undone' [*Daode Jing*, Chapter 38]. When a young man is sixteen, his vital seed is fully formed within and desires begin to arise.

The man who is whole and powerful is to be able to care for this seed and keep it whole without wasting it. Moreover if he can meet an enlightened teacher, who transmits to him the method of 'non-action and absorption' [*wuwei xiushe*], he can perpetuate his life. This is the scholar 'who leaves nothing undone'. This is what is meant by the 'most powerful' and complete man. It is the non-action of the sages which effects transformation; it represents the great individual who achieves his task through non-action.

The 'least powerful' reveals a man who 'steals the catch of creation'. He is the scholar who 'robs from the myriad creatures' [two phrases from the *Yin-Shadow* scripture]. All men, when they are just sixteen years of age, possess a vital seed which has not yet begun to be spent. This is what is meant by being purely Qian ☰.

Once feelings of desire begin to stir, the central line of Qian travels and enters into the palace of Kun ☷. Qian can then no longer keep itself pure. Its centre has emptied out and it turns into Li ☲ and, from this moment on, day and night, the Yang leaks out.

But if one can protect and retain it, how much of the Yang might one not be able to return?

Only one adept at this – who goes to no extremes – can travel the path of the sages and be made whole again. Then he can make his body one with the Immortals. This is what is meant by the 'least powerful' scholar; he is the individual who 'steals the catch of creation'. It is the method used by the sages who follow their inborn nature and it represents the spiritual person whose task lies in action.

The 'most powerful is non-action' for then nothing is left undone. [*Daode Jing*, Chapter 38] You achieve the position of the 'supreme pole' [*taiji*] and keep your body whole, finishing the task given you in the postnatal outer world. Thus the text says, 'nothing is then sought'.

The 'least powerful is action' and activity. You snatch from the work of creation to finish the task of the prenatal inner world. Thus the text says, 'Its use is never-ending.'

Our Immortal teacher in the book *Awakening to the Truth* says:

> That it starts in activity man finds it difficult to see,
> Then it comes to non-action and he begins to understand.
> But if he only sees non-action as subtle
> How can he understand activity to be its basis?

These words which generally describe the work of the Golden Elixir are not easy to understand. The adept only uses words when he has no other choice. It is Laozi who said: 'Sharp weapons are unlucky to have around – use them only when you have no choice [*Daode Jing* Chapter 31].' The implication is the same.

The 'most obstructive' is called 'being'. The 'most obstructive' is the trigram Kun. When Kun exerts its power, it is settled in and contracted. The 'being' is the Wu-soil which lies in the central line of the trigram of Kan, wherein lies the true single energy of the prenatal inner world.

The 'least obstructive' is termed 'nothingness'. The 'least obstructive' is the trigram Qian. When Qian exerts its power, it is settled in but diffused. The 'nothingness' is the Ji-soil which lies in the central line of the trigram Li, within which is stored the spontaneously arising 'water' of the postnatal outer world.

He continues: the *Book of the Double-Functioning Cavity* says:

> Ever without desire you see the mystery; ever without desire you see the cavity. These two come out from the same source, but differ in name. Both signify darkness. There is darkness even within the darkness, the gateway to all mysteries! [Cf. *Daode Jing*, Chapter 1]

The sages never practised duplicity – yet dark words and strange phrases were never far from their hearts. The world will never fathom what they meant if they lack a teacher who can transmit their meaning. If the noble and sage Yellow Emperor had not been taught by Master Guangzheng, how could he have understood the Path? Without something like this 'cavity', what could the sages have done? All their descriptions point directly towards it.

When Fuxi first drew the trigrams, he used the two images of Qian and Kun to settle this 'cavity'. King Wen did not neglect the work; he doubled up the trigrams as hexagrams in order to explain it. In the 'Wings' and commentaries to the Book of Change, Confucius developed his ideas directly from Qian and Kun. And it was Laozi who spoke of 'the gateway to the Dark Female, the root of heaven and earth' [*Daode Jing*, Chapter 6]; and the Buddhists who, in order to illustrate the Storehouse of the Eye to the True Dharma, spoke of the Mysterious Heart of the 'muddied Coil' [a literal translation of the Sanskrit *ni-pan* or 'nirvana']. It is obvious that all these directly point into this 'cavity'.

If the highest student can turn his light towards this 'cavity' he will find there – revealed within – power in action. But he must have a teacher to turn this light on within him.]

He continues: The two phrases – 'this is the law of the 'double-entranced cave', where 'the gold and inner energies assist each other' – form the key to the gateway into the *Can Tong Qi*.

Yuyan comments: The *Daode Jing* (Chapter 38) says: The most powerful is non-action, nothing is then left undone. The least powerful is action, much then remains to be done.

Now the text says, 'The most powerful is non-action, for nothing is then sought' – for the mind is guarded at the 'dark palace' and little by little nothing is left undone. And it also says, 'the least powerful is action, for its use is never-ending' – for the breath mounts up into the 'dark treasury' continuously without interruption. Here the ideas of Laozi are borrowed to express the two secret offices of the trigrams Kan and Li.

The 'most obstructive' being called 'being' describes how the 'true water' is stored visibly in Li's palace; the 'least obstructive' being termed 'nothingness' describes how the 'red dragon' is hidden invisibly at the door to Kan.

For 'nothingness raises one on high, on high where spiritual values dwell', which means the 'original mind' is resting in its own palace above and all energies follow and ascend. The mystery lies on high at the 'eight gates', which are barred, chained up and obstructed.

> Know the white but guard the black,
> The divine light comes of itself;
> For the white is the fine gold,
> But the black is the water taken as a basis.
> Water is fundamental to the method,
> To the whole world it is known as One.
>
> Being the source of Yin and Yang,
> Its darkness cherishes a yellow shoot;
> Being the ruler of all metals,
> From the north its chain-pump rolls.

Thus the lead is black outside
Yet within it carries a golden flower,
Like a slab of jade being concealed
By someone coarse, dull and wild.

This section explains how the 'true lead' is the mother of the inner Elixir. Inner alchemy takes 'mercury' to illustrate the activities of the mind and heart within the body. The mind and heart belong to the element 'fire' and store up within themselves the inner vitality of the true Yang, namely the 'true mercury'. The 'lead' is taken to illustrate the function of the kidneys. The kidneys belong to the element 'water' and store up within themselves the inner energies of the original Yang, namely the 'true lead'.

As the lead and mercury are combined, so they start to form an Elixir. Continuously you 'extract the lead to eke out the mercury' dispelling the Yin and increasing the Yang, until gradually all the Yin is transformed into pure Yang and the inner Elixir fully formed.

The 'white' is stored within the 'black' Kan-water as the fine gold. 'Water is fundamental to the method' because, although according to the sequence of the cycling five gold (metal) can produce water (become liquid), the water itself is the key – and the gold lies concealed within the water. You 'know the white' but must 'guard the black'.

The foundation of all alchemy lies in this, in the 'gold within the water', namely the 'true lead'. Again this is not the common lead of the world. As the *Mirror to Entering into the Medicine* says: 'The lead which exists in the region of the water is no more than a merest taste.'

Finally the book *Awakening to Reality* states: 'The white lying within the black is mother to the Elixir.' This is to put it in a nutshell!

Master Shangyang says: Earlier on, this book only outlined Qian and Kun, and the principle of the creative processes formed by the sun and moon. Now it settles on this 'dark gate' to explain further the two material substances of 'gold' and 'water'. The order of this writing is quite intentional.

Once the student who is developing the inner Elixir, has understood the 'cavity of knowledge', he can consider what kind of things the 'gold' and 'water' are, and how they function by assisting one another. If he can clearly understand these two materials and how they work, he can smelt an Elixir. Then he 'knows the white but guards the black'.

To know the very essence of all essences – which exists as pure and spotless clarity – is to truly 'know the white'.

He continues: The foundation lies in 'guarding the black'. To await the moment the water is born is to 'guard the black'.

When water first brings things to life, it may be termed 'prenatal'. Then it contains what is most utterly real, which may be named the 'divine light'; there is both white and black tallying together, as 'gold' and 'water', shining out most brilliantly.

Then they meet with the Ji-soil, it subdues the flowing water and you can scour out the gold. The gold and water are made whole over the furnace and the 'divine light comes of itself'.

Why is 'water fundamental to the method' and why is it to the whole world 'known as One'? Because water is produced from the oneness of the sky [the heavens] and thus forms the very beginning of Yin and Yang.

He continues: The great darkness forms the water; the 'yellow shoot' forms the Elixir; within the water lies the Elixir. Thus the analogy is with 'darkness cherishing a yellow shoot'. Inside the 'black lead', there ravels the 'white metal'; carried inside the 'chain-pump', there is hidden the 'yellow shoot'. This is just like a student who harbours a piece of jade stone at his breast so that harm might not befall him, whilst his clothing is rough and ready [cf. *Daode Jing*, Chapter 70].

Yuyan comments: The white is the 'gold'; the black is the 'water'. The Elixial method uses water as its basis; but the fine gold is born from out of the water so the text says, 'Know the white but guard the black.' If you 'guard the black', the 'white' reveals itself.

What is this like? It is like a cat guarding a hole to catch the mouse; its body does not move, nor its eyes blink. Its mind is totally tied to the mouse, with no other thoughts intruding.

The 'divine light' reveals the workings of heaven's ways. If you wish to rob its workings, you must first empty out the heart. As the heart empties, the mind comes into focus; as the mind comes into focus, so the breathing settles; as the breathing settles, so its boundaries advance and combine together as one – and the 'divine light [revelation] comes of itself'.

He continues: The 'darkness cherishes a yellow shoot' as the 'lead' is born from out of the water. Lead is the 'ruler of all metals', as it dwells in the dark and dim north. As it acquires the element of 'soil' so a 'yellow shoot' germinates.

The 'yellow shoot' is the same as the 'golden flower'. The 'golden flower' is the fine eminence of the 'lead'. Thus the outer body of lead is black, with a 'golden flower' hidden within it – just like a precious jewel being harboured in the bosom of someone poor.

He concludes: This 'true lead' is born from out of the water; it finds the 'true fire' to smelt and refine it, so it appears. Then one dare not interrupt or break off from turning the chain-pump for an instant, as it transports the fluid upwards to irrigate the Kunlun hills at the crown of the head!

> Gold is the mother of water,
> The mother hidden in her little child;
> Water is the child of gold,
> The child stored in its mother's womb.

> What is the uttermost real in man is fascinating –
> As if there, and as if not . . .
> It feels like toppling into the great deep,
> Now being in the shallows, and now in the depths.

> Withdrawn and separated out,
> Each part retains its own state,
> When plucked out, it is classed as white,
> When treated it becomes red;
> When refining it, it is guarded outside,
> So the white can stay real within.

Here we touch on 'the uttermost real in man' – which is another name for the 'true lead'. As the 'true lead' is heated, it takes on the characteristics of a chemical substance changing form within the cauldron. The brewing of an inner Elixir uses the language of outer alchemy but it really describes the fashioning of an inner medicine.

The true 'lead' is sunk nearly out of reach, 'as if there, and as if not'. The book *Awakening to Reality* says, 'If you wish to retain the mercury in the Golden Cauldron lining it red, first find the sunken silver under the surface of the White-Jade pond.'

This can feel 'like toppling into the great deep', now understanding 'the shallows', and now 'the depths'!

As the 'true lead' is withdrawn from the water it 'separates out'; originally being close to 'white' in colour, when put into the fire it glows brilliantly 'red'. The imagery of outer alchemy is again employed.

Also because lead ('black') is a soft material substance and easily impressed upon, when refining it, it must be guarded from outer influences. Then it can be put into the furnace and the gold ('white') can 'stay real within'.

Master Shangyang says: Gold is the mother of water. Generally speaking the Dui-gold [metal] gives birth to the Kan-water [following the usual order of the cycling-five], and yet the line within the trigram Kan belongs to gold. Thus the text speaks of 'the mother hidden in her little child'.

Water is the child of gold. This is the Ren and Gui-water [postnatal] born from the west and yet the line within the trigram Dui belongs to Kan. Thus the text speaks of 'the child stored in his mother's womb'.

'What is the uttermost real in man is fascinating'. What is 'the uttermost real in man' is the body of the trigram Qian. When Qian fashions material things, it acts in a manner utterly divine and fascinating as it gives them form. Perhaps 'it is there', perhaps 'it is not'. The 'great deep' is the image of Kun. When Kun fashions material things, at times it is 'in the shallows' and at times 'in the depths' as it gives them form. At no time is it seen or heard.

Therefore as Qian and Kun change and are transformed, it is Kun's power to stand by and assist in the birth. Once they give birth in transformation, Qian and Kun are 'separated out', although 'each retains its own state'.

Yuyan comments: Scholars, if you understand the real meaning of the 'gold born from out of the water' then you understand how the medicine is born amongst 'streams and springs'. The book *Awakening to Reality* says: You should know that to give birth to the medicine is to live near streams and springs – only in the southwest lies such a neighbourhood!

He continues: The Elixial method advances from midnight on and retreats from midday on. Advance and retreat are 'separated out' but 'each part' retains its own boundary 'without interference, the one from the other' [cf. Chapter 2]. The saying goes: Midnight and midday before the furnace, draw out advance and retreat; Qian and Kun within the cauldron, part the shallows and depths.

He continues: The white is the white gold, the red is the red mercury. 'When plucked out, it is classed as white' because the white gold plucked out from the northern palace of Kan is the mother of the Elixir, and white gold and red mercury are in the same class and family. 'When treated it becomes red' because each day the fire is conveyed to 'extract out the lead and eke out the mercury' at the same time.

He concludes: 'When refining it, it is guarded outside', as the fire is directed and used outside the actual furnace. 'The white can stay real within', as the Golden Elixir is safely lodged inside the actual furnace. Inside the furnace there is an Elixir. You must effect the fire outside the furnace, working away and tending to it night and day. Then the medicine will approach maturity.

> Circular and an inch in diameter,
> Disordered, yet adhering together,
> At first when heaven and earth gave birth,
> And they stood majestic on each side
> There were spreading battlements and towers
> Like twisting vines, tangled trails
> On every side turning in, shut in –
> Throughout the track uncertain, unsure,
> Protected by hindrances, dense-packed,
> Blocked-off and twisting pathways,
> False side-doors leading through
> To each other to guard 'gainst intrusion.
>
> Their passage is possible without thought,
> But difficult if approached with anxiety;
> For if a spiritual energy fills the room
> Nobody then can detain it.
> Guard it and you shine with light,
> Loosen it and you perish.
> For as all movement ceases
> It stays with man always.

This section describes the work of the furnace and cauldron. As the 'lead' and 'mercury' combine, so the Elixir is formed in the cauldron – no more than an inch in diameter.

The perception of this happening involves 'tangled trails' – thoughts rise and fall like 'spreading battlements and towers'.

Often the track seems 'uncertain and unsure', with false leads taking you back where you started. This is to 'guard 'gainst intrusion' into the process.

Hence once the Elixir is formed you must carefully protect and take care of it. The passage of these paths is 'possible without thought'. Every worry must be put out of your mind and no new projects must be begun. Like a dragon protecting a pearl, like a chicken guarding an egg, you 'gently support' and keep hold of that holy babe. If the Golden Elixir is not guarded it will slip from your grasp!

Master Shangyang comments: 'Circular and an inch in diameter, disordered yet adhering together'. Now when there is something born within this dark confusion and the 'supreme pole' [*taiji*] has not yet split apart, there occurs an instant of the prenatal inner world. Within this instant there ravels the one single energy of the prenatal inner world, dwelling there before the 'supreme pole', in the very shape of the first Ruler of us all.

He continues: This chapter directly identifies the significance of the 'doubled-up cavity' and reveals the usage of 'water' and 'gold'. When the spiritual fellow who works away at chanting the Can Tong Qi arrives at this point, he knows in a flash what is meant by it. So therefore this can be a difficult business to achieve and it is the least powerful way of working. It is a method which involves action and its successful completion depends upon the inner discipline of the self; and if the inner discipline is perpetuated too long, the divine light will never arrive.

Yuyan comments: In general as the heart reaches the point of non-action, so the energies within the body find peace. As the energies within the body find peace, so the 'ultimate jewel' is formed.

As the heart becomes tied in action, so the energies within the body become disturbed. As the energies within the body become disturbed, so the 'golden flower' is snapped off its stalk and broken. It is 'possible without thought' but it is 'difficult if approached with anxiety'.

As what is real is built up and strengthened over a long period, the Great Harmony fills out and overflows. And as 'all movement ceases', it regularly needs to be protected. 'Guard it' and you shine with light; 'loosen it' and you perish. You cannot depart from this path for an instant.

11

DEVELOPING THE SELF WITHIN
TO BUILD A FOUNDATION

This chapter continues the theme of the 'double-entranced cave' begun in the previous chapter. It forms the core to Wei Boyang's writings. The fostering of the self is illustrated here in general terms which suggest the practices of the Daoists. The last few hyperbolic lines tell of the legendary ascension often associated with Daoist Immortals. This and the previous chapter are both crucial to an understanding of the *Can Tong Qi*, dealing as they do with the central alchemical process.

> Nourish yourself thus within,
> Tranquil and still in the void,
> While at source concealing the brilliance
> Which illuminates within your whole body.
> Shut and close up the mouth,
> Repressing within the spiritual trunk,
> The senses all swallowed up
> To gently support that pearl so young.
> Observe it there, the unobvious —
> So close by and easy to seek.

The opening section describes the first task in the development of an Elixir – the building of a firm foundation. What is implied by a 'firm foundation' is that the body's and mind's resources are turned back within, so that they can advance along their restorative process. These lines should be compared with the later passage in Xu Congshi – 'The ear, eye and mouth, these three jewels, block and stop them up, do not let them gape.' (Chapter 25)

Within the human body, the heart (fire) corresponds to the sun, the kidneys (water) to the moon, and the spleen (soil or earth) to the northern Pole Star in the constellation the Dipper. Once 'water' and 'fire' have conjoined at the central soil and the senses are all 'swallowed up' within, the water and fire knot together to form a precious jewel, the 'pearl', that 'holy babe'. The 'holy babe' rests in the lower belly, depending on the 'true fire' for nourishment and support; yet its eyes are not yet opened while it draws its nourishment from its mother.

The book *Awakening to Reality* stresses: 'What is useful, we cannot see; what is seen, cannot be used.'

Master Shangyang comments: What is meant by to 'nourish your-self [yang ji]' is all your life to develop yourself within [*lian ji*].

Confucius [see the Great Appendix I.8] *says*: The one of true virtue stills his body and then moves, he simplifies his heart and then speaks, he settles his relationships and then sets out his demands. If the one of true virtue cultivates just these three he will become whole.

The sages' first real concern was with providing a training for the circumstances of being human. For every movement, every spoken word and every wish to accord with the principle of the sages – this is the true meaning of to 'nourish yourself'.

Treasure truly lies in the inner vitality or seed, and wealth in inner energy; this again is to 'nourish yourself'. To 'stand opposite a mirror and forget the mind' is to develop yourself within; 'to be constantly still, but constantly responsive' is to develop yourself within; 'to accumulate power and reach achievement' is to develop yourself within.

The bitter practice of these methods of meditation is to develop yourself within; while the long experience of these methods is also to develop yourself within. A student of inner alchemy must first develop himself within so that through bitter practice and the bearing of disgrace, he may find time to retreat into his own room. Then all his senses, each and every pore of his body, reach a stillpoint [*dading*]; he reaches a perfect maturity, while his experience tends to ripen. Then he forgets, without needing to forget, and the method is complete.

Yuyan comments: Generally if the mind is quiet and empty, the method will come of itself and dwell within. 'Utterly empty, with a profound sense of peace' the original Yang energy will return of itself [cf. *Daode Jing*, Chapter 16].

He adds: To 'return to the source and to travel back to your original nature' [*fanben huanyuan*] and to 'reflect back your brightness to light up within' [*huiguang neizhao*] – these are the great clues to the inner development of the Elixir.

Former scholars spoke of these methods as the Daoist method of the 'nourishment of one's health [*yang sheng*]'. You withdraw your gaze and turn back your sight, just like gold and water submerging their light within. Do believe them, these are true and valid words!

He concludes: The great medicine of the Golden Elixir is simply there before your eyes. How could it not be close by? But it lies in observing the 'unobvious'! As you grab for it, you lose it, although it is close by, it is also far away.

If you are able to have a plan as you search for it, then, in no more than the time taken to eat a meal, the work will be achieved and then, right before your eyes, the 'yellow flower' is revealed. So how could it be far away?

In the book *Awakening to Reality* [the poem 'Moonlight on Western River'] it says: The task is easy – the medicine not far away, divulge it and people will laugh out loud!

They laugh out loud because of how close it is and how easy to seek. But men tangle themselves in all kinds of high and lofty schemes. The book *Returning to Life* says: Understand clearly that it only exists there in front of your very own eyes. Because of this, the followers of fashion will never be able to see it.

Indeed this medicine only exists in the 'unobvious'. Thus you must contain the world within, whilst attending to it without. Perhaps you get up and breathe in the glorious rays of the sun and moon, or find time to brew up minerals, rocks and plants, or indulge yourself in the arts of the bed-chamber. Properly the path is made up in you yourself – but you are searching for it far, far away. The method lies in taking an easy line – but you search out all the tangles and complications. Oh dear, how sad you are!

Master Zhuxi comments: This section refers to those 'inward affairs' which are so very crucial to the book. Again the text describing 'the senses all swallowed up, to gently support that pearl so young', are the most crucial of the most crucial!

When a comparison was made earlier with 'that which is foremost in managing government, the 'power of the throne', and the 'linking-feature of change' [Chapter 6], it properly referred to just this.

Diligently practised then,
Day and night unceasing,
A subdued appetite over three years
Develops lightness and far you roam –
Pass through fire without getting burnt,
Enter water without getting soaked,
Able to choose either care or neglect,
And to grow in happiness without being sad.

The path comes to an end, the power is attained,
And secretly subdued, you await the hour
When Great Oneness himself summons you
To reside upon the Solitary Isle;
Then your work realized you rise above,
Borne upon the List of Immortals.

As the 'holy babe' matures so it grows in strength and power, and we should do all we can to help in its gradual progress. Very generally, within 100 days, the foundation is laid; within ten months, or 300 days, the babe is fully formed; and then, over three years, whilst it is properly tended and cared for, the process is complete and the body becomes transcendent.

The peak of achievement within Daoist folk-history has always been the attainment of blatant physical immortality.

Master Shangyang comments: Supposing there is a clear and intelligent scholar, who hears in his mind the words exchanged between him and his true teacher. He is boundless in his pursuit of their meaning and diligently practises without any disrespect. Day and night he unceasingly seeks out the medicine. Singlemindedly he 'subdues his appetite' for the world and works in secret, dwelling in some 'fairy grotto' lacking any sadness for the world which he has left behind.

He sits still by his clear-jade pool, which shines like green jasper, and grows in happiness. The path comes to an end, but he is 'secretly subdued', accumulating his power within and awaiting the hour when his fame will travel the world.

Then Great Oneness summons him to take up his post in an office of the Immortals and to move his residence to the 'Solitary Isle'. Then perhaps, if he further merits this high position, his body 'slips its traces' and he moves beyond the 'triple worlds'; then his work further suits advancement in rank and he becomes borne upon the List of Immortals.

Yuyan comments: The development of the inner Elixir only takes the time taken to eat a meal. But here a 'subdued appetite' is mentioned 'over three years'. Why is this? The old saying goes: In the time taken to eat a meal, its cultivation is easily seen. But to be well-matured takes longer than three years.

The 'time taken to eat a meal' is the time taken to first form the Elixir. 'Three years' mean that, after you have retreated away into your room in the first year, you must further work at it and gently support and revive it. It is not permissible to leave it alone or move far away from it.

He concludes: This method of gentle support and revival [*wenyang*] is quite distinct. You should also be 'secretly subdued' whilst in the human world, building up your work and accumulating inner virtue that you might see the limits of the many false paths. Then you can lightly take them for what they are – and leave them alone.

12

THE WISE SAGES' SECRET
REFINERY

This chapter begins the last part of Wei Boyang's writings. It describes the oral tradition behind the inner alchemy. It states that its transmission became lost, its original meaning obscured and that Wei set himself the task of reaffirming its truths. True alchemy always necessitates a teacher, as it is essentially a craft, and a taught, oral tradition. Its terms are specific to their study, and their interpretation and understanding demands experience. It is said, 'If you want to know the way to the mountain, ask those who have been to the mountain.'

Those wise saints and sages of old
Cherished the mystery and treasured the truth,
They secretly refined at Nine Cauldrons,
Covered their traces and were lost to the world.

Filled with vitality, they nourished the spirit,
Understanding the power of the sun, moon and stars,
They moistened their skin and flesh,
And softened and strengthened their tendons and bones.

All sickness cast out and eliminated,
Their health was constantly preserved;
Until accumulating over a long time
It transformed their bodies until they became Immortals.

This section explains how the development of a nine times refined inner Elixir can expel disease and prolong life. The sun, moon and stars in the heavens are as the spirit, the inner energy and vitality within the body.

The *Yellow Emperor's Book of Medicine* states, in its first chapter, 'If you guard your vitality and energy within, how then can disease arrive?' And a little later, 'If the proper vitality is kept within, the poisons of disease cannot intrude.' Eventually through self-nourishment and inner discipline, your strength becomes as that of the Immortals.

Master Shangyang comments: The Yellow Emperor, who resided at Cauldron Lake, secretly refined the nine times smelted supreme Elixir. Thereafter he mounted on a dragon and ascended above.

But it is not the forging of metals, minerals, and plant materials that is referred to here; it is just the secreting of the prenatal inner-world energies in order to complete the formation of an internal Elixir. Thus it is said, 'Secretly refine, do not sup what you refine!'

What is meant by 'secretly refine'? Each case is different. For instance there is 'cherishing the mystery', there is 'treasuring the truth', there is 'covering your traces', there is 'being lost to the world', there is 'getting filled with vitality', there is 'nourishing the spirit', and there is 'understanding the power of the sun, moon and stars'. These seven methods are set as the first task. They are what are spoken of as 'brazier-fire' methods and referred to as the 'development of the self within [*lian ji*].

If you can develop yourself inwardly then the true energy rises within you like steam, circulating around the whole body; like the fire in a brazier, its warming energy radiating within, almost as if you had a fever. This is what is meant by the 'brazier fire' and the 'development of the self within'.

To 'moisten the skin and flesh', to 'soften and strengthen the tendons and bones', to 'cast out all sickness' and to 'preserve health', these four are what are spoken of as the 'secreting of the inner energies'. They are what are meant by the 'development of an Elixir within [*lian dan*]'.

Generally to 'cherish the mystery' means to cherish within one-self the real energy of the 'dark unity of all'; while to 'treasure the truth' means to sustain through one's efforts the truth of the 'great Oneness of all'. To 'cover your traces' means to obscure your light and silence your steps, so that men have neither sight nor sound of you. Thus knowledge of the self is rare – and recognition of the self must be honoured.

To 'be lost to the world' means to perish in anonymity, so that men never recognize you. Thus the best among the ancients were the scholars who dwelt alone in their mystery, with a silent understanding – indeed so profound was their wisdom it was never recognized.

To be 'filled with vitality' means to saturate the inner body, with the development of 'true mercuric' vitality within. To 'nourish the spirit' means to support the whole body without, by harbouring the energy of the whole body's spirit within.

Through an accumulated effort all these aims are achieved. Their great secret lies in an understanding of 'the power of the sun, moon and stars'. This power is the most important factor in one's development. To follow the path of development but not to develop this inner power is to have the Yin without the Yang. Both the path [*dao*] and the power [*de*] complete one's development – just as Yin and Yang match each other.

If one who is concerned with this power says he has power but really has none, it results in crazy schemes and ideas. Power cannot be properly and consciously understood. If a scholar during his development has a deep and solid appreciation of this power, he really has no idea of it himself. The divine light of heaven and earth arises in the sun, moon and stars, but their power lies totally concealed within themselves.

It is just as Zhang Ge says: 'If you accumulate it within yourself, if you develop it within yourself, the heart really has no longing for it.' This is to 'understand the power of the sun, moon and stars'.

Once the development of the self is diligently carried out within, you not only accumulate a power, you arrive at a true understanding of it and are able secretly to refine the supreme Elixir. As it moistens the skin and flesh it creates a 'jade moisture', as clear as white snow. Its fluid is the 'golden fluid' which generates the 'yellow shoot'. The 'jade moisture' and 'golden fluid' move out into our marvellous mansion of skin and flesh, softening and strengthening all the body's tendons and bones. Then all sickness harboured in the joints and clefts of the body is cast out and eliminated.

Our health is derived from the Yang of the prenatal inner world and as this is constantly and yet unconsciously preserved, it accumulates over a long time, transforming our bodies until they become immortal. When the Yellow Emperor secretly refined the nine times refined supreme Elixir, this is just what he did.

Yuyan comments: 'Sightless and soundless, he enwrapped himself in stillness' – so did Master Guangzheng 'cherish the mystery and treasure the truth [*Zhuangzi*, Chapter 10].'

'Attending to his breath, making it soft and gentle, like that of newborn babe' – so did Laozi 'cherish the mystery and treasure the truth [*Daode Jing*, Chapter 10].'

He continues: This method is extremely easy and straightforward. Through every hour of the day and night, simply allow the mind to lengthen and manage the breath – then the attention and the breath become one. The body is long preserved and entirely re-turned to the sun and moon; it becomes united with the milky river of heaven, revolving and turning without tiring. Revolving and turning without tiring, one's life is then long-lasting and without end.

The book *Pointing into the Dark* says: If you can only, breath by breath, bring all into choice harmony, you exchange this bundle of sun-dried bones for a clear-running sweet-jade spring!

This is it entirely. If you breathe out without attending to it, then the breath is incomplete; if you breathe in without attending to it, then again the breath is incomplete. You must have the mind and the breath constantly following one another, the attention and the breath always guarded together.

By applying constant and continuous thought, over a short period, the body and mind gain an altogether subtle quality and become one with the Dao.

He continues: If the source is held firm, the original breath [*yuan qi*] will not fade away; then, during the breathing, you will move on to snatch the true breath of heaven and earth. But if the source is infirm, the inner vitality dies, and the breath weakens. Then it has dissipated above, while its original dwelling below lies in dis-repair. What you inhale from the true breath of heaven and earth follows the outbreath and is gone.

The original breath of the body is not the breath which is already there – it is instead the true breath you snatch from heaven and earth.

He continues: Anyone who can develop an Elixir within himself and lengthen his life achieves this through being able to rob the true breath of heaven and earth. Anyone who manages to steal the true breath of heaven and earth achieves it through his own breathing.

The outbreath is as the root, the inbreath is as the stem. Thus if you are able to steal the true breath of heaven and earth and return it to the Elixial field [*dantian*, the lower belly], the outbreath and inbreath of man is just the same as the inbreath and outbreath of heaven and earth.

He continues: Transforming the body successfully into the purest Yang begins by altering the breath. Next it moves on to altering the blood, next to altering the blood vessels, next to altering the flesh and muscle, next to altering the marrow of the bones, next to altering the sinews and tendons, next to altering the bones themselves, next to altering the hair on the head, and next to altering the whole body.

If you build these up over nine years and pass through these nine alterations, then afterwards the Yin is finished totally and the Yang is made pure; and your life processes along evenly with heaven and earth. Herein lies the transcendent method of living out a long life.

What does Wei Boyang mean by 'all sickness cast out and eliminated, their health constantly preserved'? He is implying that if you circulate around the fire, day and night, then through your inner development you exhaust the Yin energies and transmute them into the purest Yang, until your health is constantly preserved and you can achieve everlasting life.

He concludes: When the business of being human has been exhausted, then you can leave this world behind and stand alone. You take flight and ascend above to become an Immortal. But this is all achieved through an accumulation that occurs through an extended period of time.

Perhaps you think, 'It is not necessary to accumulate any work over a period of time, I can just spring into immortality from anywhere.' But this is the same as shovelling out a spadeful of earth and calling it a 100-foot well, or taking a single step and thinking of climbing a 1000-foot city wall! This cannot be right.

The *True Scripture of the Dark Truth* says: Stepping inch by inch without stopping, the lame tortoise can manage 1000 miles. Through piling up soil without resting, hills and mounds can be built. To wait on the river-bank, wanting the fish, is not as good as going home to weave a net!

Therefore anyone who makes a true study of the Elixial method does not worry over success, he only worries over forgetting to apply himself. If he does not worry over forgetting to apply himself, he only worries over not having a mind which can hold its attention over a period of time.

So then the real difficulty lies in having a mind which can hold its attention over a period of time.

Yet grieving for later scholars,
Those who loved the natural order of the Way,
They followed their inspirations,
And recorded the truth of the ancient writings,
Set it down in books and diagrams,
Spread it out for all posterity.

They revealed the twigs and branches,
Whilst keeping the real roots hidden;
Entrusting them with a host of names,
And defeating them through a mass of writings.

Those learned scholars may have gained something,
But still they ended up encased in a coffin,
Sons carried out their fathers' instruction,
Grandsons walked the way of their forebears.
They bequeathed to all doubt and confusion,
Until finally nothing was understood.
This being so, officials left their posts,
Farmers abandoned their fields,
And merchants cast away their wares,
All determined men who ruined their families.

The 'wise saints and sages' often spoke about alchemy through using metaphor, which later generations found confusing. Thus, as the oral tradition became lost, signs and terms also lost their meaning and only served to create difficulties. Men turned away from the real task and lost themselves in their passion.

Master Shangyang explains: Those who came later and were clear-sighted, still had the books but not the people.

He continues: These scholars, although they had the books, never received any instruction from a teacher or saw the work in progress. So they twisted and exaggerated the truth, and made up all sorts of crazy schemes. How could they then succeed?

I was so much affected by these affairs,
I decided to put this down in writing,
Keeping the text easy to understand,
And the work brief and uncomplicated.

I separated the twigs and branches
That the kernel of the fruit might be seen,

Divided them by due weight and number
That the whole might make sense.

So then what was a muddled text
Opened up its dark doorway –
Those who understand will examine it
And make time to consider it.

Now the motive behind Wei Boyang writing the *Can Tong Qi* is explained. He wished to enable us later scholars to understand clearly the true practice behind the inner development of an Elixir. The real crux of the matter is contained in the last two lines. Through individual effort and zeal, all troublesome problems of interpretation are overcome and the transmission between master and apprentice is complete.

Master Shangyang comments: Our gentleman Immortal here feels touched with pity. At least craftsmen such as potters and founders have a stove with which to begin. So he puts this down in writing to serve as a model for all 10,000 later generations. The text is kept easy to understand and the work is kept brief.

Yuyan comments: The thirty-ninth chapter of the manual on *Penetrating the Dark* says: In your search for immortality, if you cannot quite remember the meaning of the 'lead' and 'mercury', then at your leisure, pull out one of the thousands of alchemical books and texts.
   In general, what is described as 'lead' and 'mercury' in the alchemical texts is all done through metaphor. If you are involved in study, you become stimulated by one kind of thing and then merely extend its idea. You must never grasp onto the text and lose the image. This is to reject your inner self and to search for the meaning afar.

He concludes: Those who understand and who can honestly 'make time to consider' these ideas will – through their own consideration – certainly bring themselves to true enlightenment.

Master Zhuxi comments: This chapter explains that the Immortals of old, who composed writings in order to reveal their ideas to mankind, did not clearly describe their work. Their 'courtesy names' for the several minerals were titles for the Yin and Yang within the body. Therefore scholars mostly mistook their true meaning.

Now Wei Boyang has composed this text, being sparing in his use of words, and keeping them concise and easy to understand, again because he feared the loss of their true meaning. So then, what was mostly a muddled text, 'opened up its dark doorway'.

13

THE MILD-MANNERED MAIDEN
AND THE YELLOW SHOOT

These next two chapters both illustrate the close kinship that exists between Yin and Yang, and their part in the alchemical proceedings. This first chapter describes how the 'mild-mannered maiden' (one's own inner vitality, akin to 'mercury' or fire), needs the control of the 'yellow shoot' which grows within the 'true lead' or water. Both Yin and Yang are thus vitally involved in the act of creating life.

> On the river lives the mild-mannered maiden,
> Marvellous she is and spiritually fine,
> But as she bursts into flame, she flits away,
> Not to be for this dusty world.
>
> Just as ghosts and dragons, she lies concealed,
> Where might she be hidden?
> If you would control her
> The yellow shoot is your basis.

This section explains how having the 'lead' controlling the 'mercury' is the true basis for founding an inner Elixir.

The 'true mercury' is the spirit, evident in the quintessential nature of thought and the burgeoning emotion of the heart, both of which are ever-moving, ever-changing – just like mercury. Our tenuous grasp of this material can only be strengthened by the 'yellow shoot', which sprouts from the 'true lead' (just as yellow, orange or red litharge springs from lead upon heating).

As Master Shangyang notes, the theme of this and the next chapter, 'The Unstable Pearl and the Golden Flower', is the same.

Master Shangyang says: The river here casts an image of the 'love of all rivers and their desire for the sea'. The mild-mannered

maiden stands for our own Yin mercurial secretions including our
vital seed [*jing*].

Why are these secretions described as 'spiritually fine'? Because
their achievement is the production of human life – but they can
also cause the destruction of life. Furthermore they may be combined into an Elixir.

One moment we are sitting still and at rest, with this single
marvel nourished within us, then without warning it affects us; in
an instant running through and coming upon us, suddenly and
violently, like something intruding in from another world. Our
circumstances are shaken, feelings are produced, happiness follows, passions spoil us, ideas and thoughts arise, the mercury
following the fire and flying up like so much dust or dirt which can
never be swept up.

'Ghosts' are hidden in these secretions and 'dragons' lie concealed in their form; clouds scatter across the firmament and then
the heavens are revealed to us, as all colour and passion!

He continues: If you would control her, the yellow shoot is your
basis'. These lines have the same meaning as 'Unexpectedly there
blooms a Golden Flower, the one turning into the other [Chapter
14]'.

Generally if the mild-mannered maiden is allowed to have her
way, and you go along with her, you will easily become lost. If it
were not for this single Yang force coming from out the yellow
shoot, you could not control her. The yellow shoot is the energy of
the prenatal inner world – also called the 'lead of the true One'.

Yuyan comments: 'On the river lives the mild-mannered maiden' –
examine intently where it is she arrives from. In general it is in the
empty mind that the spirit condenses and you find her.

Truly the mild-mannered maiden arises from within your own
mind. She is what is known as the 'marvellous mercury', or else the
'spiritual mercury'. She is by nature extremely volatile. Once she
meets fire she flies up and away, without leaving a trace of her
presence. Similarly with concealed ghosts or dragons, nobody
knows where they are hidden.

If you cannot use the yellow shoot as your basis, then how can
this situation be controlled? The yellow shoot is the 'true lead'.

> Something without either Yin or Yang
> Is unnatural, it neglects creation;
> If a hen lays its own egg

A baby chick will never hatch.
And what is the reason for this?
Mating has never taken place.

If the three fives have never joined
The firm and yielding lie apart,
Their skill in effecting transformation
Rests in the natural ease of natural things.
Fire leaps and blazes upwards,
Water oozes and seeps below,
They need no teacher's guidance,
To act just as they do so;
Their gifts at first are truly whole,
And cannot be made anew.

This section illustrates how, if the 'true lead' and 'true mercury' are to be used, they need each other; and even more so, their very natures depend on one another. The *Zhou Yi* says: 'One Yin and one Yang are what are meant by the Dao' (Great Appendix, I.5). This is the underlying message of the whole of the *Can Tong Qi*.

As for the 'three fives', they are water and gold (4+1), fire and wood (2+3), and the soil (5): only if you have water and fire joining together in an 'earthenware pot' can you form the 'holy babe'.

Master Shangyang comments: If you heat up this leaden inner energy as a foundation for the Elixial work then the mercury itself will not abruptly depart. Why is this so?

It is because as Yin and Yang fit together they may be used. If there is something without either Yin or Yang it is unnatural; it turns its back upon the creative process which lies behind all living things.

When you develop an Elixir, you cannot escape Yin and Yang being taken as the foundation. And supposing the inner energy of the true One has returned – once the Elixir is already complete and matured, it will scurry away beyond the confines of Yin and Yang.

The ignorant people of this world do not read alchemical books, and when they speak of developing an Elixir, they think it must mean dwelling deep in the hills, or first going on a retreat, or abandoning their wives and children, or else that they should fast, or join in the practice of 'non-action', or sit still with their minds at a single point; and they take all these as legitimate methods. How ignorant they are!

Yuyan comments: One Yin and one Yang are what is meant by the Dao. Being determinedly Yin or determinedly Yang is a disease!

He continues: If someone can 'reflect back his brightness to light up within [*huiguang neizhao*]' then, once the Yin and Yang have joined together within him in sexual union, the firm and yielding fit together and the three fives return to become one. Why should he seek anything further?

He continues: Generally the Golden Elixir means the path of 'quietness and non-action [*qingjing wuwei*]'. Perhaps some people, drowning in dissolute and unorthodox ideas, see it as necessary here to use some sexual technique to fashion their Golden Elixir. Oh, how wrong they are!

He concludes: In the creative transformation of heaven and earth, water and fire blaze upwards and seep below. How can man's strength make use of this? Simply through being quite natural in his behaviour, that is all.

Within my own body there is a heaven and earth, and I contain within myself both water and fire. In their creative transformation they blaze upwards and seep below. Again how can man's strength make use of this? Entirely through being quite natural in his behaviour, that is all.

The book *Pointing Into the Dark* says: You must understand how to join together all paths and press everything entirely into a mish-mash unity!

Generally speaking the single human body is modelled on heaven and earth. The head represents the heavens above; the belly represents the earth beneath.

Simply submerge the mind and guard it within, neither forgotten, nor aided; and harmonize the breath at the nostrils, holding it neither too loosely nor too tightly. Then naturally the lungs will open and close, donating and receiving, without differing in any way from the creative transformation of heaven and earth.

> Now see how this cock and hen
> Join in sexual union,
> Their firm and yielding flesh
> Bonds together and cannot be released.
> Just like matching sections of a tally
> No art or skill is involved in managing this.

As the son begets he crouches,
While the daughter lies down on her back.
This action is endowed to us in the womb
With the very first spark of life.

Not only when living
Is this seen, plainly and obviously,
But also when drowned
Our bodies behave just the same.

We were never taught this by our parents,
Its learning is quite natural,
Its basis lies in the sexual act,
Decided and established at the start.

The metaphor here is of the sexual union of man and woman which illustrates further the principle of this chapter. The Chinese believed that when drowned the male body floated face downwards while the female faced upwards, and that the same thing happened with animals.

The desire for union between the sexes is natural, it is the longing for each separate element to be bonded again. The wider implication is that through the act of love – in its fullest sense – we may return to the infinity of creation. This 'turning back of the senses' as Master Shangyang would see it, an art transmitted through the corrective training of the sages, is the truly great secret of the Golden Elixir of everlasting life.

Master Shangyang concludes: When vulgar eyes are set upon these words, they see them as insignificant and trifling. But fundamentally they express the central meaning of this book. If you can properly penetrate into the true principle of Yin and Yang, an understanding of these words is immediately imminent – all this should not be a worry to you!

Yuyan comments: Why is 'no art or skill involved in managing this'? Because it is so, it simply is so. I do not understand why it is so, but it is so! Such a mystery indeed!

Zhu Yuanyu comments: Once you recognize the laws of this world, you understand how, in the prenatal inner world, Qian above and Kun below are the father and mother within our own bodies; while, in the postnatal outer world, Li above and Kan below are the son and daughter within our own bodies [see Figure 4].

Fire blazes upwards, which shows the temperament of a son and the trigram Kan, and water seeps below, which shows the temperament of a daughter and the trigram Li. The temperament of the son [Kan] and daughter [Li], is also the temperament of the father [Qian] and mother [Kun].

Now Qian is originally positioned above and Kun positioned below – until the father and mother join together in sexual intercourse to fashion the children Kan and Li. But although the places of Qian and Kun alter, their temperaments are the same. Because there is fire within Kan, it still longs to 'blaze upwards'; and because there is water within Li it still longs to 'seep below'. Each is thinking to 'return to its source, to travel back to its original nature [*fanben huanyuan*]' and revert back to its own kind.

In the case of the son [Kan] and daughter [Li], again, as they fuse together in sexual union, they recreate the constant pattern of heaven above and earth below – and the life of the prenatal inner world returns.

Master Zhuxi comments: The lines which follow after 'something without Yin and Yang' all show the pattern which lies within all material things. They explain this single rule – that one must have the Yin and Yang conjoined to form any kind of basis.

14

THE UNSTABLE PEARL AND THE GOLDEN FLOWER

This chapter continues on the same theme as the last. It describes how the inner vitality of man mixes with the 'unstable pearl'. It asserts the interdependence of the 'cycling five', the 'three fives', 'midnight and midday', and the 'dragon and tiger'; and the tendency within all natural phenomena to confound and mingle.

> The Great Yang, that 'unstable pearl',
> Constantly longs to leave man;
> Until unexpectedly there blooms a Golden Flower,
> The one turning into the other!
> Transformed it becomes a clear fluid,
> But when congealed, it is extremely solid.
>
> The Golden Flower is first to show,
> And in a second is loosened,
> Dissolving into a liquid — with horse's teeth
> Sticking out of it, as on a rough-cut gem,
> The Yang departing peaceably,
> Its temper becoming quite natural.
>
> So on hurries the darkest hour,
> And clutching at the 'forbidden gate',
> 'Kind mama brought me up',
> The obedient child shows its gratitude;
> While stern papa gives the order
> To educate his children and children's children.

This first section introduces the idea of a condensed Elixir. The Great Yang includes Li ☲, which contains within itself the 'true mercury', that 'unstable pearl' which, if not subdued and constantly guarded, will be lost. The Great Yin includes Kan ☵, and within Kan lies the 'true lead', which is naturally peaceful and quiet, solid and congealed. It is only the tranquillity of the 'true lead' which can control the volatility of the 'true mercury'.

Suddenly there appear the first petals of a Golden Flower. The setting of the Elixir proceeds as the lead is dissolved and the mercury fixed. So the lead and mercury fuse together: at first irregular and 'rough-cut', later solidifying and condensing 'something like a chicken's egg, in which white and black mutually tally' (see Chapter 7)'.

The 'darkest hour' is the hour of the 'Yin-shadow'; while the 'forbidden gate' is the 'dark opening of the mysterious female'. She is the mother Kun, in whose arms 'are the past, present and future, her children kept close and fed, for to this world she is mother-in-kind' (see Chapter 4). The 'stern papa' is the father Qian.

Master Shangyang comments: One Yin and one Yang; one Qian and one Kun. The 'kind mama' is the metal [gold], and metal produces the Kan-water. The water is the 'golden duke', who can be termed the 'obedient child'. The 'stern papa' is spoken of as the wood, and wood produces the 'red sand' mercury. Also the children produce more children, and succeeding children follow in their footsteps. Worrying they will not prove capable-bodied, their stern father gives the word of command.

Yuyan comments: The Great Yang, that 'unstable pearl' is the marvellous mercury. The song on the *Great Pathway to the Marvellous Source* says:

> Has this substance ever had a fixed position?
> When the time comes to transform, it will follow its own mind.
> When the body gets warm, it turns to sweat,
> When the wind blows, the nose produces mucus,
> When the loins are stimulated, sperm is made,
> When the eyes are touched with grief, it generates tears.
> You see that every time it constantly longs to leave man.

When the mercury is caught by the 'true lead', they turn round and follow one another, and naturally it can no longer sublimate or flow away. It stays attached within and so transforms into a golden fluid, which congeals to become extremely solid.

The true lead is generated from the position of Kan. First it is fluid, later it congeals – it congeals to make the 'yellow shoot' [see Chapter 13]'. Thus the metaphor of a 'horse's teeth sticking out' is used, which gives it the appearance of a rough-cut gem.

He continues: The lead is the lord, the mercury is the servant. The lead first moves and the mercury responds – just as a lord leads out and his servant complies. The lead is connected to metals [gold]; the mercury is connected to plant materials [wood]. It is in the nature of plant material to 'dote on' metals [minerals], the feeling within minerals [metals] is to 'cherish' plants [wood]. Yin and Yang agree together, and naturally unite as one.

He continues: The 'true lead' is born in the womb of its mother Kun, just as any kind mother rears her child. When it flies up to the Qian palace, it captures the true mercury and knots together with it to form the Elixir. Then it is returned again to the house of its mother Kun; this is how 'the obedient child shows its gratitude'. It occurs just as a kind mother crow disgorges its food for its fledglings.

But if the blazing fire is not fierce enough to reach the end of the forging process, then the 'true lead' cannot fly up. This is the 'stern papa' who gives the order and instruction.

> As the cycling five alternately rule,
> They interlock in order to stay alive;
> So fire will naturally fuse metal,
> And a metal axe will fell a tree.
>
> The three fives together as one,
> Are the very seed of heaven and earth.
> This idea can be told in secret,
> It is difficult to transmit in writing.

This short section develops the idea of the cycling of the 'five elements'. There is a saying, 'From the coarse you get the fine, through pretence you keep the truth.' This is a pointer to the whole concept of alchemical transformation.

Fire can fuse and mould metals. But later the metal can be formed into an axe, which will cut into the wood of a tree. Later perhaps the wood can be formed into ploughshares, which can be dragged through the earth and its soil heaped up to redirect the flow of flood-water. But water can subdue and dowse fire, and a controlled fire may be used to gently heat and mould metals, and so on.

It is only as they 'alternately rule', through their extraction of 'fineness' from 'coarseness', that the cycling five stay alive.

Through the alchemical inversion of the elements, by 'the wood being taken out of the fire' and 'the gold being plucked out of the water', can the Golden Elixir be found and life restored.

Signifying the reappearance of the Yang Elixir, the book *Awakening to the Reality* says:

> I may know how to turn on their heads the family of Kan and Li
> But who else? Who recognizes the current of the Age, or can rearrange
>   Host and Guest?
> If you wish to retain the Mercury in the Golden Cauldron lining it red,
> First find the Sunken Silver under the surface of the White-Jade Pond.
> The achievement of the Sages is to circulate the fire, and before midday
> A 'wheel of sunlight' appears – immersed in a Dark Pool.

The three fives are fire and wood (2+3), water and metal (gold) (1+4), and the ubiquitous soil (5). As the three fives merge into one, so the inner Elixir is complete. Again the *Awakening to the Reality* says:

> 'Three', 'five', 'one' – it lies entirely in these few words,
> Yet those that have understood this have always been few.
> The east – three, the south – two, they make up five,
> The north – one, the west – four, together the same.
> The soil of itself, in its own position produces five,
> The Three Families gaze upon one another to fashion a little child.

Master Shangyang comments: As the cycling five 'alternately rule', they turn upside down to capture one another. Lead, mercury, sand and silver all interlock together in the soil. A great fire burns down to produce soil; and soil is the mother of all metals. When fire is strong, it melts down metal; and wood dreads the punishment of metal. As metal is chastened by fire, so the wood is sufficient and happy.

The south and east join together to form five; wood is three and fire is two. The north and west join together to form five; water is one and metal [gold] is four. The central region is formed of the Wu- and Ji-soils [also five – see Figure 16]. These are the three fives.

If you count from one you arrive at 10,000, a million is passed, then 10 million added to it, the numbers come together to enclose heaven and earth. Thus you reach out, exerting yourself to touch 'its very seed'. You touch 'here' and it comes together 'there' – this can only be told and understood as a secret.

Yuyan comments: Gold [metal] produces water; wood produces fire. This is the usual way of going along with the cycling of the five elements. Now the Elixial method is described and wood and fire pair off, the fire instead producing wood; and the gold [metal] and water join together, the water instead producing gold [metal]. Thus the text says, 'As the cycling five alternately rule, they interlock to stay alive.'

Master Zhuxi comments: The 'cycling five' are mutually born through the love which exists between mother and child. The fire and the gold are mutually overpowered through the order of a stern father.

The three fives refer to fire, gold and wood. They are all endowed with the inner energy of the soil. One idea is that the three fives are the other chapter's [Chapter 32] 'midnight, midday, Wu-soil and Ji-soil'. Here the meaning is not explained in detail.

At midnight, to the right they turn,
At midday, then revolving to the east,
While dawn and dusk act as limits between,
And as host and guest divide up the two.

The dragon blows out at the tiger,
The tiger sucks in the dragon's seed,
Both drink and devour each other,
Totally greedy to succeed –
Each bites and gulps the other down,
Each bolts and sucks the other down.

Shimmering Mars guards the west,
Constant Venus is clear in the sky;
When baleful forces strike
Who may not be overthrown!

The dog will catch the rat,
Small birds fear the hawk;
Each of them acts as it can,
How dare they lay claim to greatness!

If you cannot see this pattern,
Then difficulties create wild ideas,
You squander your family's possessions,
And impoverish your wife and children.

From olden times to the present
Many, many have been devoted;
But they have ended their lives unfulfilled,
For very few may complete this work,
Searching wide outside for the famous medicine
They have turned from the path and gone astray.

This section contains the idea of the natural appetite of each thing for another in the world. It also illustrates the important way they control, confound and mingle with each other.

Midnight and midday, as water and fire, mix and mingle together, and so dawn and dusk as wood and metal act as 'limits between' them – the one acts as guest and the other as host.

Likewise the dragon (wood) 'coming out from within the fire' and the tiger (metal, gold) being 'born from out of the water', illustrate the idea of 'inversion' – the natural tendency within each element to be turned on its head and confounded.

Mars and Venus, the dog and the rat, the small birds and the hawk also show the control each creature exerts upon another.

Master Shangyang says: 'At midnight, to the right they turn' and as if boldly hurrying forward, the Yang-gold is born at midnight. 'At midday, then revolving to the east', the Yin-mercury [wood] is born at midday, enwrapped tightly with Yang vitality.

Dawn and dusk, east and west, as host and guest divide up the two. The gold which originally was set apart and sent away 10,000 miles, is now cherished and loved dearly and the gold [metal] yields to wood's kindnesses. The dragon blows out, the tiger sucks in, the gold doting on the wood's attentions; the one the host and the other the guest, they lovingly drink and devour each other; the one the crow and the other the rabbit, they are totally greedy to succeed; the one male and the other female, they bite and gulp each other down; the one the tortoise and the other the snake, they bolt and suck each other down!

The spirit of the southern direction is the scarlet bird which signifies the planet Mars; whilst the inner energies are depicted by the planet Venus which constantly travels the ecliptic. As it stays over for a night under the roof of Qian, if noxious forces strike, it within generates itself an energy which diffuses outward.

Just as 'the dog will catch the rat' and 'small birds fear the hawk', each of them acts as it can, so how dare they lay claim to any greatness? But if this secret is not transmitted to you by word of mouth, how will you ever guess at what it means?

Yuyan comments: 'At midnight, to the right they turn', means turning from the west to the position of north [midnight]; so then 'the tiger is born from out of the water'. 'At midday, then revolving to the east', means turning from the east to the position of south [midday]; so then 'the dragon comes out from within the fire'.

Midnight and midday mean north and south; north and south mean water and fire. Dawn and dusk mean east and west; east and west mean wood and metal [gold]. Turning to the right, revolving to the left [east], one comes down and the other rises up; so the water and fire interlock, and the wood and metal [gold] are no longer set apart.

Now both 'east' and 'west' along with 'dawn' and 'dusk' must be seen as different names for 'wood' and 'gold'. They do not refer to set directions in the sky, nor to either side of the human body.

He continues: The dragon is the Li-dragon of the south; the tiger is the Kan-tiger of the north. When you create an Elixir, you urge the dragon to blow out and down on the tiger, while the tiger sucks and swallows down the dragon's seed. One blows out, the other sucks in; and the two drink and devour each other.

He continues: When 'shimmering Mars guards the west', it is as fire entering into the neighbourhood of gold [metal]. When 'con-

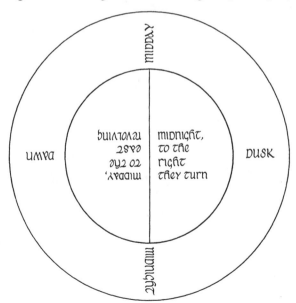

Fig. 19 '*To the right they turn . . . revolving to the east*'

stant Venus is clear in the sky', it is as gold visible and crossing the southern region of the sky, where midday is established.

When you create an Elixir, you transfer the spiritual fire so that it lights up the neighbourhood of the gold. When the gold meets the fire, it is quickly stirred into life and it mounts up, becoming visible in the southern region of the sky.

He continues: The gold is the 'true lead'. 'When baleful forces strike, who may not be overthrown!' The 'true lead' flies upwards, capturing the 'true mercury'. The 'true mercury' submits and offers itself to the 'true lead'.

The song on the *Great Path*, by Master Primal Yang goes: Once the white tiger has got itself excited, which part of the 'unstable pearl' will not follow?

This means just the same thing.

The mind enters the breath-energy to form a foetus, just as a 'dog catches a rat'. When the medicine is fired and heated to finish the Elixir, it is just as 'small birds fear the hawk'. Because these kinds of creatures exert control over each other, when one sees the other it is natural for it to pounce and hold it down. How dare they lay claim to greatness!

15

THESE FOUR IN MAKESHIFT CHAOS

This chapter again illustrates how it is 'closeness in kind' which is of supreme importance. This idea also entails the meeting of opposites – which here specifically refers to the joining of the inner vitality and energy of the body. Again this depends on the ubiquity of the ground-element 'soil' being established solidly within.

> This Elixial sand, wood's secretion,
> Obtaining the gold, they are mixed together.
> The gold and water are paired in position,
> And wood and fire make close companions.
>
> These four create a makeshift chaos,
> Each one either a dragon or tiger;
> The dragons are Yang, their numbers odd,
> The tigers are Yin, their numbers even.
>
> The liver, green, is father,
> The lungs, white, are mother,
> The kidneys, black, are her children,
> The heart, red, is their daughter,
> The spleen, yellow, their grandparent.
> At midnight forms the cycle's beginning;
> The three materials all of one family,
> Are returned to either the Wu- or Ji-soils.

This section illustrates the principle of 'the three materials returning to the One' (*sanwu guiyi*), which is followed in the completion of the Elixir. The discussion is derived from a consideration of the cycling five elements.

The 'Elixial sand' is the red sand, which belongs to fire; and fire is the 'illustrious secretion' of wood. The black lead belongs to water; and water forms the original source of energy for the gold. Because of this, water and fire find similarities in both bringing life to this world, and wood and gold are alike in that both may be made into useful utensils. Metal can produce water (become fluid), and metal may also be hidden within water; wood can produce fire, and fire must also contain wood.

From this it is obvious that gold, water, wood and fire are so closely knit together that they can never easily be separated. These four form the creative 'makeshift chaos' of the 'four images', which can again be divided into two – gold and water united in the tiger, and wood and fire joined together in the dragon.

The dragons, being Yang, signify odd numbers; the tigers, being Yin, are the even numbers.

Heaven has five elements; likewise man himself contains five organs. These five organs and five colours directly correspond. The liver (just like wood and all vegetation) forms the colour green; the lungs (having sympathies with all metals and minerals) form the colour white; the heart (like fire) forms the colour red; the kidneys (belonging to water and fluids) form the colour black; and the spleen (akin to the soil) forms the colour yellow.

During the inner development of an Elixir, water and fire play the central role. Wood belongs to the Yang, and wood can produce fire, therefore the liver (wood) is called 'father'; whilst metal is Yin, and metal can produce water, therefore the lungs (metal) are called 'mother'. Water is born from metal, hence the kidneys (water) are called the 'children'; fire is born from wood, hence heart (fire) is called the 'daughter'; both metal and wood are produced from the soil, and they generate water and fire, hence the spleen (soil) is called the 'grandparent'.

Lastly, the 'generated' and 'completed' numbers of heaven and earth all begin with 'one', and the cycling five elements have their beginning in water. The oneness of the firmament (heaven) above generates water; water corresponds to the north and midnight. Therefore 'at midnight forms the cycle's beginning' (see Figure 6).

Wood and fire form one substance; gold and water also form one substance; but the soil forms one substance on its own. Therefore as the three families stand together, they see their mutual resemblance – they all return to the oneness of the soil. As the three families join so they form an inner Elixir together – which depends entirely upon the ubiquity of the soil.

This chapter should be compared with Chapter 32, 'The Two Soils Complete the Work'.

Master Shangyang comments: The most utterly marvellous and treasured possessions in man's body are his inner vitality and energy. The *Heart Seal Canon* calls these the 'ultimate medicines'. Zhang Boduan [in his book *Awakening to Reality*] calls them 'life's jewels'.

Now what our Immortal has described in this book, the *Can Tong Qi*, is 'sameness' and 'difference'. What is meant by 'sameness'? When the text says that once the gold reverts to its source in the water it may be declared the 'restored Elixir' [Chapter 33]. This very simply is what is meant by 'sameness'.

What is meant by 'difference'? It is Qian and Kun, Kan and Li, male and female, the pipes and bellows; open and closed, 'being' and 'nothingness' Yin and Yang, the sun and moon; the dark female, the Wu- and Ji-soils; the firm and yielding, the cock and hen; the pivot of the Dipper, the bowl of the Dipper; the crow and rabbit, the Hun- and Po-souls; the gold and the inner energies, the spiritual light; the yellow shoot, the chain-pump; the lead and the silver, the sand and the mercury; the floating and sinking, the black and the white; the teeming void, the flurried confusion; the proper compass within, the pivot and lynchpin; the empty void, the dark obscurity; the truth in man, the great chaos; the battlements and towers, the tangled trails; the red bird, the tortoise and snake; the white tiger, the green dragon; the nodal point, the unstable pearl; the golden sand, the watery silver; the eight stones, the yellow soil; the 'double-entranced cave', where 'spiritual values dwell'; the 'moon on its back' as the furnace, the suspended womb-cauldron; the red-coloured gate, the 'dust in the window-light'; the upturned and downturned bows of the moon, the mild and fierce firings; the Elixial sand and wood's secretion, the 'mild-mannered maiden' on the river; the citadel and the city wall, the 'horse's teeth' and 'rough-cut gem'; the forbidden gate, the knife-point; the Golden Flower, the autumnal stone; our feelings and our nature, the host and the guest; the white snow, the yellow carriage; the dark pool, the Herdboy star; the cooking pot and the gnomen of the sundial; the 'dog's-teeth set against each other' and the green dragon's secretions; the three fives and both sevens; the minutest share and the line's tokens, and so on.

Each appearance is alike; one and all, they are jewels of the self. They either represent the 'door and gateway of Change' [see

Chapter 19]; or else describe the 'spiritual energy filling a room' [see Chapter 10]; or else are speaking of the cauldron vessel; or else are used as metaphors of the body's functioning; or else are various images, perhaps relating to advance and retreat.

Yuyan comments: Heaven, as one, produces water, which is established in the north, and its family is of the 'dark warriors'. The earth, as two, produces fire, which is established in the south, and its family is the red bird. Heaven, as three, produces wood, which is established in the east, and its family is the green dragon. The earth, as four, produces minerals [metal], which is established in the west, and its family is the white tiger. These four each occupy a single direction; each one identifies a separate family, originally independent of the others [see Figures 6 and 16].

Now the text says, 'The gold and water are paired in position, and wood and fire make close companions', which means that the Yang dragon finds its source in the palace of Li and the Yin tiger is reborn at the position of Kan.

Now since each one identifies a separate family the text should mention and commend all four images. But the red bird [fire] and 'dark warriors' [water] are not mentioned – only the tiger and dragon. This is because north and south form the warp, while east and west form the weft.

What is meant by the 'gold and water paired in position' is that the western number four, the white metal-tiger, is sent down into the water; while what is meant by 'wood and fire make close companions' is that the eastern number three, the green wood-dragon, is hoisted up into the fire. Henceforth the gold is not in the west but 'paired' with the water in the north, and the wood is not in the east but in 'close company' with the fire in the south. The white tiger is changed into a black tiger and the green dragon is transformed into a red dragon!

Generally if these four – gold, water, wood and fire – are collected together and become as one, they form a state of complete and utter 'makeshift chaos'. It is as if the 'supreme pole' [*taiji*] had not yet split apart and formed into Yin and Yang (see Figure 2); so that the Zhen-dragon 'mercury' appears in the neighbourhood of Li, while the Dui-tiger 'lead' is born from the direction of Kan.

He continues: The Golden Elixir is the mysterious process whence something is born out of nothing. This can never be performed with anything which has any particular form or substance. Now Wei Boyang is speaking of the five organs of the body. Why is this?

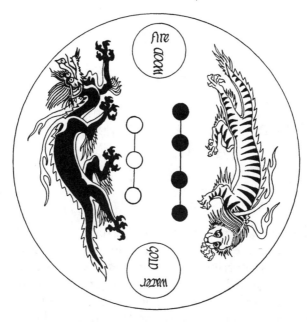

Fig. 20 The dragon and the tiger

He is not making use of the five organs. He has only borrowed
the idea of the organs because of their likeness to the five elements.
The liver being green and the lungs being white, signify wood and
metal; the heart being red and kidneys being black, signify fire and
water.

He concludes: The gold and water are 'paired in position' and the
wood and fire make 'close companions'. They both join together
with the Wu- and Ji-soils of the central region to form the 'three
materials'. Generally the four images and five elements rely totally
on the soil. Without the Wu- and Ji-soils they could not form an
Elixir: thus here 'the three materials, all of one family, are returned to either the Wu- or Ji-soil'.

16

DAWN AND DUSK, PENALTIES AND POWERS

In this chapter we find a description of the actual instant the Elixir is acquired, as the source of our inner-world congenital energy. The last lines describe the revival of life, which is ultimately mysterious – gained through assimilating the idea of how the firm and yielding alternate, invert and interweave with one another. The time of midnight stands for the birth of the Yang, which represents a genesis happening during a time of darkness.

> Now firm and yielding arise alternately,
> As their order is changing, spreading out:
> The dragon to the west, the tiger to the east,
> Now set up at dawn and dusk.

> Their penalties and powers are assembled together,
> And they co-operate together, tamed and at ease:
> Penalties ruling over submissions and destruction,
> Powers commanding life and new beginnings.

> In the second month the elm-seeds fall,
> As the stars of the Dipper come down near the east;
> In the eighth month the wheat sprouts,
> As the bowl of the Dipper seizes the west.

> Midnight in the south and midday in the north,
> They are linked by a single guiding thread;
> Their destiny is of one to nine,
> In the end returning to its origin;
> Buried within, at the very first weak and perilous,
> Sown as young seed at midnight.

This chapter explains the principle of the Yin and the Yang combining to form the One and similarly describes the linked functioning of penalties and powers.

The inner development of an Elixir uses water and fire as its materials, and metal and wood as the tools. But whilst midnight and midday form the warp, and dawn and dusk the weft to this process, now these opposite posts are inverted and engulfed, responding to the body of the heavens above. Thus the firm and yielding forces, the Yin and the Yang, arise successively, pushing and pulling upon each other. Now, contrary to their usual positions, the dragon (wood, dawn, the east, powers) arrives in the west and the tiger (metal, dusk, the west, penalties) occupies the east. The dragon's powers turn to penalties and the penalties of the tiger become powers.

Thus in the spring months of the year, when all is coming into life, the elm-seeds fall; and in the autumn, when all is dying, the wheat sprouts. The significance is similar to 'the elm-seeds falling down, returning back to their roots', and 'penalties and powers turning their backs as night and day draw apart' (Chapter 5); and also compare 'at the second month of autumn, then lay by the young grain that the withered may yet return to life', and 'the

Fig. 21 The inversion

shepherd's purse and wheat both shoot, for as they prosper so they stay alive (also Chapter 5).

These examples demonstrate the 'single guiding thread' linking all creation and destruction. In the tapestry of the sky, dawn to the east and dusk to the west form the weft, and midday to the south and midnight to the north form the warp. But in this chapter these positions are inverted and turned upon their heads.

These guiding pointers all variously interlink, finding their source at midnight, in the quiet and the stillness, when the inner vitality and energy of the body returns once more, coming together at its origin.

Master Shangyang says: The green dragon belongs in the east and the white tiger to the west. These are their proper places. As 'their order is changing, spreading out', so the green dragon sets up transversely at dusk [west], while the white tiger sets up transversely at dawn [east]. Thus, their 'penalties and powers assembled together', they 'co-operate together, tamed and at ease'.

If they are turned head over heels and interweaved, the dragon and tiger are turned to face each other. They are joined to each other in position, the two creatures 'tamed and at ease'; and thereby they command life and create powers.

If the dragon in the east and the tiger in the west were fixed – each in its own position – they would be self-willed and think only of themselves. Then the two creatures would disturb each other and quarrel, and thereby command destruction and create penalties.

He continues: Penalties mean going along with the course of the cycling five; powers mean interweaving with the course of the cycling five. Penalties mean the Yin dispersing the Yang; powers mean the Yang joining up within the Yin. Penalties mean the Yin is the greater and the Yang the lesser; powers mean the Yin is the lesser and the Yang the greater.

Moreover this situation is just the same as when there are four Yang and two Yin lines in the hexagram of the second month of the year ☱. The Yang is growing and the Yin is shrinking, but although there is more Yang there still remains some Yin. The greater Yang are the powers while the remaining Yin rule over destruction.

Therefore during the three months of spring, as all the myriad creatures come back to life, the elm-seeds fall down – returning to their roots.

It is the same in man. During the vigorous part of his life there is more Yang within his body and less Yin. Each day he feels full of vigour. But during this time, the sea of desire is greatly inflamed and, although there is more Yang, it is all used in dispersing the Yin. If the surplus Yang cannot take control, then sickness and disease crowds in and ultimately the Yang is lost, just as thoughts invade and there comes a return to the world of desire.

Use your utmost strength to seek out the Yin. If the remaining Yang meet up with the Yin, they all become lost and the Yang will ultimately perish. This is what is meant by 'powers turning back into penalties'. Grasp hold of the remaining Yang and use them in an orderly fashion, hastening along the path of the restored Elixir. Then you are able to return to eternal life.

This is what is meant by 'penalties and powers assembled together'. They are 'co-operating together, tamed and at ease'.

Also this is just the same as when there are the four Yin and two Yang lines in the hexagram of the eighth month ䷠. The Yang are being dispersed by the Yin, but although there is more Yin there stilli remains some Yang. The greater Yin are the penalties while the remaining Yang rule over life.

Therefore during the three months of autumn, as all the myriad creatures are stripped of life, the shepherd's purse and wheat both shoot and prosper.

It is the same in man. As his years draw close to sixty, there is more Yin and less Yang in his body, and each day the remaining Yang declines. If during this time he takes command of the re-maining Yang and fashions it – following the path of the Golden Elixir – then he can make the Yang anew. This is what is meant by 'turning back old age and restoring youth', or 'everlasting life and eternal vision'.

He continues: 'The Yang numbers start at one and end at nine. When the Yang numbers reach nine they come to an end. At the end they return again to one. This is what is meant by 'their destiny is of one to nine, in the end, returning to its origin'.

'Buried within, at the very first, weak and perilous, sown as young seed at midnight'. The completion of the whole task of fashioning an Elixir lies here in these two lines.

In general it is the trigram Kan which represents the 'weak and perilous'. On the earth it is represented in the sun and moon becoming reunited and repaired – like an ancient jade badge of rank.

It is as when the single Yang is first born, wherein the tortoise and snake lie coiled around one another [as 'dark warriors']. This great Oneness contains within itself the prenatal inner-world original energy and its true seed is encountered at midnight, when it is bestowed upon the earth.

He concludes: During the glorious springtime how many creatures do not bring to birth? Nevertheless the elm-seeds are dispatched to the ground. Similarly you should protect against penalties within powers, and defend against destruction during a time of bringing to birth.

During the weather of the autumn, how many creatures do not wither away? Nevertheless the shepherd's purse and wheat put forth shoots. Similarly within penalties there are powers, and during destruction there is a coming to life.

In the writing this theme is continually mentioned. Little by little, you will come to understand it – although its central idea must remain a mystery. It is only therein that you will find the prenatal inner-world energy.'

Yuyan comments: The images are inserted here in order to act as illustrations. Wei Boyang has concocted them in order to teach people. His idea is for them to be totally absorbed by their own self-illumination. What use is it if they 'grasp hold of the text and let fly the images'? Often they only search these pages, thinking they mean no more than their own thoughts and ideas. As a result they lead themselves grievously astray, and nothingness and being are denied!

Then they will certainly never understand that when Wei Boyang speaks of 'the dragon to the west', 'the tiger to the east', 'midnight in the south' and 'midday in the north', he means heaven and earth being turned upside down and inverted within our own bodies.

If they can clearly awaken to this mystery of heaven and earth being inverted within their bodies, they establish east and west as the weft and the linked north and south as the single guiding thread. All these directly and precisely identify the workings of our heavenly self-nature. How then can we waste our time seeking anything else besides?

He continues: The destiny of 'one to nine' is to honour the nine-fold destiny of the One. 'In the end, it returns to its origin'. It proceeds from one to nine, from nine to one, coming and going, rising and falling, circulating about without cease.

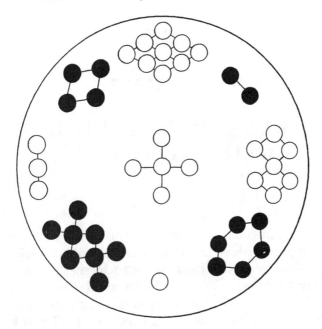

Fig. 22 One to nine

He concludes: The mystery of the Golden Elixir lies buried, at the very first, in the prenatal inner world, while it is 'sown as young seed' in the postnatal acquired world. Silent and without moving, hidden away and unseen, this is the moment when the 'supreme pole' has not yet split apart [see Figure 2].

What is it like, the postnatal and acquired world? When it is touched, then it follows and opens out. It is the moment when, in a flurry of confusion, the 'supreme pole' actually begins to split apart. The prenatal and inner world concerns only one single energy. After it has become postnatal and acquired, it enters the outer world and is assumed as the seed of our own true vitality.

17

YOU BEGIN THINKING ON SOMEONE YOU MEET

An oral transmission demands the strictest attention, especially when comparing ideas and thoughts. Only similars will respond together – dissimilars will antagonize each other – so how absurd it is to think otherwise and resort to chemical elixirs in your search for everlasting life! The natural world is straightforward. If you take the true Yin and true Yang, which are similar in kind, and mate them together, how could you be without an Elixir for long?

> You begin thinking on someone you meet –
> Watch for any clues and begin unravelling them.
> You take all sorts of things and compare them,
> In order to sort out their source and their end.
>
> See how the cycling five subdue one another,
> Altering to become either father or mother;
> As mama holds within her stimulating juices,
> So papa grants his endowment.
>
> Their condensed vitality streams into a form
> Shaped as pebbles of gold that will never decay,
> Watch out especially that they do not spill,
> Or you will never complete the work.
>
> Set up a pole and you see its shadow,
> Shout across a valley and you hear the echo;
> Surely this is miraculous,
> The very image of the universe!

This section underlies the great care needed for the successful completion of the alchemical work. As you compare what you hear and observe in people, and what you see and understand of the world, so you combine various kinds of things together and sort out their source and end.

The cycling five bring forth and restrain each other in turn, acting both as father or mother. The usual rule of the cycling five is that of mutual production, whereby each in turn gives birth to the other. But if you do not also have control and subjugation, you do not have life, because within destruction lies birth and new beginnings.

A mother cares for and nourishes us; a father bestows his vital spirit. The significance here is the same as in the passages 'kind mama brought me up', 'stern papa gives the order', and 'the cycling five alternately rule, they interlock in order to stay alive' (see Chapter 14).

Both the shadow thrown by a pole and the echo returning from a call are phenomena which appear miraculous and yet are quite natural. It is the same in the ways of heaven: they are obvious and straightforward for all to see.

Master Shangyang comments: This chapter is speaking of the possibility of someone meeting a teacher. He should first examine fully all he says, watching for any clues and unravelling them. Which are true? Which are false? In this manner the *Can Tong Qi* asks us to compare them all.

If you have found a true teacher there are no questions he cannot answer and he will explain to you how to begin without stopping or obstructing you. But if he is a false teacher he will only answer one question in ten. All the clues he gives you are made up and do not ring true. He guides you – but the path turns out to be a mean and dispirited one.

Perhaps he advised you that 'not using words is the Dao', or tells you only to practise 'sitting silently and gazing into the void'. If you question him on the 'sand and mercury', or the 'dragon and tiger', or the 'gold and wood set apart', or the 'shape of the Zhen-thunder on the third day', or on 'turning back to the prenatal inner world', he has not read and fully understood the alchemical books. He looks foolish and cannot reply.

The simple people of this world only hear rumours about how someone sat silently for several years, or about how so-and-so left and went to such-and-such place, and further confused tales about the 'Dao'. How can they understand about the teacher Mazu [709–88, one of the greatest patriarchs of Zen] sitting at Southern Hillock and ridiculously 'polishing a tile'? How can they comprehend Yin and Yang holding in their jaws the reasons for life and destruction? There has been generation upon generation of these usual masters with their general sediment of ideas drawn from the mouths of men.

Yuyan comments: The petty arts of the uninitiated make the work seem complicated and tricky. They are easy to find but difficult to complete. The supreme method of the Golden Elixir makes the work seem concise and simple. It is difficult to find but easy to complete.

As 'you begin thinking on someone you meet, watch for any clues and begin unravelling them'. This is to 'take all sorts of things and compare them, in order to sort out their source and their end'.

So then, in the interval between heaven and earth, as things appear and things transform, peer into the heights and depths to see what is happening and what is not. It is all quite clear and straightforward. Everything can be singly identified and ideas developed. For instance the crane cries out midway through the night, while its young call out at the fifth watch [cf. Hexagram 61, 'Inner Truth']. What is the cause of this? It is because there is a mutual response within the energies of heaven and earth.

It is just the same as when the cicada falls silent in cold weather or the rhinoceros gazes at the bright stars, or the old oyster holds inside itself a moon-lit pearl, or a mere block of stone contains jade. It is the same as the butterfly straightening and bending its wings, or the glow-worm brightening and dulling its light, or the closing and opening of the cat's eyes. It is just the same as the turning one way and then another of the deer's tail, or the taken-in breath of the tortoise in hibernation, or the spat-out sand of the turtle. It is just the same as the windsock blowing in the wind, or the drip-tile on a roof dripping water, or the lodestone pulling at a needle, or amber attracting small particles. It is just the same as the turning well-sweep which brings up water, or the sweet flag in the rice-fields which collects the dew, or the snake entering into hibernation, or the fish resting in still water, or the dung-beetle rolling his ball, or the solitary wasp driving out its young, or the baby chick contained in the egg, or the young rabbit harboured in the womb. It is just the same as the ox having a yellow hide, or the dragon harbouring a pearl, or plums and walnuts producing kernels, or the sweet melon shedding its skin. It is just the same as the banana-tree woken by spring breezes, the parasol-tree hanging with autumn drizzle, the evening moon seen over the clear blue lake, or morning mists shrouding the green hills. All these are revelations of the Golden Elixir. It is as Zhang Boduan says, 'To smelt the Golden Elixir you must deeply delve into Yin and Yang and fully comprehend the ways of creation.' How true this is!

He continues: The essential in the method of the Elixir is attained in the cycling five and the mystery of the cycling five lies entirely in the trigrams Kan and Li.

The trigram Kan means water, and metal and water are 'paired in position' with the metal [gold] within the water; the trigram Li means fire, and wood and fire 'are close companions' with the wood within the fire [see Chapter 15]. These are the four images. In addition Kan inherits the Wu-soil and Li inherits the Ji-soil. These make up the cycling five.

He continues: The Elixial method takes the fire to smelt the metal, and the metal to fell the wood. If fire is too strong then water is poured onto it, while if the water is too strong then earth is built up to check it. This is what is meant by 'the cycling five subdue one another'.

Metal produces water, but if water has gold [metal] as its child then the gold is born out of the water. Wood produces fire, but if fire has wood as its child then the wood is born out of the fire. This is what is meant by 'altering to become either father or mother'.

The father is similar to heaven; the mother is similar to the earth. The energies of the skies descend to the earth and the earth receives them to complete its task of the generation of life. Thus the text says, 'As mama holds within her stimulating juices, so papa grants his endowment.'

He concludes: If the scholar who works on his inner development can create an intercourse within his own heaven and earth, and have his own five elements clustering together there within him, then each will mix up, chew at, and bolt down the other – and each one will have a joint passion for another. And it is then that you begin to feel the sense of a 'something' being born out of a 'nothing', forming within you that little 'holy babe'!

Supposing you take an inch of wild creeper,
Or an ounce of croton bean,
Thrust it into your throat
And abruptly you stiffen and fall down.

> At that moment could Duke Zhou or King Wen,
> With their various stalks of divination,
> Or Confucius foretelling through his diagrams,
> Or Bian Que grasping his needle.
> Or the Wizards of yore shouting and drumming –
> Could any one of them command you to get up alive?

This section ridicules the work of the outer alchemists. They will as easily poison you as help you – and then none of the saints and sages will be able to come to your aid. Yet if the Golden Elixir is gathered solidly within your own belly, although you may remain stupid and unable to explain it, it will still lengthen and strengthen your life.

Master Shangyang comments: Most certainly, the inner energy of the true Yin and Yang comes through things which occur in the same kind of circumstances being merges and matched together. How could you ever then be without the marvellous Elixir for long!

18

WEI BOYANG'S OWN POSTFACE

The author charmingly portrays himself and explains how he was drawn to the present work. He exorts us to 'embrace the One and not to forsake it', and emphasizes how the true alchemy of everlasting life lies in an acceptance of the interchanging aspects of Yin and Yang. Through setting up this natural process, our own spiritual vitality ultimately guides not only ourselves but the whole world into peace.

> In a state of Kuai, a common man,
> Alone in a valley barely existing,
> Clasps to his bosom rough simplicity,
> And pleasures in neither circumstance nor honour.

> In rude habit he spends his time,
> Careless of either fame or profit,
> Grasping onto the quiet and solitude,
> Those rare times, so tranquil and still.

> So there, dwelling in idleness and ease,
> Then I composed this work,
> To sing of the order of Great Change,
> The Three Sages' forgotten words . . .
> I looked at their obvious meaning,
> And saw one thread connecting them all.

This whole chapter explains the writing of the text of the *Can Tong Qi* by Wei Boyang. The first section, in humble fashion, states the intention of explaining the texts of the *Zhou Yi* (Changes of Zhou) – to 'sing of the order of Great Change' – and his avowed idea of the 'one thread connecting them all'.

It is based upon the principle of acceptance,
Which is dazzlingly displayed as spiritual vitality.
Transforming, this spirit fills out
To guide the whole world ultimately to peace.

Outside it lies in the calendar,
And 10,000 generations follow without cease.
But for order to exist in government
Your actions must be uncomplicated.

Guided within, thus nourish your nature
On the naturalism of Huangdi and Laozi.
Holding your power solidly within,
Return it to the root, to the source.

And then quite close by in your own heart,
Not apart from your own body,
You embrace the One – do not forsake it,
For thus you may be long preserved.

Pairing up through this inner cultivation,
As the cock and hen take up position,
As the four images remember their support,
The cycling five come back and follow.

Do away with forced embellishment,
The 'eight stones' utterly reject.
To examine the use of fabricated things
Is to honour what everyone prizes.

This section describes the main teaching of the *Can Tong Qi*. Its central tenet is the focusing of attention on the harmony and acceptance existing between the Yin and the Yang. Extending the same idea to oneself, it signifies the marriage of one's inner vitality and one's spirit – nurtured through a resolve which turns them back 'to the root', returning 'to the source'.

This is displayed without in the progress of the heavenly calendar, and within during the process of our own inner development. The tradition of Huangdi (the Yellow Emperor) and Laozi (author of the *Daode Jing*) exists within Daoism as a 'quietist and non-active' (*qingjing wuwei*) school.

The *Daode Jing* says, 'Holding your power solidly within, you become like a new-born babe – poisonous insects will not attack him, wild beasts will not seize him, birds of prey not swoop down upon him (Chapter 55).' It also says, 'Returning to the root means stillness, stillness means returning to life, returning to life means to be always preserved (Chapter 16).' This is the gist of the meaning here.

The idea is of maintaining life, without tampering with external procedures. In the mutual accord of Yin and Yang, activity and rest intermesh, just as the 'true lead' and 'true mercury' properly intermix during the cultivation of the Elixir.

Yuyan comments: Fu Xi drew up the eight trigrams. Following on this, they were doubled up and King Wen devised the hexagrams; while, through observing their shapes, he attached texts to them to explain good fortune and misfortune. Confucius also collated the ten 'Wings' [appendices] to the book. Thus they all three accepted the principle of their inner natures and destinies, and made good any deficiencies in the Dao of heaven and earth.

Therefore 'outside it lies in the calendar' where it can be quite openly followed. This has been the rule for '10,000 generations'.

'For order to exist thus in government', 'your actions must be uncomplicated'. This means that if it is capable enough to form the model for a hundred kings, the Dao of Change must indeed be called great!

The Yellow Emperor 'observed the ways of heaven, and grasped the actions of heaven' [the opening lines to the *Shadowy Tally* scripture]. Laozi, 'holding his power solidly within, may be compared to a new-born babe [*Daode Jing*, Chapter 55]. If the 300 or more characters of the *Shadowy Tally* and the 5000 or more of the *Daode Jing* are turned over and over again in discussion with others, there is nothing then that will not be made clear in the mysteries of creation.

> Set out in order then just three ingredients
> As branches and twigs all joined together,
> They may appear with different names,
> Yet they all emerge from out of one gate.

> Not vainly have I tied up these verses,
> And sounded out harmony in these lines,
> In them the truth can almost
> In all its detail be seen.

> Had I pushed myself to produce more,
> It would be pretence and repetition.
>
> The work is entitled 'The Threefold as One',
> Now minutely inspect its doctrines;
> Its phrases are few but its method is great,
> You are its later heirs and you should honour it.

This section explains the 'threefold path' as being one, which is one explanation of the title to Wei Boyang's work – *can tong qi* can translate as 'the threefold as one'.

First comes change, as it is displayed in the ancient book of the *Zhou Yi* – which gives the idea for the material ingredients for the Elixir; secondly there is the 'quietist and non-active' Daoist tradition of nourishing one's inner nature – which yields the idea of the inner 'furnace' and 'cauldron'; lastly comes the alchemic tradition of firing metals – which completes the process, bringing in the idea of the firing times for the Elixir.

These three, the *Zhou Yi*, Daoism and alchemy, are all brought together here as three paths which yet emerge from one single gate. Thus they are the 'threefold' as 'one'.

Yuyan comments: The great *Book of Change*, Huangdi and Laozi, and the alchemical fire. If these three ingredients are 'set out in order, as branches and twigs all joined together, they may appear with different names yet all emerge from out of a single gate'. This is what is meant by being 'three of the same kind'.

> Abandon the world, flee from its hurts,
> And follow your mission onto the hills.
> There you may roam solitary and alone,
> Neighbour only to sprites and pixies.
> You transform your body to become immortal . . .
> And become engulfed, silent and unknown.
>
> Then in a hundred generations you descend
> To wander among the men of this world,
> Displaying your 'feathered wings'
> And bending south, east and west.
>
> In turbulent times and when in distress,
> It is as in a plant when the water dries up,

The stalks and leaves cut off will wither yellow,
And lose their flowering splendour.
Yet if each sustains itself from the other,
Tranquil and secure they achieve everlasting life!

Here Wei Boyang sums up his message to the human world. In our activities we 'bend south, east and west', but the northern direction – corresponding to water and the 'true lead' – lies hidden and unspoken of. Accordingly, Wei Boyang imitates this idea by mischievously hiding his own name within the text.

The first character in the first line, *wei* ('abandon'), is a pun; and it combines with the character *gui* ('ghosts', 'sprites', 'pixies') to form the two halves of the character for his family name 'Wei'.

In the next stanza, *bo* ('hundred') is a pun on *bo* ('white') which, along with *ren* ('men') forms the two halves of the character 'Bo'. Then the left-hand part of the character for 'displaying' is combined with the right-hand part of the character for 'turbulent' to form the character Yang. Thus the lines of poetry reveal the name of the author as Wei Boyang.

Finally he uses the image of a plant in which the need for water is illustrated in the plant's stalk and leaves. If the one sustains itself from the other, tranquil and secure, the whole plant perpetuates its life. It is the same within all things – Yin and Yang together in harmony bring everlasting life.

XU CONGSHI'S TEXT

19

THE OVERALL ORDERING OF
GREAT CHANGE

This is the first chapter of the text said to be written by Xu
Congshi, disciple of Wei Boyang, and he begins in the manner of
his reputed teacher. The first chapter illustrates how the method of
refining an Elixir possesses a cyclical form, with its own consti-
tuent markers, or 'tokens' – the hexagrams or trigrams. Managing
to refine an Elixir is like managing 'a team of horses' – in like
manner, phenomena in the natural world echo phenomena in the
human world.

> Qian and Kun are the door and gateway to Change
> Father and mother to the various hexagrams;
> Thus Kan and Li are greatly assisted
> In turning the hub on a proper axis.

Qian and Kun, either as hexagrams or trigrams (the terms are
interchangeable), stand for heaven and earth, Yin and Yang. Qian
and Kun occupy a position of special importance within the eight
trigrams because they lay the foundation for all phenomena within
the natural and human world. They are the 'door and gateway to
Change'.

The trigram Qian ☰ is made up of three single Yang lines and
its body is purely Yang; the trigram Kun ☷ is made up of three
single Yin lines and its body is purely Yin. As Yin and Yang act on
each other, so they produce the six trigrams Kan ☵, Li ☲, Zhen
☳, Dui ☱, Gen ☶ and Sun ☴. As the eight trigrams are doubled
up, so they form the sixty-four hexagrams. The *Zhou Yi* is made
up of these sixty-four hexagrams, which are founded on the Qian
(Creative, Hexagram 1) and Kun (Receptive, Hexagram 2). It is in
this fashion that they act as 'father and mother'.

As the trigram Qian ☰ acquires the central line of Kun ☷, it forms the trigram Li ☲; it belongs to the Yang, its form is fire and it is represented by the sun. As the trigram Kun ☷ acquires the central line of Qian ☰ it forms the trigram Kan ☵; it belongs to the Yin, its form is water and it is represented by the moon.

Qian is thus represented in the heavens above, and Kun shown in the earth beneath. Through their separation they 'greatly assist' Kan and Li, the moon and sun, to rise and fall between them. Thus Qian and Kun form the image of the axle of a carriage, while Kan are Li are represented by the hub which turns upon the axle. As there is an axle for the hub, the carriage can proceed.

The hexagrams Qian and Kun form the body of Change, Kan and Li make up their function, and all four of them – through their mix and interplay – give rise to change and transformation.

Within the human self, Qian and Kun form the 'cauldron and furnace' of Change, whilst Kan and Li make up the ingredients for the Elixir. The rest of the sixty hexagrams symbolize the 'firing times' for the Elixir.

As in Wei Boyang's first chapter, the analogy is with driving a carriage. There are many similarities between the chapters.

Master Shangyang comments: Qian moves out directly and is Yang; at its uttermost point it then produces Yin. Kun moves out and bursts forth as Yin; at its uttermost point it then produces Yang. Yin and the Yang interleave to complete the trigrams Li and Kan.

Confucius said [Great Appendix I.11]: In Change there is the 'supreme pole' [*taiji*]. This gives birth to the 'two forms' [Yin and Yang]. The two forms give birth to the 'four images'. The four images produce the eight trigrams.

When Qian makes use of the 'nines' [Yang lines], it first rides onto Kun ☷ to form Returning ䷗, and Returning is pregnant with Zhen ☳. Returning then forms the Army ䷆, and the Army is pregnant with Kan ☵. The Army then forms Humility ䷎, and Humility is pregnant with Gen ☶. Humility then forms Enthusiasm ䷏, and Zhen ☳ is born out of Enthusiasm. Enthusiasm then forms Relating ䷇, and Kan ☵ is born out of Relating. Relating then forms Tearing Apart ䷖, and Gen ☶ is born out of Tearing Apart. So then you have the three sons,

Zhen ☳, Kan ☵ and Gen ☶, all borne as children within the belly of Kun ☷.

When Kun makes use of the 'sixes' [Yin lines], it first rides onto Qian ☰ to form Encounter ䷫, and Encounter is pregnant with Sun ☴. Encounter then forms People At One ䷌, and People at One is pregnant with Li ☲. People at One then forms Treading ䷉, and Treading is pregnant with Dui ☱. Treading then forms Small Cultivation ䷈, and Small Cultivation gives birth to Sun ☴. Small Cultivation then forms Great Possession ䷍, and Great Possession gives birth to Li ☲. Great Possession then forms Breakthrough ䷪, and Breakthrough gives birth to Dui ☱. So then you have the three daughters, Sun ☴, Li ☲ and Dui ☱, all borne as children within the body of Qian ☰.

'The cock and hen mess around together, each kind assisting the other [paraphrasing Chapter 8].' So then Qian again joins with Kun to form Approach ䷒, Approach then Flourishing ䷊, Flourishing then Great Vigour ䷡, Great Vigour then Breakthrough ䷪. This is the Yang chasing after the Yin.

Kun again stimulates Qian and they form Retreat ䷠; Retreat then Decay ䷋, Decay then Observance ䷓, Observance then Tearing Apart ䷖. This is the Yin flirting with the Yang.

Such is the way the hexagram Qian gives birth to three daughters and three sons. The sons thence depart – the three sons and three daughters alternate as husband and wife, and the sixty hexagrams are produced in order. This is the meaning of Qian and Kun acting as 'father and mother to the various hexagrams'.

What is meant by 'Kan and Li are greatly assisted'? The Yang rides over the Yin, and within Qian ☰ is produced a hollow which forms Li ☲. The Yin rides over the Yang, and Kun's ☷ belly is filled to form Kan ☵. The trigrams Kan and Li inherit their bodies from Qian and Kun, and their 'great assistance' is found in Yin and Yang. In like manner, Qian and Kun exist with Kan and Li – just like a carriage-wheel exists with a hub and axle. Qian and Kun form the proper wheel of Kan and Li, while the centrepiece of Kan and Li is the hub Qian and Kun.

Laozi says, 'Thirty spokes share the single hub of a wheel [*Daode Jing*, Chapter 11].' In all things the significance of the elder Yang is the same.

Yuyan comments: This single human body is modelled on heaven and cast in the form of the earth; it unites together Yin and Yang with heaven and earth. If man understands how this body unites together Yin and Yang with heaven and earth, he can partake in any discussion on the method of the restored Elixir!

Kan is the moon; Li is the sun. The sun and moon travel the path of the ecliptic, and night and day arrive and depart; following around ceaselessly, as if greatly assisted at every turn.

The hub is like the body; the axis is like the mind. If you want to turn the hub you must have a proper axis. When cultivating the restored Elixir, you turn around the sun and moon within your body until they follow the same course as the creative powers of heaven and earth. If you do not correct the mind, then how can this be done?

Master Zhuxi comments: 'Qian and Kun represent the whole universe put into words. So then Qian-heaven is situated above and Kun-earth is situated below; and the change and transformation of Yin and Yang and the beginning and end of all the myriad things is situated in their midst.

If you take man's body and put it into words, the Qian-Yang is situated above and the Kun-Yin is situated below; and the single body's Yin and Yang and all the myriad things, their change and transformation, end and beginning, is situated in their midst.

So here Qian and Kun may be regarded as the 'door and gateway to Change', and the father and mother to the various hexagrams.

Generally when we speak of Change it only means the change and transformation of Yin and Yang; whilst, within the human frame, it signifies the Great Medicine of the Golden Elixir with Qian and Kun as its furnace and cauldron.

He concludes: 'Once Qian and Kun are simply set up above and below, Kan and Li rise and fall in their midst. This is what signifies Change. In the positions of the prenatal inner world, Qian is south and Kun is north, Li is east and Kan is west [see Figures 4 and 23]. This is just how it is. Therefore they represent the outer rim of a wheel – they rise and fall as if they relied on the turning axle-tree of a carriage. The axle-tree passes through the hub in order to turn the wheel. The wheel falls and then rises.

> Male and female, four in number,
> They are the bellows which revive the fire.
> Travelling the path of Yin and Yang
> Is like driving a team of horses:
> Adjust the dark reins,
> Seize bit and bridle,
> Proper as square and compasses,
> To follow the rutted wheel-tracks;
> Settled within, thereby you control without,
> Our destiny rests in the rule of the calendar.

The birth and transformation of Qian and Kun generate Kan and Li; thus the four hexagrams may be gathered into one, as Yin and Yang.

The central line of Qian ☰ has been transformed to produce Li ☲; the central line of Kun has been transformed to produce Kan ☵. Qian and Li's male nature belongs to the Yang; Kun and Kan's female nature belongs to the Yin. As Qian and Kun open and close, Kan and Li arrive and depart. The movement and activity of these four influences the whole world, just like a pair of bellows blowing, stirring up dust and ashes.

Laozi says: 'The space between heaven and earth is like a pair of bellows (*Daode Jing*, Chapter 5).' Qian, Kun, Kan and Li form the bellows – gathered into one they form Yin and Yang, spread out they fashion all the myriad creatures of the world.

If you would control a carriage you must take the reins in your hands and adjust them, seizing the bit and bridle and holding a steady course. Our destiny as human individuals lies in just this – the careful management and development, guidance and regulation of Yin and Yang. Within the self this is seen as the inner cultivation of an Elixir – represented in the outer world as 'the rule of the calendar'.

Master Shangyang comments: The sages were skilled at snatching the process of creation, they were skilled in their use of Kan and Li. The way to snatch the process of creation skilfully is similar to skilfully driving a team of horses. You adjust the 'dark reins', until they are held as properly as a square and compasses. What could not be achieved from this!

One skilled in the use of Kan and Li is similar to one who seized the 'bit and bridle' in order to follow the rutted wheel-tracks. What could not succeed from this?

The sage acts as if the whole universe rested in his hand and all the myriad changes of creation were born out of his own body. He is skilled at being 'settled within' – and thereby 'controlling without'. He understands 'the rule of the calendar' and thus knows his destiny.

Yuyan comments: Qian ☰ is purely Yang; it is the male trigram. Kun ☷ is purely Yin; it is the female trigram. Kan ☵ is the Yang within the Yin; Li ☲ is the Yin within the Yang. These are the trigrams of the male and female joining together.

The method of the Elixir is to position Qian and Kun above and below and to divide Kan and Li left and right, so that Qian and Kun open and close while Kan and Li arrive and depart [see Figure 23]. This is entirely to copy the shape of a pair of bellows.

He continues: In general the empty vastness of the Great Void is akin to the body of a pair of bellows. The energies of the universe arrive and depart – as the Void opens and closes – copying the action of a pair of bellows. To know this is to be more than halfway towards the idea of the method of a restored Elixir!

Master Zhuxi comments: Qian is the moon at its full and Kun is the moon at its new, while Kan and Li rise and fall in their midst. Zhen is born in the brightness of the moon and Dui at its upturned bow; Sun is born in the gloom and Gen at its downturned bow. The moon is just like a bulging bag, either slack and empty or taut and full.

There is a saying: Qian and Kun establish the positions, above and below; Kan and Li separate as doorways, left and right. The primary trigrams of the *Can Tong Qi* are here set out. Each one occurs once and only once.

He concludes: This speaks of how man's heart may be ruled through the Yin and the Yang. The turning of the hub on the axletree thus fashions an Elixir. The 'bit and bridle' signify the means by which we order the Yin and the Yang, and the 'dark reins' signify the firing times of the Elixir. The 'rutted wheel-tracks' are the cause of its rise and fall. 'Within' refers to the heart; 'without' refers to the breath. 'Our destiny' occurs in later sections of the text as the firing times of the sixty hexagrams.

The month is broken into six lots of five days
With the warp and weft each day presented;
In all there are sixty, with the firm and yielding lines
Occurring equally throughout.

At the new moon's light, Sprouting Forth takes up the
work,
Towards the end, at eventide, Innocence is fitted to
receive.
Day and night each hexagram
Is applied in turn,
Until reaching the end with Already Over, Not Yet
Over,
The whole returns to the beginning.

Herein are described the 'firing times' for the 'small circuit' (*xiao zhou*) of the heavens, represented by the passage of the moon during the month. After the hexagrams Qian, Kun, Kan and Li are taken away, there remain sixty hexagrams out of sixty-four – two for each day of the month.

On the first day when the moon is new, Sprouting Forth (Hexagram 3) 'takes up the work' in the morning, while Innocence (Hexagram 4) 'is fitted to receive' in the evening.

The sixty hexagrams are assigned and follow in pairs, through the month: Sprouting Forth and Innocence; Waiting and the Lawsuit; the Army and Relating; Small Cultivation and Treading; Flourishing and Decay; People At One and Great Possession; Humility and Enthusiasm; Following and Festering; Approach and Observance; Biting Through and Grace; Tearing Apart and Returning; Unerring and Great Cultivation; the Jaws of the Mouth and Great Excesses; Influence and Duration; Retreat and Great Vigour; Advancing and the Darkening Light; Family People and Separation; Obstruction and Release; Decrease and Increase; Breakthrough and Encounter; Gathering and Ascending; Oppression and the Well; Transformation and the Sacrificial Cauldron; Shaking and Resting; Gradual Progress and Returning to Marriage; Abundance and Travelling; Bending and Joyful; Dispersion and Restraint; Inner Faith and

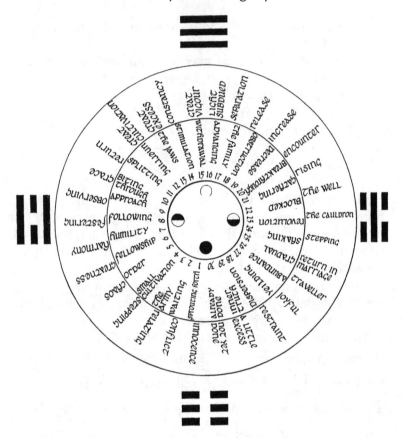

Fig. 23 The sixty-four hexagrams of the moon

Small Excesses ䷽; Already Over ䷾, and Not Yet Over ䷿.

As the sun and moon interweave, their warp and weft are shown in the moon-phases – the moon's shape waxes and wanes, according to the influence of the sun. Each day is represented by two hexagrams, one for the morning, one for the evening. As these two hexagrams are paired up, their firm and yielding lines reflect and oppose each other. Sprouting Forth (Hexagram 3) takes up the work and Innocence (Hexagram 4) receives and carries it on. After the very last two hexagrams, the whole process repeats itself. But this should not be taken as a hard and fast rule – it is only given as an analogy.

Master Shangyang comments: Zhen ☳ beneath with Kan ☵ above forms the hexagram Sprouting Forth ䷂. Zhen is the eldest son who can return the Yang within Kan ☵, thus bestowing the virtue of careful nourishment. Thus the text says, 'Sprouting Forth takes up the work.'

Again Gen ☶ above with Kan ☵ beneath forms the hexagram Innocence ䷠. Gen is the youngest son who can gather together the Yang within Kan ☵, thus achieving the merit of a 'gentle support' [a term from Chapter 11]. Thus the text says, 'Innocence is fitted to receive.'

Yuyan says: The *Can Tong Qi* sees Qian and Kun as the cauldron and furnace, and Kan and Li as the medicinal ingredients. Therefore the rest of the remaining sixty hexagrams stand for the firing times.

Each day there are twelve double-hours; two hexagrams are made up of twelve lines, and so each day uses two hexagrams – in the morning Sprouting Forth and in the evening Innocence, in the morning Waiting and in the evening the Lawsuit, until Already Over and Not Yet Over finish the process off.

If Sprouting Forth ䷂ is turned upside down it becomes Innocence ䷠, which gives the image of rising and falling. On the inside of Sprouting Forth ䷂ there is rising, morning, daytime, spring and summer; on the outside of Innocence ䷠ there is falling, evening, night-time, autumn and winter. All the hexagrams are just the same as this.

Thus as the sixty hexagrams are divided among the thirty days, they represent a single month. But this is slightly limiting, so why is it done in this fashion? Because it is only a metaphor. They are not meant to refer directly to the thirty days.

Master Zhuxi comments: In general there are sixty-four hexagrams, but, besides Qian and Kun, Kan and Li, which are used as the furnace and range, only sixty hexagrams are used in the firing times of the Elixial medicine.

The above [the two examples of hexagrams, Sprouting Forth and Innocence] serve as an example of the usage of all the sixty hexagrams. Each single moon is one single round. In general, day by day, through the hours and quarter-hours, the merits of each single hexagram are used at some time or other.

The sun and moon measure out the year
And movement and quiet bring about dawn and dusk,

Spring and summer receive a substance within
From midnight reaching out to late morn',
Autumn and winter match their use outside
From midday to late evening.

Reward and punishment echo spring and autumn
Confusion and understanding come as heat and cold:
Righteousness and human-heartedness are spoken of in
the lines,
Joy and anger arise with the times.
Respond in such a manner as the seasons
And you match the pattern of the cycling five.

Herein are described the 'firing-times' for the 'great circuit' (*da zhou*) of the heavens, represented by a single year. In the section above the 'small circuit' was calculated through the use of the moon; now the 'great circuit' is calculated through the passage of the sun through the year.

The sun represents brightness, morning and the Yang; the moon represents darkness, night-time and the Yin. The Yang moves, bringing an increase in the flame; the Yin brings quiet and a decrease in the flame. At first, advancing the flame brings about the 'dawn'; then next, withdrawing it brings about the 'dusk'. During the spring and summer, the Yang energies are advancing, just as in the first part of the day; during the autumn and winter, the Yang energies are declining, just as in the latter part of the day.

The 'substance received within' is the trigram Zhen ☳ on the inside of the hexagram Sprouting Forth ䷂, which brings forth the Yang-fire from within. The 'use matched outside' is the trigram Gen ☶ on the outside of the hexagram Innocence ䷘, which ushers in the decline of the fire without.

Innocence ䷘ is a complete inversion of Sprouting Forth ䷂; thus it shows the 'matched use' of Yin for Yang, of Gen for Zhen, of the Yin-shadow for the Yang-light.

In similar fashion, reward and punishment, spring and autumn, confusion and understanding, heat and cold, righteousness and human-heartedness, joy and anger all show a relativity. They function implicitly through following the natural fluctuations of the 'firing times' for Yin and Yang – they can never be managed through effort.

Only through acting in this manner can you cause the cycling five elements to gather together into one and thus complete the development within yourself of an Elixir.

Yuyan comments: Now heaven is set above and the earth is set below, while the two energies circle around in their midst, ceaselessly rising, falling, arriving and departing, just like a pair of bellows.

Man receives this soft and gentle breath – born between heaven and earth – and is never separate from heaven and earth. What if he can awaken to this mysterious opening and closing of the bellows of heaven and earth? Then his mind becomes empty, clear and silent, naturally at one with this breath. It streams around him, above him and below him; he opens and the breath escapes, and closes and the breath comes in. It escapes like the rising breath of the earth, it comes in like the falling breath of heaven, and he himself can exist and endure along with heaven and earth.

Master Hua has said:

The ancients knew the way to do it – they raised earthworks as fortifications, they traced the spring to protect its source, and sunk themselves in safe and settled homes. They found nothing that opposed them, all intercourse ceased whilst they remained at one with their own thoughts. Their innermost souls they kept guarded, whilst they prudently showed tact in speech; they kept themselves thus undivided, whilst the true energy was preserved; above and below it poured through them, streaming on and on, as unhindered as trickling water – like the sun and moon turning unceasingly, the Yin protected and hidden, and the Yang kept solid and treasured. From its source it flowed out and on unchecked, it filled them through and through without ever overflowing. It poured into them on and on without ever filling them full. This is what is meant by everlasting life.

20

HEAVEN AND EARTH SET THE
STAGE

In this chapter the author Xu Congshi glosses his own writings
concerning heaven (as Qian) and earth (as Kun), Kan (as water)
and Li (as fire). Kan and Li, fire and water, are the two main
ingredients used in fashioning the inner Elixir.

> Heaven and earth set the stage,
> Whilst Change travels in their midst.
> Heaven and earth take as images Qian and Kun,
> They set the stage for the fitting together of the separate
>   Yin and Yang.

> Change is shown through Kan and Li:
> Kan and Li are the two functions of Qian and Kun.
> These two function beyond established lines,
> Altogether streaming through the six empty spaces;
> Coming and going without settling,
> Rising and falling without regularity.

This section describes how the ingenious ravelling of Kan and Li
must be based upon the setting in position of the hexagrams Qian
and Kun. Before there was heaven and earth, and the sun and
moon, there was one 'great teeming mishmash chaos', which filled
the Great Void (*tai xu*) to overflowing.

As the Great Void gave birth and produced Qian and Kun, so it
formed the 'supreme pole' (*taiji*). As Qian and Kun were born, the
'supreme pole' split into two forms – the Yin and the Yang. Qian
was positioned above, the image of the heavens; and Kun was
positioned below, the shape of the earth.

The first two lines of this chapter are derived from the Great
Appendix (I.7) to the *Zhou Yi*: 'Heaven and earth set the stage,

whilst Change travels in their midst.' These lines became the watchword for the later alchemists, although they gave it new scope in their writings.

The trigrams Kan and Li are born as Qian and Kun, the father and mother, who act upon each other. Thus Qian and Kun describe the essence of Kan and Li, whilst Kan and Li are the two functions of Qian and Kun. Put another way, Kan and Li are the visible application of Qian and Kun. Kan and Li, water and fire in their ceaseless movement and activity, describe the 360 lines, which are endlessly active throughout the six 'empty spaces' of the sixty hexagrams, never settling and never stopping in their constant change and transformation.

Master Shangyang comments: The Great Appendix [I.1] says: The heavens are honoured above; the earth is humbled below. Qian and Kun are set in place.

Our Immortal explains this thus, saying, 'Heaven and earth set the stage whilst Change travels in their midst.' Then he comments on his own text, saying: 'Heaven and earth take as images Qian and Kun, they set the stage for the fitting together of the separate Yin and Yang.'

Again he says: 'Change is shown through Kan and Li; Kan and Li are the two functions of Qian and Kun.' His terms are described here in detail; his mind one with the All. How could it be said that the people of this world do not believe them? They may be simple-minded but if they meet with his words they will understand them.

The Wings ['Shuogua', or Eighth Wing, Chapter 2] say: Divide out the Yin, divide out the Yang, and they function successively as the firm and yielding. Henceforth, in Change, there are six positions which complete the shape.

The 'two functions' are the 'use of the nines [moving Yang lines]' in Qian ☰ and the 'use of the sixes [moving Yin lines]' in Kun ☷. These lines possess a function but no established positions.

Qian's text [in Hexagram 1] 'using nines: see a flock of dragons without a leader, good fortune' means the true-hearted person walks the middle path, and his power is ultimate. Kun's text [in Hexagram 2] 'using sixes: favourable for eternal devotion' describes the power of the Kun; it is the way of the earth, the way of the wife and the way of the minister.

If the way of the earth is incomplete, it becomes irregular and comes to an end – and so using Kun ('the use of the sixes') must mean the Yin is alone and incomplete. For this reason 'using sixes' signifies following Qian and going along with its own kind. Then as 'the use of the nines' mates with Kun, 'to the south-west they gain friends (see *Book of Change* Hexagram 2 text)'.

Qian and Kun change and transform, each finding its proper destiny. At the very beginning Qian's 'use of the nines' ☰ means it rides on into Kun ☷, and the Yang lines ☰ have an empty Yin line lodged within them to form the trigram Li ☲. The great unifying force of Kun's 'use of the sixes' ☷ is encouraged by Qian ☰, and the Yin lines ☷ have a solid Yang line lodged within them to form the trigram Kan ☵.

Thus the trigrams Kan and Li acquire the unique body of Yin and Yang, and change and transformation then take place.

Yuyan says: Qian is heaven; Kun is the earth. They form the cauldron within my own body. Li is the sun; Kan is the moon. They are the medicinal stuffs within my own body.

In the prenatal inner world diagram of the eight trigrams, Qian is south and Kun is north, Li is east and Kan is west [see Figure 4]. North and south separate out heaven and earth, which fit together in their positions; east and west divide apart as the sun and moon, which exit and enter through their own gate. Turn about and seek them within your own body, then you can cause them to unite.

Qian and Kun represent them in essence; Kan and Li represent them in use. The two, Kan and Li, stream through, rising and falling into the six empty spaces – they come and go, above and below, but without established positions for their lines.

Kan and Li circulate within the cauldron of my own body, hidden away from the heavens yet finding the heavens, hidden away from the earth yet finding the earth. How then could their lines have any established positions?

Master Zhuxi comments: This chapter takes a line from the *Book of Change* and then comments upon it. Thus it clarifies the functions of Qian and Kun, Kan and Li. It tells of Qian being above and of Kun being below, of Li falling and Kan rising.

The 'two functions of Qian and Kun' means the Qian 'using nines', and the Kun 'using sixes'. The nines are the old Yang lines; the sixes are the old Yin lines.

The two hexagrams, Qian and Kun, each have six lines. Each nine [an old Yang line, which moves] and each six [an old Yin line, which moves] has its set position. Only when 'all the lines are nines [all moving]' and 'all the lines are sixes' [all moving'] are they without set positions – and then the six lines of nines and sixes 'stream through, rising and falling'.

Throughout the rule of the Inherited Stems, Qian inherits Jia-wood and Ren-water and Kun inherits Yi-wood and Gui-water, Zhen inherits Geng-metal and Sun inherits Xin-metal, Gen inherits Bing-fire and Dui inherits Ding-fire. All these have set positions. (See Figure 25 p. 182)

But Kan inherits the Wu-soil and Li inherits the Ji-soil, and they have no set position.

Generally the Yin and Yang of the six trigrams – Qian, Kun, Zhen, Dui, Gen and Sun – signify the lines within Kan and Li which 'stream through, rising and falling'.

21

THE SUN AND MOON, THOSE SUSPENDED IMAGES

This chapter describes how the movements of the sun and moon illustrate the passage of Yin and Yang – 'as the Yang departs, so the Yin arrives'. The crucial moment to consider is when the first-born Yang appears, the instant the trigram 'Zhen arrives, and its token is received'. This illustrates the coming together of the medicinal ingredients used to fashion the Elixir.

> What changes are the images:
> 'Of those suspended images which send forth light
> None are so great as the sun and moon.'
> Daily they unite the vitality of the five,
> Six times monthly the law of the calendar;
> Five sixes making thirty divisions,
> So in the end they repeat again the beginning.

> Probe these marvels in order to understand
>   transformation,
> For as the Yang departs, so the Yin arrives.
> The spokes spinning, revolving, appearing,
> Disappearing, rolling up and unspreading.

This section describes how the simple juncture of the sun and moon happens quite naturally. It is the prime object of the work in cultivating the Elixir.

The two lines, 'of those suspended images which send forth light, none are so great as the sun and moon', occur in the Great Appendix (I.11) to the *Zhou Yi*. 'The five' are the cycling five, which stand respectively for each day of the five-day week; this sequence is passed through six times in a single month, making thirty days in all. Then, in the end, the process is repeated.

The idea of the carriage-wheel, with its thirty spokes, is continued from Chapter 19. The uniting of the trigrams Kan and Li, the moon and the sun, represents the turning of the hub on its proper axis. As they join, the Yin and the Yang, the firm and the yielding lines, also turn and interchange, and the carriage advances forward.

Master Shangyang comments: Confucius said [Great Appendix I.11]: Of those things that change and influence others, none is so great as the four seasons; of those suspended images which send forth light, none is so great as the sun and moon.

Our Immortal reiterates these words and explains them. After quoting them, he expands on them. This passage is modelled on the imagery of the sun and moon, which are taken to illustrate the workings of Yin and Yang. The sun and moon cling to the heavens and there is the partnership of new and full moon; Yin and Yang are present in the world and there are the ways of 'going with' [*shun*] or 'turning against' [*ni*] generation and completion. The sun is formed of a purely Yang inner energy, which is why it is called the 'great Yang'; the moon is formed of a purely Yin vitality, which is why it is called the 'great Yin'.

He concludes: When the Yin reaches its extreme, the Yang is born; as the Yang departs, so the Yin arrives. It is just as if the Yin is attached to the Yang, as the spokes of a hub are attached to the wheel. The spokes meet at the hub and the wheel turns, the Yin curls up and the Yang extends.

Yuyan comments: Wei Boyang [Xu Congshi] wants to describe clearly the Yin and Yang within the body, but they exist within the body and have no outer form which can be sought.

The saying goes: 'The common people use them daily without knowing of them.' If he did not use metaphor and imagery to stand in the place of Yin and Yang, how could he explain and enable people to 'probe into their marvels' and 'understand their transformation'?

On this account, gazing about him into the space between heaven and earth, he saw the brilliant and obvious images of the sun and moon – which send forth their light. Thus he took their brilliant lights to proclaim to people and enabled them truly to understand the Yin and the Yang of heaven and earth. Then through precisely recognizing the mysteries of their marvellous transformation, those who 'use them daily' within their own bodies 'without knowing them', can be shown how they work by illustration – although they are not spoken about directly.

In Change, there are 384 lines:
Rely upon these lines to reveal the tokens,
By 'tokens' are meant the sixty-four hexagrams.

When the dark of the moon meets the new moon's light,
Zhen ☳ arrives and its token is received –
At this time, at this juncture,
Heaven and earth lie together,
The sun and moon grope for each other,
As cocky Yang sows upon the dark bestowing earth,
So henny Yin transforms it through her yellow covering.

In makeshift chaos they open to one another,
And in such a temporary stance lay the foundation,
There to build and maintain the citadel,
A marvel condensing to form the human frame.
And so the multitude of men step forth,
Wriggling insects stir, and they all emerge . . .

The juncture of the sun and moon at the new moon gives birth to the single Yang energy. This crucial activity is comparable with the founding of an inner Elixir.

The sixty-four 'token' hexagrams have, in all, 384 lines between them. This merging of the ideas of the tokens and the hexagrams is central to the union of the two studies of the *Zhou Yi* (the *Changes of Zhou*) and of alchemy.

At the passing of the last day of the old moon and the beginning of the first day of the new moon, the Yin has reached its extreme and the Yang is born again. This rebirth is shown in the appearance of the single Yang line beneath in the trigram Zhen ☳.

The images of the cock and the hen also illustrate the union of heaven and earth – the tussle between the sexes describes the opening of Yin and Yang, and the birth of new life. It is also mentioned in Chapter 1: 'these four [Qian, Kun, Kan, Li] in makeshift chaos, directly enter back on into the void'; and also in Chapter 15: 'these four [metal, water, wood, fire] create a makeshift chaos, each one either a dragon or tiger'.

Master Shangyang comments: At this time, at this juncture, Heaven and earth lie together, and all things draw on the void to receive life. The sun and moon 'grope for each other', the crow and rabbit bond together and are unable to be released. The Yang cock is firmly packed and he bestows change into the azure-blue; the Yin hen opens and transforms, her yellow covering releasing stimulating juices. Muddied and obscured in shape, within 'makeshift chaos', the two open to one another; within such a 'temporary stance', male and female begin coition and start to lay the foundation.

He concludes: Yin and Yang are, at the beginning, going along well together [*shun*] and thus giving birth to human life and all the myriad things. Hence the text says: 'So the multitude of men step forth, wriggling insects stir, and they all emerge . . ..'

The people of this world do not understand the active 'going along with' method of the postnatal outer world. It is also to borrow the images of 'Sprouting Forth in the morning and Innocence in the evening'; comparable to 'laying a foundation for the citadel'. But to think of this as the creation of a restored Elixir within the cauldron is wrong.

Yuyan comments: The 'lines' referred to here are the lines of the hexagrams; the 'tokens' mean the joined bodies of the hexagrams. There are sixty-four hexagrams in the *Book of Change*. The Elixial method takes Qian and Kun as the cauldron, Kan and Li as the medicines and the remainder of the hexagrams to represent the firing times for the medicines.

Now to take the view of Qian and Kun, the book begins in Sprouting Forth and Innocence [Hexagrams 3 and 4] and ends in Already Over and Not Yet Over [Hexagrams 63 and 64]. Between them each pair of hexagrams faces and reflects the other, and each one, in every instance, finds affinity with another. In this way we can see how 'a single Yin and a single Yang make up the Dao [Great Appendix I.5]' and how the ancient Immortals took hold of the lines and hexagrams in order to illustrate the cauldron, the medicines and the firing times for the medicines. Now this is what may be called 'crafted to perfection'!

He continues: At this moment, the mind [*shen*] and inner energies [*qi*] join together within, the inner energies and the mind merged together. It is like heaven and earth lying together, and the sun and moon rejoined. Thus the text says, 'Heaven and earth lie together, the sun and moon grope for each other.'

'Heaven' and 'earth' are the Qian and Kun of my single body;

while the 'sun' and the 'moon' are the Kan and Li of my single body. Heaven and earth, the sun and the moon take this chance to join up, and thus are able to mould all collected categories of things into the achievement of a single year; the trigrams Qian and Kun, Kan and Li take this chance to join up, and thus are able to snatch from the wonders of creation to form a 'holy babe'.

Wei Boyang [Xu Congshi] fears that you scholars will not understand the creative wonders of Yin and Yang, so he uses the moment the sun and moon join up as an illustration. But this does not mean that the affair will only work at the single moment which occurs between the old and new moon.

The book *Awakening to Reality* ['Four-line Stanzas'] says: The sun and moon each thirty days have one moment they meet, at this time change the day to model it on spiritual achievement.

If you scholars can understand the mystery of 'at this time, changing the day', you can pry into the workings of heaven and earth and complete the Supreme Elixir!

He continues: As the two energies of Yin and Yang open to one another, above and below, they form a confused mass which becomes one. Hence the significance of the 'makeshift chaos'. This makeshift chaos forms the outer rim of heaven and earth, and the womb of all the myriad things.

The Elixial method then takes this 'temporary stance' to be a laid 'foundation' on which to make a start. So then heaven and earth, and all the myriad things, entirely exist within my own body. It is no use to seek for them outside.

The 'citadel' forms the base or footstalk. The Elixial method is to build and maintain there while you 'reflect back your brightness to light up within [*huiguang neizhao*]'. Then your mind hankers after the inner energies which are condensing and the energies hankers after the mind which is resting still. They naturally join and knot together to form a 'holy babe'.

He concludes: The method of Yin and Yang opening to each other is the source of all change and transformation. This is not the case merely for man but for all living beasts and creatures. Even in the case of crawling, flying or wriggling insects, which creep along with jerking antennae, even for these very small unimaginable things, it is the same. Thus the text says, 'The multitude of men step forth, wriggling insects stir, and they all emerge.' This is just the way it is.

Bestowed on human life they produce humanity; kept inside

yourself they produce the medicine. This is merely the clear divide between the 'saintly' and 'worldly' paths – between 'going along' [*shun*]' with things' or 'turning against [*ni*]' them.

Chen Xianwei comments: The trigram Zhen occurs when the Yang is born, and the fire advances its token by a single Yang. At this time, in your own spiritual room, you cultivate a vitality within your own body – and the gold and the fire act upon each other.

The 'cocky Yang' is the dragon; the 'henny Yin' is the tiger. 'Sowing upon the dark bestowing earth' means the dragon mounts up into the dark heavens to send down rain; 'transforming it through her yellow covering' means the tiger enters in amongst the deities of the earth to produce gold [metal]. Rising into the heavens and entering into the earth symbolizes a comparable twining within the 'makeshift chaos'. Hence 'such a temporary stance' is set up to 'lay the foundation', on which to 'build and maintain' the inner 'citadel'.

Once this marvel is condensed, it forms itself into the 'human frame'. At once it is great, great as heaven and earth; and minute, minute as wriggling insects.

Having a shape and an energy, all things must result from this. It is only one single occurrence produced outside, yet from the lower roots it streams out to the very tips of the branches – the inexhaustable process of generating life.

It is only one single occurrence produced within, yet it 'turns back to the source, travelling back to its original nature [*fanben huanyuan*]' – the transcendent process of everlasting life.

Master Zhuxi comments: This section describes the time the new moon's light begins to function in Zhen, formed by the sun and moon. Yin and Yang initiate a love-match and thus promote the work of our inner cultivation.

22

THE WISE OF OLD OBSERVED
THE SKIES ABOVE

This lengthy chapter first mentions how Confucius sought out the ways of the ancient people of old in his amalgamated writings. The ancients observed the world and recorded the beginnings of all things. They watched the movement of the moon in the sky and used Qian and Kun that the world might distinguish Yin and Yang and recognize their advance and retreat. The passage of the 'small circuit' of the heavens, or a single month, is described in detail.

And so Confucius placed emphasis on the 'teeming void',
And on 'Qian and Kun's' power to penetrate emptiness;
He sought out the 'ancient ways' of the very first rulers;
And with the 'osprey's cry' began all poetry;
When 'youth first marries' its vigour binds as one;
It is just as shoots stir at the 'very start of the year'.

In this section, Xu Congshi identifies the sources of each of the five Confucian classics by quoting their opening lines. The rule in laying a foundation for the Elixir and in discovering the fundamental origins of all things is the same. The phrases recorded in the above lines begin each of these books – the *Book of Change* (*Yi Jing*), the *Book of History* (*Shu Jing*), the *Book of Songs* (*Shi Jing*), the *Book of Rites* (*Li Ji*) and *Spring and Autumn Annals* (*Chunqiu*) respectively.

The 'teeming void' (*hongmeng*) contains within it the natural, original and vital energy of life. In the Daoist *Huainan Zi* book (second century BC) the 'teeming void' is said to be like the 'sun breaking the horizon at dawn'. Compare this with Chapter 4, where it states that 'in the matching of the moon-phases, an activity occurs within, as chaotically, through a teeming void, the male and female tail one another'.

The emphasis throughout this section is on first beginnings.

Master Shangyang says: The Wings [Great Appendix, I.11] state: In Change there is the 'supreme pole [*taiji*]. This gives birth to the 'two forms' [*liangyi*, the Yin and Yang].

Thus did Confucius commend the 'teeming void'. Qian and Kun's power lies in the 'empty mystery of makeshift chaos [*huntun xumiao*]'. The very first rulers came down to us from Pan Gu [the mythological creator of the universe] who separated heaven and earth. Thus Confucius sought out their ancient ways. The osprey's cry defines the correctness of man and woman, and all human relationships – a husband and wife in their youth initially come together in marriage.

When Confucius arranged the *Book of Songs* he began with the idea of husband and wife in order to set out the way of the unerring Yin and Yang; when he began his Wings to the *Zhou Yi* with Qian and Kun, he wanted to illustrate clearly the principle of the necessary match between the firm and the yielding.

Thus the Great Appendix [I.4] says: The *Book of Change* is a mirror-image of heaven and earth; it reveals microscopically the ways of heaven and earth. Look above to observe the astronomy of the heavens and beneath to examine the geography of the earth; thus you comprehend the cause of the seen and unseen. The original beginning returns at the end; thus you comprehend the meaning of death and life.

What is meant by the 'original beginning'? Generally it means the way of going along [*shun*] with Yin and Yang, which gives birth to men and all living creatures. Therefore the text says, 'When youth first marries its vigour binds as one.' This is what is meant by 'comprehending life'.

What is meant by 'returns at the end'? If you can reverse [*ni*] your actions into the method of the prenatal inner world then you step over the worldly and enter into the sagehood. Therefore the text mentions 'shoots stirring at the very start of the year'. This is what is meant by 'returns at the end'.

Zhu Yuanyu says: Here our Immortal borrows from these human documents and compares them with the rule of the Elixial method.

The 'teeming void' signifies the single energy within the void. Qian is the cauldron, which hides within itself the root of our nature; Kun is the brazier, which hides within itself the stalk of life. Between them, the sun and moon come and go, the image of them 'penetrating emptiness'.

The 'first rulers' illustrate the first beginnings of ancestral power;

the 'osprey's cry' illustrates the two materials' mutual stimulation; and the 'binding as one' of youth illustrates the two inner energies joining together. As 'shoots stir at the very start of the year', so the single Yang stirs and the true seed comes alive.

Master Zhuxi says: The sages wrote the Six Classics [including the lost *Book of Music*] entirely with the purpose of giving things a beginning – this really sums up the whole significance of this chapter. When 'cocky Yang sows upon the dark bestowing earth, and henny Yin transforms it through her yellow covering' [see Chapter 21], it also sums up entirely this single section. Both explain what is meant here.

> The wise of old never led empty lives,
> They observed the evidence in the skies.
> As the heavenly tokens advanced and retreated,
> They adjusted their moves accordingly.
>
> Thus Change governs the core of the sky,
> Whilst the hexagram Restored ☳ sets the start.
> The eldest takes his body from his father,
> Relying on his mother as foundation.
>
> Ebb and flow accord with the rule
> Of the yellow goblet, the moon;
> Rise and fall rely on the turning
> Of the Dipper, the crux in the sky.

This section's main concern is with how the single returning Yang line within the hexagram Restored (Hexagram 24) lays the basis for the cultivation of the Elixir.

The sun and moon govern change, and 'change governs the core of the sky'. The tokens in the sky advance and retreat following the natural order. The hexagram Restored ☳ has the trigram Kun ☷ above and the trigram Zhen ☳ below. The trigram Qian ☰ is the father, and Kun ☷ is the mother. Zhen below takes its first Yang line from its father, thus he 'takes his body from his father'; while Kun above supplies the source for the rest of his nourishment, thus he 'relies on his mother as foundation'.

The moon-phases, which also 'accord with the rule', summarize the progress made in the smelting of the inner Elixir, which is also depicted in the turning of the handle of the Dipper around the northern Pole Star.

Throughout this chapter, the bright full moon above in the heavens (which represents the Elixir) shows the triumph of the Kan-water (moon) risen above, and also reflects the glory of the Li-fire (sun) sent beneath. They both stand together as a symbol for the interpenetration of Yin and Yang, depicting the innate inner-world 'true fire' of our bodies mellowed and softened by the 'true waters' of the moon – thus returning us to our natural, prenatal birthright.

Master Shangyang says: The Qian-Yang is first born beneath the two Yin lines as the trigram Zhen ☳; Zhen ☳ is the eldest son who is born again in Kun ☷. Being in the hexagram Restored ䷗ means there is a single Yang line crouched beneath the five Yin lines. Kun is the mother, so the text says he 'relies on his mother as foundation'.

Yuyan comments: The perfect men of old 'observed the ways of heaven, they grasped the actions of heaven' [opening lines of the *Yin Shadow* scripture]. Thence they borrowed the advance and retreat of the heavenly tokens and the movement of Yin and Yang; they constructed a model of the firing times for the Elixir in order to inform the people.

In general heaven and earth are similar to a cauldron, while the sun and moon represent the medicinal ingredients placed within. The sun and moon travel the breadth between heaven and earth, coming and going, appearing and disappearing. These create the 'firing times'.

Man also has the capacity to do just this. If he turns back to seek these objects within his own body, he himself may truly realize the mystery of the advance and retreat of the 'firing times'.

He concludes: In general, a year and a month are simply one and the same, a month and a day are simply one and the same, and a day and an hour are simply one and the same. The spectacle of a year appears within a whole month, the spectacle of a month appears within a whole day, and the spectacle of a day appears within a whole hour. Any single hour contains within itself the 'catch' whereby the single Yang returns.

This 'catch' does not exist at the winter solstice, nor at the dawning of the new moon, nor at the hour of midnight. If you do not comprehend fully heaven and earth, Yin and Yang, you will never understand its silent catch. In such a fashion it works, so secretly.

The father Qian goes down to engage with the line at the beginning of the mother Kun and form Zhen. Zhen is the eldest son, so the text says, 'The eldest takes his body from his father.' Zhen is born from out of Kun's body, just as a little child is born from out of its mother's belly, so the text says, 'relying on his mother as foundation'.

When the book *Awakening to Reality* says, 'Duke Gold was originally a boy from the eastern troupe, given over to his western neighbours to board there for his needs', it means just the same. If you can understand this, you can also understand not to search at

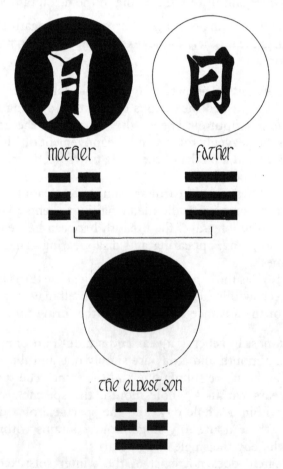

Fig. 24 Zhen, the eldest son

the winter solstice for the development of the inner Elixir. Within your own body there is a single Yang being born – do not neglect the influence of the year, the month, the day and the hour!

Master Zhuxi comments: Here again the single moon is regarded as divided into twelve sections. Taking the hexagrams Restored, Approach, Flourishing, Vigour, Decisive, Creative, Encounter, Withdrawal, Stagnation, Observing, Tearing and Receptive as the correct order, there is a single division made each two and a half days.

The hexagram Restored then donates inner substance to the first six sections of the moon's division through the trigram Zhen. The eldest son is Zhen, the father is Qian and the mother is Kun. The next section, which follows immediately, describes its restoration at the new moon.

On the third day, it appears directly
As Zhen at Geng-metal, received in the west;
At eight days Dui receives Ding-fire,
Its upper arc stretched taut as a bow;
At fifteen days, Qian's body is complete,
Full to the brim at Jia-wood in the east.

Now the striped toad and spirit-rabbit
Pair up as the sun and moon in brightness:
The toad exhibiting the trigram's divisions,
The rabbit exuding the living light.
At fifteen days, the track ended
It bends about, turns below and descends.

On the sixteenth comes the first tug on the reins
And Sun at Xin-metal is seen at dawn,
Gen appears faultlessly at Bing-fire in the south
And by the twenty-third day, the lower arc is strung.
Kun receives Yi-wood on the thirtieth day
. . . ' to the north-east, losing friends' . . .
The divisions used up, they abdicate
Allowing Restored to inherit – bringing forth the dragon!

This section uses the rule of the Inherited Stems (*najia*), described within the prenatal inner world diagram (Figure 4), in order to introduce the idea of the 'firing times' within a single month or the 'small circuit' of the heavens (see Figure 25).

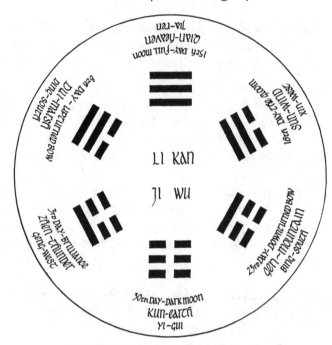

Fig. 25 The Inherited stems and the moon

The rule of the cyclical Inherited Stems was originated by Jing Fang (77–37 BC). It is based upon the principle of heaven and earth bestowing nourishment upon all things. The ten 'heavenly stems' are Jia, Yi, Bing, Ding, Wu, Ji, Geng, Xin, Ren and Gui – there are two for each of the cycling five elements. Altogether they catalogue precisely the directions of the compass, the cycling five, and the eight trigrams. Qian inherits Jia-wood and Ren-water, Kun inherits Yi-wood and Gui-water, Zhen inherits Geng-metal, Sun inherits Xin-metal, Kan inherits Wu-soil, Li inherits Ji-soil, Gen inherits Bing-fire, and Dui inherits Ding-fire (see Figures 25 and 32).

Above, the fluctuations in the moon's body, as it appears in each aspect of the sky at a different time of the month, are depicted by the cyclical stems. The new moon (Zhen ☳) is seen in the evening in the west (Geng-metal), the first quarter (Dui ☱) is seen in the evening in the south (Ding-fire), the full moon (Qian ☰) is seen rising in the east (Jia-wood), the moon just past full (Sun ☴) is seen falling at dawn in the west (Xin-metal), the last quarter (Gen ☶) is seen at dawn in the south (Bing-fire), and the old moon (Kun ☷) is seen at dawn in the east (Yi-wood).

The trigrams Kan and Li themselves represent the sun and

moon; thus they are not directly included. But the matching of the Wu-and Ji-soils is entirely necessary for the functioning of the other signs.

At the interval of the new moon, the sun and moon (Kan and Li) combine together; after they combine together, they gradually draw apart. Then after the full cycle of the moon they come together again, Zhen ☳ appears and the hexagram Restored ䷗ inherits – 'bringing forth the dragon!' Again, for this whole section, compare Chapter 4.

Yuyan comments: The moon at the third day brings forth its light. In the evening it is positioned in the west at Geng-metal, shaped like the trigram Zhen ☳. Accordingly it inherits the stem Geng of the trigram Zhen. Spoken of in terms of the firing times within your own body, it signifies when you 'dare not for a moment interrupt the water-pump! [a line from the book *Awakening to Reality'*.

Zhen at Geng-metal
In the evening-in the west

Fig. 26 Zhen at Geng-metal

When the moon arrives at the eighth day it forms an upturned bow. In the evening it is positioned in the south at Ding-fire, shaped like the trigram Dui ☱. Accordingly it inherits the stem Ding of the trigram Dui. It illustrates the Yang-fire halfway ascended above within your own body.

When the moon arrives at the fifteenth day it is as full as the sun. In the evening it is positioned in the east at Jia-wood, shaped like the trigram Qian ☰. Accordingly it inherits the stem Jia of the trigram Qian. It illustrates the time when the Yang-fire is full and strong within your own body.

Dui receives Ding-fire
in the evening-in the south

Fig. 27 Dui receives Ding-fire

QIAN's BODY COMPLETE AT JIA-WOOD
in the evening ~ rises in the east

Fig. 28 Qian's body complete at Jia-wood

He continues: The elixial method takes the first half of the month as Yang, and belonging to Zhen ☳, Dui ☱ and Qian ☰; it takes the last half of the month as Yin, and belonging to Sun ☴, Gen ☶ and Kun ☷. Thus the text says, 'The toad [moon] exhibits the trigram's divisions.' The moon is the great Yin; the sun is the great Yang. The Yang controls emission; the Yin controls taking in. The moon originally has no light of its own; it receives the light of the sun to become bright. Thus the text says, 'The Hun-rabbit [sun] exudes its living light.'

When the moon arrives at the sixteenth day a portion of it is already showing dark. In the morning it is positioned in the west at Xin-metal, its light partly waning, and shaped like Sun ☴. Accordingly it inherits the stem Xin of the trigram Sun. Spoken of in terms of the firing times within your own body, it signifies when 'the Yin is taken in and the Yang resigns, the peak is toppled and the path diverted'.

sun at xin-metal
falling in the west at dawn

Fig. 29 Sun at Xin-metal

gen at bing-fire
in the south at dawn

Fig. 30 Gen at Bing-fire

When the moon arrives at the twenty-third day it forms a downturned bow. In the morning it is positioned in the south at Bing-fire, its light partly waning, and shaped like Gen ☶. Accordingly it inherits the stem Bing of the trigram Gen. It illustrates the Yang-fire halfway descended below within your own body.

When the moon arrives at the thirtieth day it forms the old moon. In the morning it is positioned in the east at Yi-wood, its light completely lost, and shaped like Kun ☷. Accordingly it inherits the stem Yi of the trigram Kun. It illustrates when the 'shadowy token' [or Yin-shadow *yinfu*] is exhausted completely within your own body.

Master Zhuxi comments: At the full moon it is the inner energies [*qi*] which have filled it full. The sun has sunk down below while the moon's disc is in the heavens above. At the new moon, the sun

KUN receives YI-WOOD
IN the east at dawn

Fig. 31 Kun receives Yi-wood

and moon have truly joined together above – which is the kind of thing meant by 'the raising of water intimidates fire' and 'gold reverts to its original inner nature [Chapter 33]'.

> Ren-and Gui-water match Jia-and Yi-wood,
> Qian and Kun embrace both beginning and end.
> Seven and eight make up fifteen,
> Nine and six follow suit.
> These four combine to form thirty,
> The Yang energy bound up and extinguished in hiding.

This section continues the theme of the Inherited Stems. Ren- and Gui-water, and Wu- and Ji-soils are not used in the above cycle of the moon-phases. These lines explain how Ren-water matches Jia-wood, and Gui-water matches Yi-wood; how Ren is inherited by Qian, and Gui is inherited by Kun. The ten cyclical stems begin at Jia- and Yi-wood, and end at Ren- and Gui-water. Qian inherits Jia-wood and Ren-water; and Kun inherits Yi-wood and Gui-water. Thus 'Ren- and Gui-water match Jia-and Yi-wood'. The ten stems begin at Jia- and Yi-wood and end at Ren- and Gui-water. In this fashion 'Qian and Kun embrace both beginning and end'.

Seven is the completed number (5+2) of fire, eight is the completed number (5+3) of wood, nine is the completed number (5+4) of metal, and six is the completed number of water (5+1).

Both these pairs of elements, wood and fire, metal and water, add together to make up fifteen, and both fifteens pair up to make the thirty days of the month. At the end of the month, as the Yin is full, the Yang energy is 'extinguished in hiding' and about to return.

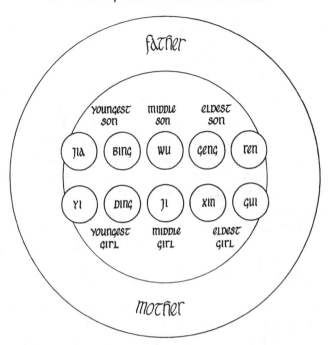

Fig. 32 The family of Inherited Stems

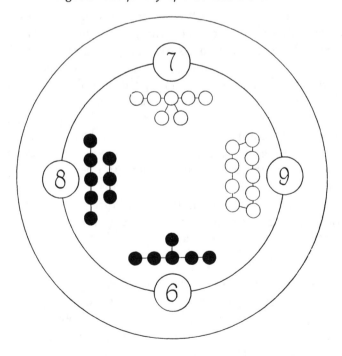

Fig. 33 Six, seven, eight, nine (2)

Yuyan comments: In general the Inherited Stems signify the selection of images during the timing of the firing. The 'extracting and eking out' of the firing times is no different from the waxing and waning of the moon.

Here the six trigrams are distributed throughout the single month so that Zhen represents the third day when the moon appears at Geng, Dui represents the upturned bow seen at Ding, Qian represents the moon facing the sun when first full, Sun represents the sixteenth day when the moon is waning at Xin, Gen represents the downturned bow when the moon is fading at Bing, and Kun represents the old moon when it is lost in Yi.

This illustration is merely taken on the pretext of discussing the advance and retreat of the six trigrams which time the firing within the body. They are not meant to be taken literally as to what happens during the thirty days of each month.

He continues: This does not literally mean that you should advance the fire when the moon first appears at Geng-metal; nor that you should retract and shade it when the moon begins to wane at Xin-metal.

The scholar who only observes the waxing and waning of the moon's body should turn back and seek within himself. Then the single Yang is born within his own self, represented by Zhen ☳ – and the moon appears on the third day. The second Yang grows and appears like Dui ☱ – becoming the moon's bow on the eighth day. The three Yang are full and like Qian ☰ – the round moon of the fifteenth day. The single Yin is born and it appears like Sun ☴ – the waning moon on the sixteenth day. The second Yin grows and it appears like Gen ☶ – the moon's bow on the twenty-third day. Lastly the three Yin are complete and become like Kun ☷ – the moon lost on the thirtieth day.

But must you adhere rigidly to the differing positions of the moon's appearance and disappearance and be ruled by the numbers of lines within the trigrams' bodies, basing it all on the kinds of calculations made by astronomers?

He concludes: Seven is the number of fire; eight is the number of wood; and they join together to make fifteen. Nine is the number of metal; six is the number of water; and they join together also to make fifteen. These four combine altogether to make thirty, a number which corresponds to the number of days in a single month [see Figures 16, 17 and 33].

This is to copy the period of deepest winter,
When all vegetation is stunted,
The ruler of men holds back travellers
And keeps himself hidden to assist the Yang.

He copies the season, obeying the time,
Closing up his mouth to halt all discourse;
The ways of all nature are exceedingly vast,
They occupy a great darkness without shape or form,
A silent emptiness, unobserved –
To try and aid them is at once to be lost.

Interference only bungles their work
For your words fly back and injure you;
Separate out the order of the four images
And they are a light dawning on later generations.

This section describes the idea of the quiet sublimation of activity which forms a basis for cultivating the Elixir. The four images are seven (fire), eight (wood), nine (metal) and six (water). As mentioned above, 'seven and eight make up fifteen, nine and six follow suit'. Separate them out and they appear as four images – draw them in and they form one. The unity of the moon's cycle is identical with the work of refining the Elixir.

This section probably does not belong here. Most earlier editions regard it as apocryphal and place it at the end of the work.

Yuyan comments: Whether the Elixial method refers to the winter solstice or the interval of the new moon, it is comparable to the moment when the Yin is at its extreme and the Yang is born.

In terms of the month this is the night of the darkest moon, when the moon's light is scattered and extinguished in hiding. In terms of the year it is the period of deepest winter, when all the plants and vegetation are scattered and broken. In each case the significance is the same.

The *Book of Change* says: Thunder within the earth: Restored. Thereby the former kings on the solstice closed the passes, merchants and travellers did not go forth, nor did the ruler inspect the regions [Hexagram 24, 'great image']. Such is the quiet and stillness which nourishes action and welcomes the ways of nature.

However although the ways of nature are 'exceedingly vast',

their true workings lie buried within each instant; and although they 'occupy a great darkness without shape or form', they dwell subtly in silence and seclusion. Therefore in the middle of the day on the winter solstice you should first close up your mouth, quieten your passions and guard them, turning them back to a single point. This enables the gold and mercury to run and return back into the furnace.

It is the same as when the sun and moon rejoin, hiding away their aid. Engulfed deep within and penetrating into the emptiness, the mind comes into focus, the inner energies contract, and a 'golden fluid' congeals within.

However, in the event that you forget to keep silent, your burden becomes insurmountable and overwhelming. If you then go out, you inflict injury on yourself.

Chen Xianwei says: At the period of deepest winter, all the myriad creatures return to their roots. At this moment, at this juncture, it is very difficult to fathom creation. Observe the ways of nature – they are stopped off, without anything coming through, they are 'exceedingly vast' and unknowable; look into that great darkness – it is silent, empty and lost, without any observable shape or form. Really what basis can we use now to fathom the catch of creation?

The princely Wei [Xu Congshi] here 'separates out the order of the four images' in order to inform us later generations.

> The eight trigrams spread out dazzle the eyes,
> Crossing the sky without losing their centre,
> They are finely poised and tricky to observe,
> So look into them to verify the tokens;
> Observe their images from your own position,
> And exactly determine their shape and form.
>
> What stands outside may be regarded as model,
> Divine from the times to settle good luck and bad.
> As a sign is sent out, accord with its moment
> And do not mistake the shifting of the lines.

The eight trigrams, as depicted in the prenatal inner world and postnatal outer world diagrams (Figures 4 and 5), describe the whole round of the sky – yet in their passing they never lose order. Kan and Li, the sun and moon, inherit the Wu- and Ji-soils, which remain intact at the centre.

Master Shangyang says: Qian and Kan remain in the north, Gen and Zhen return to the east, Sun and Li are recycled to the south, and Kun and Dui are restored to the west. They are jointly spread out and dazzle the eyes, crossing and progressing over the sky, without losing their centre. Their centre lies at the very core of the sky, like something finally poised at the central pole of the heavens and tricky to observe.

Heaven gave birth to the sages, and they looked especially into the task of measurement, seeking verification through comparison and taking the heavenly tokens as their evidence. They observed the images cast by the sun and moon, and determined their shape and form.

What 'stands outside' and casts a shadow may be regarded as a proper model. In their divination and knowledge of the times, they inspected the eight trigrams in order to settle the good luck and the bad. If a sign is sent out you should accord with its moment and exactly determine the shifting lines. Then you may understand the birth of the Yang.

Yuyan comments: When creating the Elixir, only fear that the heart – like a untamed monkey – will scamper around outside. If you can 'withdraw your gaze, and turn back your hearing [*shoushi fanting*]' you focus your attention for a short while, enabling the two materials to return to the Yellow Track without losing their centre.

Then the 'enshrouded mists' of heaven and earth feel their way into each other's presence, in order to fashion a single drop of dew-like pearly fluid – which rapidly settles within the Elixial field. It lies finely poised and borne within a silent dimness – insignificant and unobserved. The *Daode Jing* [Chapter 21] says: Oh, silent and dim! And yet within it lies vitality. This vitality is very real and within it lies true faith.

In general the method of the Great Elixir tallies with the ways of natural creation. As a true faith in heaven is attained, the 'red-veined stone-clock' strikes the hour and the 'door to the jade cave' moves with its double-action opening. This is why its action is so obscure.

He concludes: 'When the thunder within the earth shakes open the gateway of the trigram Sun and a dragon energetically arises from out of the Eastern Lake, this is the moment the single Yang line is stirring within the body. At this moment, the pliant energy merges and fuses. If your mind starts to lose its grip and gets confused, just advance the fire slightly. Do not delay!

Above examine the outline of the Milky Way,
Below the progressive contours of the earth,
Between them delve into the human heart,
And combine these three talents together as one.

In your movement follow the trigram's divisions,
At rest, draw upon the commentaries' instruction;
With Qian and Kun in use and circulating
The whole universe is then at peace.

This chapter concludes that to advance the inner cultivation of an
Elixir, the three powers – heaven, earth and man – must be
combined together as one. The text is derived from the Great
Appendix (I.2), which says: 'When the true-hearted person is
living quietly, he observes the images and ponders the explanations; when beginning any movement, he observes the changes and
ponders the prognostications.'

Only as movement and rest both meet in measure according to
the ways of nature, will heaven and earth be put to use in Qian and
Kun, the Elixir be made whole and the universe at peace.

Master Shangyang says: Above you examine the Milky Way and
are clear on the shape of Qian as it appears at the entwining of Yin
and Yang; below you see the contours of the earth, judging carefully the mysterious transformation of gold and water within the
body of Kun. Between these two you delve into the human heart
and read the signs sent out accordingly.

In your movement you 'follow the trigram's divisions' – in the
hexagram Restored, Zhen travels out at the fore. At rest you 'draw
upon the commentaries' instruction'. Great indeed is the original
power of the Creative! 'Clouds pass, the rain does its work and all
material things flow into their forms [from the 'Tuan' commentary
to Hexagram 1]'. Its bestowal is magnanimous, its light is magnificent. It yields and follows through 'favouring devotion'.

Once the outline in the heavens is examined, the contours of the
earth are in order and the heart is also corrected, then out of the
gate of Qian and Kun runs the pathway of Yin and Yang –
enabling heaven, earth and man together all to gain peace.

Yuyan comments: Although heaven and earth are great, and the
ways of nature mysterious, the light sent forth from the sun, moon
and stars and the spread-out ring of the elements and trigrams, is

all gathered together by me into my own self. It forms either my own cauldron and furnace, or my own medicines, or my own times for the firing of the Elixir.

When I turn to myself and observe these three powers – heaven, earth and man – they are all there complete within me. There has never been anything else to be sought besides what lies there within my own self.

23

THE THREE SAGES' FORMER CONCEPTIONS

Here Xu Congshi outlines his tradition. He explains how the former sages were moved to honour later generations and how defamation of their name and knowledge may be seen to be a crime. Yet the business of explaining the refining of an Elixir is still a tortuous process. By writing this he will merely 'hand on a glimpse of its guiding thread'.

Of all the greatest sages of old
None surpassed Fu Xi –
Beginning by drawing the eight trigrams,
He modelled them on heaven and earth.
King Wen, our ancestral Emperor,
Consolidated the extensive line-texts;
Whilst Confucius, the bravest of sages,
Added, to give support, the Ten Wings.

These three sovereign rulers all stood out,
And each one improved upon the management of the times –
But although their works have followed at length,
Their achievements are not really different from each other.
In my writings, I have followed in their footsteps
And examined their work in the minutest detail.

Where there is form, Change is easy to reflect upon;
Where there is nothing, things are difficult to devise.
The matter of this work can now have a model,
To set the world to rights through its texts.

Originally I had no former knowledge to help me
Then from my teachers I understood –
Gleaming brightly, as at the picking away of the curtain
Now, with scornful eyes, I advance up on the stage.

This section tells of the historically continuous tradition of the three 'sages of old': the legendary Fu Xi (*c.* twenty-eighth century BC); King Wen, founder of the Zhou Dynasty (*c.*1122 BC); and Confucius (551–479 BC). These 'noble sages' have traditionally been credited with the amalgam of texts known as the *Zhou Yi*. In other words, the *Zhou Yi* – the Changes of Zhou – has been one single effort. More likely the work derives from the Han dynasty, drawing on the earlier Yin-Yang school. It is traditionally ascribed to antiquity to enhance its prestige.

Following the same tradition, Xu Congshi makes his own uncertain contribution in the *Can Tong Qi*. He uses the former sages' work as his model.

Master Shangyang says: Fu Xi drew the trigrams, King Wen put down their interpretations, the Duke of Zhou recorded the line-texts. Altogether these make up the two books which form the true Classic [Hexagrams 1–30, and Hexagrams 31–64].

Confucius put the ten books of 'Wings' [the *shi-yi*] or commentaries after the true Classic. These comprise the upper and lower sections of the 'running' teachings [the 'Tuan' commentaries]; the great and small 'image' teachings [the 'Xiang' commentaries]; the lengthy Great Appendix [the 'Xizi', generally philosophical]; the 'poetry' teachings [the 'Xu' or 'orderly' and 'Za', 'disorderly', groupings, in rhyme]; the 'prose' teachings [the 'Wen Yan' commentary]; and the first, middle and later sections of the 'discussion on the trigrams' [the 'Shuogua' commentary]. These are the Ten Wings, which explain the *Book of Change*. But they are not called 'explanations' but 'Wings', because they give support to the ways of Change.

He continues: When our gentleman Immortal says that the Ten Wings 'were added, to give support' his words are indeed far-reaching. The achievements of these sages have been bestowed equally on later generations. Only fear that you scholars lack their supreme happiness and power, and miss out on their great insight and wisdom. If you lack these you inherit only a thousand confusions and contradictions – you are without the sages' experience, as each improved upon the other's writings.

Examine what our 10,000 generations have had as a teaching model and submit yourselves to their ultimate path. Heaven gave birth to the clear intelligence of the sages. How can you enlighten yourselves? You must rely on what has been given to you by your teachers.

Surrender and trust to this wisdom, reflecting upon their thoughts. Supposing you have some obstacle to your progress. If you are loving and kind, and you search deep within your heart, in the end suddenly their intent is made clear and a clear understanding dawns upon you.

It is just as if the curtain within the hall were suddenly plucked back, and everything seen clearly and at once – and with half-closed disdainful eyes, you advance up on the stage. You see everything.

Yuyan comments: Fu Xi took as his model heaven and earth and created the *Book of Change*. He begun by drawing the eight trigrams as a diagram of the 'prenatal inner world [*xiantian*]'. Qian, as heaven, was situated above and Kun, as the earth, was below; Li, the sun, and Kan, the moon, were separated left and right; Zhen as thunder and Sun the wind, Gen the mountain and Dui the marsh were then positioned in pairs. How can we do other than follow in his footsteps?

King Wen consolidated the trigrams and extended the idea of Change by creating the line-texts. In his diagram of the 'postnatal outer world [*houtian*]', the trigrams Zhen and Sun, both wood, give birth to Li, fire; and this continues until Kun, the soil, covers them over. The trigrams Dui and Qian, both metal, give birth to Kan, water; and this continues until Gen, the soil, halts them. Again how can we do otherwise than follow in his footsteps?

Confucius followed on from Fu Xi and King Wen, and commended the idea of Change by creating the Ten Wings. Although he was not in the position of ruler or king, society saw him as the teacher of rulers and kings. Thus he was the bravest of all sages.

Master Zhuxi comments: Where there is form, change can be regulated – where there is no form, things find it difficult to succeed. Through relying both on Wei Boyang's [Xu Congshi's] own words and on your teachers you will understand this principle.

The Fire Records make up 600 chapters
Whose main trend is 'nothing dissimilar'!
The phrases are most tortuous to think upon,
The people of this world are not used to considering.

Yet if you seek to determine their derivation,
You find confusion and clarity occupying the same root!
If I admit to a small talent in voicing this,
Dare I be careless in writing it down?

It is as if I'm tongue-tied – unable to speak,
Yet to break-off telling of it would be a deadly sin.
To unburden my feelings now I put them down,
For fear of slighting the heavenly tokens.

Yet I sigh increasingly; still undecided,
Starting and breaking off, continuing this stupid
     business . . .
A potter or founder has a model to measure by,
But I will never know fully how to explain it.
I will hand you on a glimpse of its guiding thread,
Its merest outline may be seen as a rough guide.

Here Xu Congshi continues from the previous section by examining his own feelings as he puts down this writing. He outlines the tortuous nature of his alchemical subject, and how Yin and Yang – confusion and clarity – spring from a single root. He is resigned to explaining the little he can, leaving the reader to make up any deficiencies.

Confucius says in the *Analects*, concerning his own teaching, 'I throw up one idea and they come back with three!'

Yuyan comments: The 600 chapters of the Fire Records are just the same as the sixty hexagrams. The sixty hexagrams describe the timing of one single moon – the 600 chapters describe the timing of ten moons.

In general during the sixty hexagrams of the single moon, each hexagram occurs only once and is unique; while in the 600 chapters of the ten moons, each chapter matches with another similarly. Thus the text says, 'The main trend is "nothing dissimilar"!'

He continues: The number of works written on alchemy would fill a cart which would make the oxen sweat! There are at least 1000 terms and 10,000 different characters, while the number of quoted examples is immeasurable. Perhaps you can understand now what is meant by 'tortuous'!

However if you seek to determine the derivation of these terms and characters, you will find they amount to no more than Yin and Yang. This is all. The two come from the same source, they only differ in name.

The ancient Immortals exerted themselves to the utmost to communicate this idea to the world. But happiness and prosperity in the world create the conditions for shallowness – and many are too fully occupied to ripen their thoughts.

Wei Boyang [Xu Congshi] wrote this single work in order to describe the location of the cauldron-vessel, the 'rivers and springs' of the medicine, and the graduations of its firing times; and along with these he spoke of care and neglect, 'being' and 'nothingness', and the secrets of 'host' and 'guest', of what comes before and what after.

He concludes: The old lines go: If you meet someone and it is not transmitted, the path of heaven is lost! But a false transmission from someone wrongly will waste the heavenly jewel! To achieve a transmission means your own self is to be worked on; while a false transmission means seven generations of groping in the dark.

This is the reason Wei Boyang [Xu Congshi] felt 'tongue-tied' and unable to speak a single word. But then for him to 'break off the telling of it would be a deadly sin'!

Master Zhuxi says: The '600 chapters of the Fire Records' generally describe old books which have been lost. It cannot be known which they were.

24

THE TWO SEPARATED ENERGIES LOVINGLY TRANSFORM

This short chapter begins the central part of Xu Congshi's writings. The three chapters at the centre of his work communicate directly the message of the book: resonance and transformation through close intimacy, happening beyond thought. Here the burning mirror ('Yang Mirror') and dew vessel ('Watery Toad') of Han times are used as examples of how two separated energies, similar to Yin and Yang, are each lovingly transformed and so succeed in the process of creation.

> The Yang Mirror is used to make fire
> But if not for the sun it would have no light;
> If the Watery Toad did not view the moon and stars
> How could she collect her fluid?
>
> If two separated energies distant and afar
> Yet lovingly transform and reflect each another –
> How much more so, close by, in your own body,
> Intimately within your own breast,
> Do Yin and Yang match the sun and moon,
> And fire and water effect an equal case.

This chapter takes water and fire, and the sun and moon, which both influence and work on each other, to serve as examples of how the meeting of similars results in the formation of the Elixir. The burning mirror ('Yang Mirror') kindles fire through reflecting the sun; and the dew vessel ('Watery Toad') captures dew at night-time.

The same ideas are discussed in Chapter 34 – 'Things of the same kind make the work easier, the wrong materials make it difficult to achieve skill'; and in Chapter 27 – 'It is best to use things of the same kind.' The implication is that only an inner Elixir will perpetuate your life, and that dealing in similars is the obvious way to succeed.

Master Shangyang says: The Yang Mirror is a Yang object which contains an inner energy, so that when it is struck by the sun it can kindle a flame. The Watery Toad is a Yin object which contains an inner vitality, so that when struck by the moon it can produce water.

The sun and moon lie in the sky far away; the Yang Mirror and Watery Toad are very small. These two separated energies of Yin and Yang lovingly transform each other. How much more so then do the true Yin and true Yang within the human body, as they lie intimately within our own breast. One can relate to them, one can be familiar with them, they are close by and easy to seek, so how could they reflect each other and be lovingly transformed? It is simply because posterity has not yet discovered the Elixial method.

The Yin and Yang within the human body may be compared to the sun and moon in the sky. The water and flame of the Watery Toad and Yang Mirror may be taken to illustrate the vitality and inner energy within the human body. If things which have no feelings still reflect one another when there is feeling and spirit, then things will naturally and lovingly mix.

Moreover the most spiritual object between heaven and earth is man. Even the very poor and very stupid know the truth of the transformations of Yin and Yang. But they do not wait to be taught and carry them out. They are all misled and only know how to 'go along with things [*shun*]' to produce men and things. As for the use of 'turning back [*ni*]', if they have no teacher, they try to understand it in vain. Very generally the method of turning back Yin and Yang is to 'smelt the vitality and subdue the energy [*lianjing fuqi*]' in order to form them into an Elixir.

This chapter illustrates how the two separated energies of Yin and Yang lovingly reflect each other and so succeed in the process of creation.

Yuyan comments: How much more so, close by, in your own body, intimately within your own breast, do fire and water effect an equal case! Within your own heart lies something of medicinal quality. If you cannot 'reflect back your light to illuminate within [*huanguang fanzhao*]' then how do you seek out the mystery of loving transformation?

He continues: Generally if Yin and Yang agree together then they are naturally and lovingly transformed. Now Wei Boyang [Xu Congshi] takes the fire made in the Yang Mirror and the water made in the Watery Toad as illustrations. He wants to enable us scholars to delve deep into our hearts and awaken our innermost feelings that we might see how 'being' is born out of 'nothingness'. This also happens as a 'loving transformation'.

He concludes: If someone can empty his heart, focus his mind, and be calm and settled without a single atom of random thought, then his very own sun and moon gather together their light within, and do not scatter it. And as they endure so their energies settle, the time becomes right and a rare effect occurs.

The essentials of this ultimate method do not lie far away, but are constantly before your eyes. It is just like a lodestone attracting iron; it reaches past any obstruction and ultimately acts as if it were close by.

But the common crowd go astray and forget to turn back – and this is precisely because they cannot seek within themselves. One old song goes: Be careful to share fully your teachers' attitude, it does not lie anywhere but before your eyes! It goes on: When you pick up a phrase at your teacher's side, very quietly close your eyes and turn in on it. Now you can see exactly what is meant by acting 'close by'.

25

THE THREE JEWELS, THE REAL CRUX

This most valued section explains in detail how to intimately refine the Elixir within your own room. To learn the procedure, one must seek oral instruction from a teacher. This meditative process, characterized early on in Daoist schools as 'sitting and forgetting', is here explicitly based upon sensory withdrawal, or Daoist yoga. This chapter contains the most explicit references within the text to the physiological results of inner alchemy.

> The ear, the eye, the mouth – these three jewels,
> Block and stop them up, do not let them gape.
> The truth in man lies at the very depths,
> He roams wide yet guards a proper compass within.

> Sight and hearing are both crooked and winding,
> They function entirely together
> As the pivot and lynchpin or the self,
> Their movement never exhausted.

> Bank up and guard the sight within,
> Do not employ the ears in hearing,
> Close the mouth to chattering,
> With rare words out of the teeming void.

> These three are the crux of the affair –
> To be with a relaxed body, resting in an empty room,
> Abandon the will and return to the void,
> And without thinking thus find constancy.

> Let signs of difficulty promote your change,
> And preserve one mind without rebelling:
> In bed the spirit cradled in your arms,
> Alive and alert to its care or neglect.

This section identifies the three keys to the inner development of an Elixir – the ear, the eye and the mouth. They correspond to the internal vitality or body's essences (*jing*), the inner energies (*qi*) and the mental faculties or spirit (*shen*).

During one's cultivation, the turning back of the sensory organs upon themselves is 'the crux of the affair'; instead of going along with (*shun*) the outward flow of perception, the attention is turned back (*ni*) within. Furthermore this is not a forced act of will. The 'one mind' allows one neither to push, nor to slacken in one's efforts. The will is 'abandoned' and 'returned to the void' and so neither forgotten nor aided.

Inwardly the three jewels may be kept intact 'without thinking of them' – all quite naturally. As water will gradually find its own level, as a ripe melon separates from its stem, as the moon slowly comes to the full, the process is complete in its own time.

Master Shangyang says: This chapter details the secret purpose of our own private engagement in the inner development of an Elixir. If someone has gained personal instruction from a teacher then he must further chant this verse over and over again, until he has savoured each morsel of it and attended to each detail. He must not merely read it through once and put it aside. If even a single word is passed over and misunderstood he will not form the Elixir.

In general this single chapter combines the eye, the ear and the mouth together as one, in the 'binding up of their sharp practices'. But in mentioning this process the chapter does not discuss or divulge any arcane secrets of these most praiseworthy heavenly jewels.

For instance the nature of man in the world is always good. But as he grows up, if he does not rely on the aid of the sages, he finds himself suddenly alone – and rare indeed is the man who can preserve himself in this situation. Loud-speaking friends and wild-thinking companions entice him without, bright sounds and colours, sensations and desires seduce him within – each and every pore of his body becomes an open door, through which passions and pleasures may run riot. Daily he makes use of them, nightly he is active, and everything becomes plunder and turmoil.

The ear, the eye and the mouth are the highest and bitterest poisons. The ears hear enticing sounds, the eyes view entrancing sights, and the mouth tastes exciting flavours. This is just the way it is. Our happiness is ruined by entrancing sights; harm follows on enticing sounds, disease enters through the mouth and fantasies are born within a drunken stupor. These follow on inexhaustably. How can they ever be finished?

Often the reason why someone cannot properly succeed in the Elixial method is entirely because the ear, the eye and the mouth, these three – like close neighbours – join together and lure him out, utterly confusing the truth.

Our Immortal here considers the ear, the eye and the mouth to be 'three jewels', which should be valued highly and not frivolously played with. The practice of blocking and shutting them up is done in order not to let them gape open.

When you privately engage in this matter, the 'great task' becomes very clear. Each and every pore of the body reaches a stillpoint [*dading*] and you are able to manage your inner development.

He continues: If you are familiar with these three as the 'crux of the affair', then you can relax the body whilst resting in an empty room.

To 'relax the body' means there are neither demands on you, nor are you overtired; an 'empty room' means a private and clean room, where there are no distractions and where one can 'abandon the will and return to the void'.

Very generally, this 'void' signifies the place where the inner energy originates. This is the one single energy of the prenatal world [*xiantian yiqi*] which is naturally born out of the void. If you want to gain this energy, you must bend your will to it in prayer.

'Without thinking' of it, thus you 'find constancy': without thinking – these two words ultimately mean being comfortable in yourself.

'The truth in man lies at the very depths', and so 'without thinking', you respond to it. You 'roam wide, yet guard a proper compass within' and so without thinking, you attend to it. Your outbreath and inbreath support each other and so without thinking, you attain it. Once these three qualities have been assembled together, without thinking, you merge with the truth. If you can be responsive and attentive, attain this condition and finally merge with the truth, then your achievements are numerous and so you find constancy.

He concludes: When you are in bed and 'the spirit is cradled in your arms' the mind does not rebel. A civil life does not promote any change in this state. Any time you are lying in bed, cradle the mind and inner energy together 'in your arms': constantly be alive and alert, to attend to the 'care or neglect' of this one single energy. The achievement of the inner cultivation of an Elixir is attained through making use of strength. Now as you experience this, you understand the message contained in the teachings coming down to you of old.

Yuyan comments: Wei Boyang [Xu Congshi] takes these three essentials, these three jewels, and says 'block and stop them up, do not let them gape'. Generally if you are never restrained within, you will never let go properly outside. The image is of there being 'three jewels' within, which you take great care of and hide away.

Have you ever seen a pot cooking rice? You close the lid tightly on top, and build up a fire to heat it below. There is not the slightest gap left between the lid and outside, while the hot gases wind and whirl around and are pent up within. Then, in a short while, the rice is cooked and you have a meal.

Now someone who is engaged in this business of cultivating the Elixir must turn back his sight, take back his hearing, close up his mouth and swallow down his saliva. He should not allow the slightest gap to be left for the true energy to escape outside. Then the ultimate medicine will be brought to life and the Great Elixir fully formed and mature.

He continues: The 'truth in man' means the original spirit, the 'original mind [yuanshen]'. The 'very depths' signify the uttermost depths of the void. The 'truth in man' has been called by a multiplicity of different things. Below I mention some of them.

The Mudball Palace, the Unstable-pearl Palace, the Jade-pure Palace, the Purple-pure Palace, the Iridescent-invisible Palace, the Supreme-invisible Palace, the Supreme-single Palace; the Supreme-hidden Gateway, the Hidden Gate, the Hidden Palace, the Hidden Room, the Hidden Valley, the Hidden Field, the Gravel Field, the Number-one Gateway, the City Gate, the Heavenly Gateway, the Heavenly Gate, the Heavenly Valley, the Heavenly Field, the Heavenly Heart, the Heavenly Wheel, the Heavenly Hub, the Heavenly Spring, the Heavenly Pond, the Heavenly Root, the Heavenly Hall, the Heavenly Palace, the Qian Palace, the Qian Family, the Loving-union Palace, the Li Palace, the Spiritual Palace, the Spiritual Room, the Spiritual Gateway, the Spiritual Capitol, the Spiritual City, the Dark City, the Old City, the Old Region, the Old Hill, the Old Forest, the Old Palace, the Purple Storehouse, the Purple Courtyard, the Purple-gold Mound; the Purple-gold Cauldron, the Red-sand Cauldron, the Mercury Cauldron, the Jade Cauldron, the Jade Room, the Jade Capitol, the Jade Canopy, the Precious Peak, the Number-one Peak, the Very-highest Peak, the Blessed Stately Peak, the Kunlun-mountains Summit, the Gansu-Henan Mountains, the Fairyland, the Honoured Isle, the Honoured Capitol, the Honoured Palace, the Honoured Darkness, the Honoured Origin, the Honoured Valley, the Honoured Earthen Pot, the Elixial Field.

But although these names are numerous, they really stand for the single same thing. In the book the *Kingfisher Flashing in the Void* it says: The skies have seven luminaries and the earth holds seven jewels; man has seven openings which all empower the brain. From the *Collection of Most Ancient Sayings* comes: When the Golden Elixir was sent along to reach the mudball cave (the brain), the name first recorded for it was 'Jade City'.

The supremely single Elixial method which enables you to return to your 'original mind' means simply going against the stream of the hundred vessels of the body, and sending their energies upwards to replenish the 'mudball' of the brain. Once the brain has been solidly filled, the mind is made whole; once the mind has been made whole, the body is made whole.

What Wei Boyang [Xu Congshi] means by 'the truth in man lies at the very depths, he roams wide yet guards a proper compass within' is that if man follows the true respiration as it comes and goes, whilst allowing the true breath to rise and fall, then all day the original mind will be constantly settled at the 'mudball'.

The *Yellow Courtyard* scripture says: If you do not want to perish, build up the Kunlun! Again the song 'Tranquillity Within' goes: I build up the Kunlun hills to gain an understanding of the secret. The book *Returning to Life* pointedly tells us: Gather back at home with the family; in the family, they tend to a small, square, heavenly field.

The book *Restoring Back the Original Mind* says: My method is very clear – understanding brings broad-mindedness. When not busy, sit up properly, and travel through and out of the Heavenly Gate!

So this then is the proper method which is extremely easy. You need only move the true breath along to the topmost gate just like lifting up the string of a lute with a plectrum. Then, very evenly and silently, the true energy rises up through three stages, rising and falling, quite naturally, and all the body's joints are opened quite easily and naturally released.

It is similar to moving a 10,000-ton barge with only an 8-foot oar, or holding back the string of a 1000-pound bow with only an inch of trigger. You do not to waste any force whatsoever.

But the blind and ignorant will not believe this. If perhaps you decide to pay a visit to the 'Old Ruler' who sits in his 'Mudball Temple', then pay your silent respects to him. It you do any more, it would be like adding legs to a snake!

He continues: You should 'relax the body, resting in an empty room', then you may be able to cultivate the inner Elixir. To relax the body means there are no pressures on you to be anyone or do anything, and neither is your body tired from overwork. An empty room means a quiet room somewhere – a room without anything else in it, only a stick of incense, a lamp, a stool and a bed, and that is all.

When sitting do not have too much light, much light injures the Hun-soul; but neither have too much dark, much darkness injures the Po-soul. Generally the Hun prefers the light and the Po prefers the dark – lightness belongs to the Yang and darkness belongs to the Yin.

This is what is meant in the book *Kingfisher Flashing in the Void* when it says: A room is best by some trees, where you catch the morning light. As an opening, have a clear window which faces the evening glow.

He continues: The vitality is born at one particular moment – when this moment arrives the mind understands. For a whole single day, never deviate from the task – walking, standing, sitting or lying, continuously preserve it, like a chicken sitting on an egg, without interruption keeping it warm. This then can be called the development of an inner Elixir.

He continues: Generally this 'supreme medicine' of the Golden Elixir is fashioned through the mind and inner energies being knotted together as one. There is something substantial being born from something insubstantial – they knot together and fashion a 'holy babe'.

This long toil of caring for a 'babe' over ten months is similar to that of a young mother first falling pregnant, or a young dragon for the first time cherishing a pearl. While the mind and energies are focusing together, it is extremely easy for them to be lost.

Whilst you are in bed you should have the spirit 'cradled in your arms', making completely sure that you do not deviate from the task and fall into dreams or fantasies. When you are awake only fear that the fire will cool and the strength of the Elixir perhaps be delayed.

Thus you should watch over its 'care or neglect'. Every hour of the day and night keep your thoughts on it; just be present and think on it. Afterwards the work will be complete, the Elixir become pure and unadulterated, the quality of the medicine will not be wasted and the firing times not broached. How could you ever depart from this task for an instant?

> Your face becomes soaked through and shining,
> The bones and tendons gain in firmness,
> Discharged of the many evil toxins,
> Then to set up a true healthy strength.
>
> Practise this cultivation without interruption,
> And a mass of energy forms like clouds and showers,
> Overflowing feelings come like the spring rains,
> Trickling juices like melting ice.
>
> They flow through you from head to toe,
> Finally rising up back above,
> Coming and going reaching into nothingness,
> Disturbing and stirring all throughout.
>
> 'To turn back is to know the truth of the path,
> To know weakness is to handle its power';
> Toss over and weed out past impurities,
> And with great care you achieve clear harmony.
> In the mud there then appears the pathway,
> And the darkness finally shows forth a light.

This section explains the physical effects of the cultivation. The Elixir promotes a feeling of well-being throughout the body, eliminating disease and generally strengthening it. The physical effects are as 'spring rain over a valley' or 'ice melting on the river'. It is all one process – a harmonious brightening and gentle lightening.

Yuyan comments: 'Your face becomes soaked through and shining, the bones and tendons gaining in firmness.' This means something ultimately precious being brought to fruition within you so naturally a clear and beautiful flowering appears outside you.

Similarly when there is jade lying in the hills, the trees which grow above appear healthy; and if there are pearls in the deeps, the nearby shores are not crumbling or tumbling down.

He continues: Filling gently like mountain mists riding up into an empty space, driven hard like rich rains covering the flat fields, overflowing like spring flood-waters seeping through marshes, trickling out like river-ice about to melt away, the energies come and go through the entire body, with all its vessels merged into one.

It pervades throughout, extending right out into the limbs. The heart in the chest beats strongly, and you feel joyful and young again, as if you were slightly drunk on wine. The *Mirror for Viewing the Medicine* says: When the prenatal inner energy and postnatal outer energy agree together, it is as if you were slightly drunk!

He continues: To 'turn back' means to return. The *Daode Jing* [Chapter 16] says: Obtaining an ultimate sense of emptiness, I guard a deep feeling of peace. All the myriad creatures come into being, and I watch their rise and return.

Generally the effects of cultivating the inner Elixir arise from this 'ultimate sense of emptiness' and 'deep feeling of peace'. This is where one is allowed into the unseen union of heaven and earth. Thus the original energy returns and comes again, following on the single Yang.

But if the emptiness is not total or the sense of tranquillity not substantial, it is like being one basketful short of building a 100-foot mound. How then can you gain the effects?

To 'know weakness' means to know suppleness. The *Daode Jing* [Chapter 10] says: Attend fully and become supple, can you be as a newborn babe?

Generally the control of the cultivation of the Elixir means holding on to the aim, without forcing it. If you can know suppleness and weakness, just like 'a newborn babe', then the process is complete. But if this aim is not held to, the energy goes unnourished and nothing at all is gained while something indeed is lost! How can then this be called being in control?

He concludes: If the knowledge has been darkened a long time, it must finally come to light; when something is muddied a long time, it must eventually run clear. When this moment arrives, the energy transforms, and the news scatters through 'the nine-stored heavens' like sweet delicacies strewn from a carriage.

The spiritual water clears and deepens, the flowery pool stills, white snow swirls out up and over the four hills and the seven jewels build themselves eventually up into a twelve-storeyed gallery. Before the gallery, yellow flowers are seen blooming, over a long period of time, distinctly and intensely bright.

Now you see them all against a 'flurry of confusion', how can you stay in the darkness and remain confused?

> Gradually the Yellow Centre unfurls,
> Shining out, enriching the muscles and skin;
> Start out correctly and finally you are healed,
> The trunk established, the branches take hold.
> The One itself is covered in and shaded;
> The people of this world have never understood.

The effects of the Elixir are again explained. Once the 'holy babe' has reached maturity the inner Elixir has reached its full term. Gradually its influence spreads out to the whole of the body. This experience of Great Oneness (*taiyi*) is something the ordinary person will never understand.

Master Shangyang comments: The 'One' refers to the Wu- and Ji-soils. They assemble together in this single idea, 'the One'; with this single word you arrive at the central idea in Wei Boyang's [Xu Congshi's] mind.

Confucius said: My method is One when you experience it. Laozi has the saying: Gain the One and all things are brought to a close [*Daode Jing* Chapter 22]. The Buddhists say: 'All the thousand Dharmas return to the One.'

Thus heaven is one and gives birth to water. But you need to understand how the water is born from out of 'the centre of the One'. The 'centre of the One' means the central line in the trigram Kan ☵. But now the One is 'covered in', so you need to gather up its vitality in order to understand its magic; it is 'shaded', so you need to be clear on its magnetism in order to extend its energy.

Someone who can know the One can hold all space and time in the palm of his hand! For someone who gains the One, all things are born from within himself. The One is a mystery and if you never find a teacher you will never understand it. Thus the text says, 'The One itself is covered in and shaded, the people of this world have never understood.'

He continues: Our mysterious Immortal's Elixial method says you must first 'repress within the spiritual trunk [Chapter 11]'. This means self-discipline and focusing the mind; to 'gently support that pearl so young [Chapter 11]' means to accumulate vitality within and build up an inner energy. As you discipline yourself, the work becomes easier and you can develop the restored Elixir within.

The people of this world do not understand this important process. Moreover they only try half an hour for its benefits, and expect success. How stupid! From the canon Clarity and Purity *comes the method*:

> Gaze inwards at the heart,
> Gaze outwards at the body;
> See them from afar
> And they all appear empty.
> Empty without being empty,
> Means being empty but there not actually being nothing.
> A nothing which is also a nothing without there being actually
>   nothing,
> Is lacking nothing, since there is actually nothing!

Such profound words! One should always be silent after them, a silence in which there is no silence. When language reaches its limit, man will always see only the appearances. But if there is no great resistance, then how can there be any great release? Why is it that we are pulled down by our human state? From whence is desire born? If desire does not arise, we are in a state of pure tranquillity. In a state of pure tranquillity, we can respond to all things and inspect mere appearances.

Acting thus from within a state of pure tranquillity and in response to all things is taking on the true business of 'starting out'.

Yuyan comments: If there is something within the Elixial field [the lower belly] like a single energy coming through you, as it is harmonized within and a 'beautiful flower' is unfurled outside. When the outside is correctly done, the influence is proper; when the spring is deep within, the stream flows long. 'Gain the One and all things are brought to a close (*Daode Jing*, Chapter 22).'

The supreme Dao of our ancestors is carried totally within this one single energy which forms and transforms. Split it apart and it becomes the 'black and white', divide it up and it becomes the 'green and yellow'. It can be illustrated as the 'sun and moon', or identified as the 'dragon and tiger'. In this way it allows a profusion of names, all described by just two words, 'Yin' and 'Yang'. But really it is just the single same thing. People may call it the 'magic water within the flowery pool', or the 'earthenware pot upon the leaden furnace'. But really these are both the single same place.

Someone may speak of the 'midnight hour on the winter solstice' or the 'interval of the new moon', and if others do not know that it means the single Yang returning, they will actually wait for midnight on the winter solstice. And as for the 'sun and moon reformed together' they will actually wait for the new moon. Then they search through the calendar and vacillate over this time or that – which is to be misled in the extreme!

Who is it that knows how to gather up the years and contract them into a month, to gather up the months and contract them into a day, to gather up the days and contract them into an hour, and then – within the single same hour – to find within himself the creation of the single same year and the single same month?

Then the single same hour is the single same place and the single same place is the single same thing.

Thus what are generally known as the solstices of winter and summer, the equinoces of autumn and spring; dawn and dusk, Jia-wood and Geng-metal; the dark and new moons, the quarters and full moon; midnight and midday, and the hours just before; midnight till mid-afternoon, early dawn till evening, the twenty-four seasonal changes and the seventy-two five-day weeks (*hou*); the intercourse of the single year, and the circuit of the single moon; the hours of Kan (midnight) and Li (midday), and the months of the hare (July) and the cock (January); the hole for Sun and Qian, and the gateway for the 'two eights'; the morning of Sprouting Forth (Hexagram 3), the evening of Innocence (Hexagram 4), the day of Encounter (Hexagrm 44) and the night of Returning (Hexagram 24), all emerge totally from this single same One.

In this world, who is it that knows the One? Very few people indeed!

26

UNDERSTANDING THE
PERVERTED AND FALSE PATHS

If Yin and Yang do not join together, all methods must fail. In this chapter there is clearly illustrated the heterodox separation of Yin and Yang, which leads the individual down false and misleading paths. The twisting and confused approach is quite obviously seen – it does not rest on 'an ultimate sense of emptiness and a deep feeling of peace'.

This is not to describe any of these 'innards' methods
Where your 'inward gaze' is preoccupied with thinking:
Where you step the path of the 'Bowl Stars' of the Dipper
And choose the day and the hour by the 'Six Beginnings',
Or play in bed, tiring yourselves with the 'Nine One'
    method,
And confuse yourselves with material from the original
    womb!

Perhaps you feed only on air – and it rumbles in your
    bowels,
Or you expel the true breath and suck in sickness from
    without;
Then night and day there comes no sound sleep,
And month to month you never experience rest.

Your body and mind worn down daily, become exhausted,
And blurred in appearance, as if you are addicted;
Your blood boils and bubbles up furiously,
Unable to settle or ever find peace.

You pile up soil to stand as an altar,
And morning and evening worship at the sacrifice,

Ghostly things are seen – strange images,
With dreams and curious visions which tempt you!
There are happy rejoicings which delight the heart,
Convincing yourself that you must live for ever –
But then, still young-looking, you perish,
Your body and bones laid bare to decay!

This section presents examples of commonly mistaken approaches
to the study of caring for one's life and longevity. Not only will
they not ward off illness, they will actively encourage harm. Such a
disturbed approach should be abandoned.

Yuyan comments: There are 3600 different methods, and any
number of differing sects concerned with 'nourishing life'. They all
disagree and confuse each other, they cannot be outlined here one
by one.

   For instance there is the 'inward gaze' method of closing the
eyes and concentrating on your 'innards', or of vainly stepping the
path of the Dipper and setting the day and the hour by examining
the 'beginnings' – which they call 'the method of the Golden Elixir'!
Again there are the sexual practices of making nine shallow thrusts
and then one deep, which they call 'timing the firing'! This results
in the 'mischief of the original womb'.

   Then there is the haphazard business of feeding on air and
'spitting out the old to take in the new', which they call 'forming
the medicinal substance'! It only causes their empty bowels to
rumble.

   They sit in meditation obstinately and vacantly – and then suffer
sleepless days and nights. They overwork and instead the body
and mind are worn down daily and exhausted. Perhaps they sway
the head back and forth to shake up the brain, or rub the palms
together to increase their strength but their blood only boils and
bubbles up, causing things like ulcers and abscesses to occur.

   Perhaps they pile up soil to serve as an altar where they can
worship in the morning and sacrifice in the evening. They communicate through night-time visions and ghosts, and happenings
occur – like being entrapped by the guiles of 'bewitching mountain
bogeys'.

   At first the heart rejoices and you convince yourself you must
live for ever. Then abruptly, in the midst of your work you die
young – you cannot evade the body and bones being laid bare to
decay! This is all due to your resolute and singleminded rebellion.

Through blundering you bring up opposition,
And rebelling you lose a pivotal opportunity.
There are many, numerous, separate transmissions,
Way, way too many, far enough too many.

Pushing back the ideas of Huang and Lao,
They abridge and falsify the whole Canon.
You who understand, examine these ideas so very intently,
That you may be boundless in your knowledge of the
    source.

To summarize, in these cases neither one's plan nor one's actions
are correct. If you turn your back on the true Path, you will never
find the key to the proper transmission. It is to neglect totally the
'quiet and non-active' (*qingjing wuwei*) tradition which is central
to the Daoist Canon.

The grand 'Song on Smashing Superstition' by Wang Liangqi
(Wang the 'Perfect Vessel') goes:

To 'circulate the breath' is not the Way!
The body's fluids are not a magical water.
To 'guard the thoughts' is not the Way!
How can you eat a picture of a cake!
Sexual practices are not the Way!
When the seed has gone, life passes.

The newly born foetus is not the Way!
What is unclean has nothing to do with the true Energy.
To stop eating salted foods is not the Way!
Your food then lacks stimulating flavours.
A vegetarian diet is not the Way!
Going hungry only injures the stomach and spleen.
Abstaining from sex is not the Way!
Yin and Yang then lose their honoured positions.

So then what is the Way?
Great Oneness holding to himself the true Energy.
The Energy entwined and yet not entwined,
Rising and falling like heaven and earth.
The two materials pairing off with each other,
They arise themselves from an original beginning.

The mild-mannered maiden and newborn babe,
Paired off as Already and Not Yet Overcome.

Fundamentally they are the true Yin and Yang,
The husband and wife joined together with a single goal.
For this reason they are never to be separated,
How can the sole Yang achieve anything?

Out in this world there appears a Golden Immortal,
But his Golden Elixir is not easy to come by.
A determined individual will never discuss this truth
But hide its profundity in the deepest abyss.

If the cycling five are not let go on their way
The tiger is born from out of the water –
If the cycling five are artfully inverted
The dragon comes out from within the fire.
These words tell of the true mystery
Which is the strength of our deity Great Oneness.

Master Shangyang says: There are numerous side paths and numerous small byways, and they all lead nowhere. Once you deviate from the religion of Huangdi [the Yellow Emperor] and Laozi you can never merge yourself with the true teaching of Yin and Yang and join with them in kind. If you abridge and effectively falsify the whole Daoist Canon, what use is this, if you want to form the 'millet-sized pearl'?

This practice runs directly contrary to prolonging your life because it hurries down the path of mortality.

Yuyan comments: Clearly deviating from the refined teachings of the Yellow Emperor, you engage in deception – then you miss entirely the message of our old lord Laozi, and blindly adhere to the wrong path. You arrive at this place through your own fault so who is to blame?

This is the reason Wang Liangqi wrote his 'Song on Smashing Superstition' [see above].

27

THINGS OF THE SAME KIND ESSENTIALLY JOIN

This chapter begins the last part of Xu Congshi's text. It explains how, for man to foster life, he must understand the processes of life and penetrate the workings of Yin and Yang. Change is nothing but Yin and Yang. Combining the right things will produce the right results; combining the wrong things will produce the wrong results. Desire is really the tarnishing of our 'golden' inner nature. If we understand and practise only restraint – considering the inner alchemy – we will enter finally into the secrets of sagehood.

When the 'Persian powder' is thrown into a fire
It spoils in colour and turns back to lead.
Likewise ice and snow in a gentle heat
Melt and flow away back to nothing.
Gold's main ingredient is coarse red sand
But its disposition is to blend with mercury.
Transformation and change follow these truths,
The beginning and the end arising from one another.

If you want to perform the method of inner cultivation,
It is best to use things of the same kind:
In planting crops one should sow grain,
In breeding chickens one uses their eggs.
Take the same kind of things that help naturally,
That are easily formed and moulded into shape.

How could fish's eyes be taken for pearls?
Tea cannot be made from the wild raspberry!
The same kinds of things comply with one another,
Forcing them to serve each other is worthless.

And so the mountain-finch does not produce peacocks,
Nor foxes and rabbits suckle horses!
Streaming water does not blaze upwards,
Nor flickering fire seep down!

This section again uses examples to illustrate how 'things of the same kind' (*tonglei*) affect each other, while things of differing kinds have no effect on each other at all. If they affect each other you can form the Elixir; if they do not affect each other, or have very little effect, then the Elixir cannot be made. Things of the same kind make the work easier to complete. 'Persian powder' is a name for an oxide of lead.

Transformation and inter-transformation follow these truths. One thing divides into two, whilst two combine to make one. To 'return to the source, to travel back to the original nature (*fanben huanyuan*)' is the fundamental law to follow during the inner cultivation of an Elixir.

Both the main commentators mention the 'inner training' needed for 'gold' to retain its lustre. The smelting of metals (gold) is a metaphor for the controlling of desire, especially sexual desire, and the prevention of the loss of the sperm (golden essence) which tends to follow after the 'mild-maiden mercury' (the quicksilver mind).

Master Shangyang says: The 'Persian powder' results from smelting black lead; when it is put into fire it returns to its original state. Ice and snow are made up from frozen water; when they meet with heat they return to where they came from. When yellow gold is put with mercury it turns clear: if it is heated then it regains its red lustre. The people of this world are wholly given over to their own lustful desires, which throw their inner natures into turmoil. If their natures are kept whole, they are able to lead a long and fruitful life.

What is meant here by 'gold's main ingredient is coarse red sand, but its disposition is to blend with mercury'? The person who is on the path of inner cultivation must be clear on the process of life, and understand fully the workings of Yin and Yang. If he wants to cultivate a Golden Elixir, he first must amass together the 'red sand' and blend it with the 'mercury of the jade pond'.

Besides, you use the water within the trigram Kan ☵ to overcome the fire within the trigram Li ☲. Once water and fire overcome each other's deficiencies, gold and sand merge their bodies together. 'Transformation and change follow these truths' of combining the same kinds of things together; 'beginning and end' arise from the leadership given by the cock to the hen.

When the text says 'If you want to perform the method of inner cultivation, it is best to use things of the same kind', it is really only stating the plain truth. For example to plant crops you must sow grain and to breed chickens you must use their eggs. If you want to fashion an immortal Buddha and cannot manage to get agreement between things of the same kind, even if you enter the portals of a hundred schools and sit for a thousand years, you will never gain anything.

Yuyan comments: In my own body I have one single heaven and earth, and one single Yin and Yang. So the book *Returning to the Source* speaks of 'cracking open the bones and scooping out the marrow of that heaven and earth'! During the time they are intimate with each other, it is imperative I creep in and steal away their energies!

The sun and moon are formed of the energies of their spiritual father and holy mother; within our own bodies our blood and bone are formed of the energies of our common father and mother. Thus if we take the energies of our true father and mother to change and transform the body of our common father and mother, we will turn into a purely Yang and true Immortal; and live out our lives along with the eternity of heaven and earth.

If someone is blind to his search for things of the same kind and unaware that he himself is joined with Qian and Kun, he will persist in searching outside for 'things of the same kind' or have the mad idea of taking a young girl in order to fashion the 'true lead'. In this case he is entrusting himself to the practice of the Yellow Emperor with his many consorts.

But this is just a pretext for perversity, which has been created to indulge the desires of scholars! On this account the more well-off families and honoured officials may practise these arts, but they will mostly sink into death and depravity. This is simply what goes on.

The true classic, *Southern Flower* says: Without tiring your body! Without disturbing your seed! This is the practice to follow in order to secure everlasting life!

Abroad in the world there are many scholars,
Subtle-minded men full of outstanding qualities;
Suddenly they meet with the unforeseen,

Destruction by fire, loss of wealth and property.
Relying on a veneer of words,
Wildly and wilfully they work away,
Drawing out loose ends without any connection,
And with all degree and deliberation cast away.

They pound down hard gallstones,
Mica and magnetic alum;
Heat yellow sulphur until it flares up,
With soft mercury to help in the smelting,
And case the drum with five stones of copper
To support and hold it beneath.
But things of varying natures differ –
How can they want to join them together?

A thousand attempts must mean 10,000 failures,
Wanting to be clever you only develop an addiction,
And then luck and fortune both give out,
For only the sage knows their whereabouts.

From early youth until their hair turns white,
They work amidst doubt and suspicion,
Turn their back upon the method to keep up the
    deception,
And leave the correct path to come upon evil byways.
With tunnel vision a broad view is impossible,
And trouble arises as they guess at where to go.

This section clearly identifies the errors and pitfalls of the outer
alchemists. However many times they attempt by chemical means
to fashion an Elixir of everlasting life, they must fail. 'Things of
varying natures differ', so 'how can they want to join together'?
   Finally they are driven to guess at the direction to follow. But
ultimately they have no principle or rule and are netted and lost in
the web of the world.

Master Shangyang comments: The people of this world are only
familiar with what they are used to. They are unwilling to enquire
or ask questions themselves, and will never 'stand out of the
thicket' in order to gain a broad view. Their ears are blocked, their
eyes bowed down. Which one of them is capable of seeing or
hearing anything above or beyond themselves?

Turn your back on pomposity – which others regard as heroic. All these so-called outstanding abilities are due to a vague reliance on their subtle minds – which are merely lost in self-pride and self-satisfaction!

Yuyan comments: The book *Awakening to Reality* says: Even if you are quicker to perceive than Yanzi and Minzi [disciples of Confucius], without meeting a true teacher you will have nothing but suspicions. If you merely read books on alchemy, without receiving the spoken article, how can they teach you to form a 'holy babe'?

In general, there are not a few abroad in the world who have become subtle-minded scholars and loved study. But among these, those who have sought out a true teacher and gained the proper transmission are no doubt few.

Those who smelt the 'three yellow stuffs' and 'four divine ingredients' have a mad idea that the method somehow lies in doing this. They really do not understand that minerals and stones and all things which have form and substance in this world are, as such, dissimilar in kind. Their characters, their substances, their names all differ; how could they ever wish to join together their bodies and manage something?

Thus whoever it is that practises these arts, it means 'a thousand attempts and 10,000 failures'. Wanting to be clever they only develop an addiction to their work. What happens then? They 'draw out loose ends without any connection' and 'all degree and deliberation are cast away'. This is the cause of it all.

He continues: The holy Immortals' golden fluid supreme restorative Elixir is the ultimate medicine whereby something is born out of nothing. The 'red sand' and 'mercury' are no more than images devised for comparison, that is all. What remedy is there for those in the world who do not recognize the 'true lead' and 'true mercury'? They take them to mean common red sand and mercury and often their laboratories are destroyed by fire and their property destroyed, so that in the end they achieve nothing.

Then suddenly they are found sighing deeply, their hair turned white and all their schemes incomplete – with nothing ever finished. Oh misery indeed! The true path is simple and uncomplicated. But true words seem plain and without savour so who is it that believes them? Who is it that can put them into practice?

Finally even if they gain the proper transmission, in the middle of their work doubts arise. Then they leave the correct path to come upon evil byways. This is just how it happens.

Master Zhuxi explains: This section describes the forming of an outer Elixir. If one does not use ingredients which are similar to the medicine, one will never be able to form the Jewel.

28

THE TWO BOWS OF THE
DRAGON AND THE TIGER

The production of an Elixir is quite simply achieved through the matching of similars. This is the method which underlies all proper transformation and change: it is the same with the smelting of an Elixir.

> The Fire Records were not futilely written,
> And to expand on Change will elucidate them.
> The crescent-moon on her back is the cauldron on the furnace,
> While the white tiger simmers at the nodal point,
> The mercurial sun becomes an unstable pearl,
> The azure dragon accompanying them:
> Arising in the east to unite at the west,
> The Hun- and Po-souls are in each other's arms.

The alchemical corpus which made up the legendary 'Fire Records' probably provided the source material from which Wei Boyang and Xu Congshi constructed the *Can Tong Qi*. They used primarily the moving lines of the *Zhou Yi*, and their derived images and ideas, in order to fashion an approach.

Here Xu Congshi takes the shape of the moon to represent the cauldron on the furnace and the progress of the sun across the sky to represent the firing times for the Elixir. The 'white tiger' and 'azure dragon' represent medicinal ingredients.

The white tiger stands for the 'true lead' and the azure dragon for the 'true mercury' – they hurriedly join together on the 'central ground' (the Wu- and Ji-soils), to begin to form the Elixir. In addition the dragon signifies the east, vegetation and wood; while the tiger stands for the west, metals and minerals. The two are attracted to each other. Minerals feed into vegetation, vegetation turns back to

minerals, but the two are not easily merged – they need a true
'central mind' to help them together. Then they will fall 'into each
other's arms'.

Master Shangyang comments: To speak of the furnace and cauldron, the dragon and tiger, and both bows of gold and inner
energy, our Immortal describes the 'crescent-moon furnace', the
'white tiger', the 'upturned bow', the trigram Dui ☱, and the Po-
soul. They belong in the west and represent the 'other' or 'jade
pond'. He also describes the 'mercurial sun', the 'unstable pearl',
the 'azure dragon', the 'downturned bow', the trigram Gen ☶,
and the Hun-soul. They belong in the east and represent the 'self'
or 'cauldron of gold'.

The 'crescent-moon furnace' is the spiritual furnace belonging
to Great Oneness. It is that which is sometimes described as the
'yin furnace'. It forms an upturned crescent similar in shape to the
new moon when it first appears. The 'white tiger' is a creature
belonging to the western-region Dui-palace. As heaven and earth
begin to draw apart its original energy is first connected to 'other-
ness' – in the form of the awesome tiger. If you strike it, it will
respond. It releases itself liberally, gloriously and greatly to the
world and all material things depend on it for life. Suppose it can
injure people and kill them – still if we gather up its greatness we
may grasp hold of its true power.

King Wen, commenting on the *Book of Change*, said: Treading
on the tiger's tail, it does not bite the man, blessings [Hexagram
10, Treading]. The *Book of Change* also says: Treading the path
exactly level, a hermit's devotion brings good fortune [Hexagram
10, line 2].

Confucius comments on this hexagram: It enjoys itself but
responds to strength ['Tuan' commentary]. Again the hexagram
says, 'Treading a simple path and going forward, alone he carries
out his intent ['lesser image' to Hexagram 10, line 1]. The scholar
who cultivates an inner Elixir must know how to dread this tiger.
He must firstly subdue it and make it cower down. Once he can
make the tiger cower, it will begin to simmer at the nodal point
and not 'bite people'.

The trigram Li stands for the sun and mercury, which within
itself, carries the 'red sand', commonly called the 'unstable pearl'.
The 'azure dragon' is a creature belonging to the eastern-region
Zhen-palace. Through countless eons it has become strong – its
original energies connected to the 'self'. This is the fierce and

awesome dragon which has the ability to transform, to affect all things in the world and open up communication – 'The clouds form and the rain does its work, and all material things flow into their forms ['Tuan' commentary to Hexagram 1, Creative].

As the nine at the second line of the Creative says: The dragon is seen in the field, favourable to see the great man. Confucius comments: The power of the dragon works properly and penetrates all things ['Wenyan' commentary Hexagram 1:2]. If the people of this world do not awaken to this life-giving power which the dragon possesses, then each suffers harm. If any one of them can awaken and dread it, regulate it and subdue it, they will bring it under control and actually make use of it.

As they 'arise in the east to unite at the west', their coming together is commended and in proper-mannered accord.

Yuyan comments: As an old saying goes, 'The production of the ultimate medicine comes about through nothing but fire and water!'

Once fire and water are interconnected, the energies of the dragon and tiger are blended and melted together within the cauldron, to form a golden fluid. The idea here is very clear. When creating an Elixir, if you retain a humble heart, silent and stilled, with the mind focused and entered into the 'dwelling of the energy [*qixue*]' – then east and west join up, gold and wood match together, north and south blend into one, water and fire have overcome each other's deficiencies and the 'four images' and 'five elements' cluster each to the other. All these settle and focus themselves at a single place. So then where is the problem?

Master Zhuxi comments: The crescent-moon I suspect refers to the earlier lower part of the circle, when the latter upper part is empty. The shape is that of the crescent-moon.

The white tiger is the lead, the fire, the inner energy, the west, the Po-soul, the Yang, and it 'simmers at the nodal point'. The text describes how it scurries below and then begins to seep and steam upwards. The mercurial sun is the inner vitality, the green dragon, the water, the east, the Hun-soul, the Yin.

He continues: The categories of Kan and Li, water and fire, dragon and tiger, lead and mercury are interchangable. Actually they only describe the inner energy [*qi*] and vitality [*jing*] of the body. This is all they refer to. Our inner vitality is represented by water, Kan, the dragon or mercury; our inner energy by fire, Li, the tiger or lead. The Elixial method involves using our mental powers [*shen*]

.to help the vitality and energy to interact together and to form an Elixir. The Yang inner energy is situated beneath and at first it balances out the fluid water. But the fire smelts it and they both congeal together to complete an Elixir.

The upturned bow at Dui ☱ numbered eight,
The downturned bow at Gen ☶ also eight;
Both bows are quintessentially joined,
Forming the body of Qian ☰ and Kun ☷ complete.
Eight ounces on eight ounces, one pound –
The method of Change, proper and unfailing!

This section continues along the same theme. It notes the calculated weights of the ingredients used in forming the Elixir. The 'upper bow at Dui numbered eight' may be compared with Chapter 22, where it says, 'At eight days Dui receives the Ding-fire, its upper arc stretched taut as a bow.' This describes how the moon, by the eighth day, is shaped like an upturned drawn bow.

The 'lower bow at Gen also eight' matches with 'Gen appearing faultlessly at Bing-fire in the south and, by the twenty-third day, the lower arc is strung (also Chapter 22). Here the moon, by the twenty-third day, or the eighth after the full moon on the fifteen, is shaped like a downturned drawn bow.

At the upturned bow Yang is extending and Yin contracting; Yang is growing and Yin in decline, the Hun advancing, the Po in retreat and Yin changing into Yang. At this moment, the 'true mercury' is being produced and it must speedily be collected and taken. Below is one explanation of how this comes about.

The 'mercury' stands for the fire. The prenatal inner-world fire of the 'gate to life' (kidneys) is the Bing-fire; the postnatal outer-world fire of the heart is the Ding-fire. But despite both fires appearing at the same time, the Bing-fire alone of the prenatal inner world is the 'true mercury'. Both fires amassed together 'weigh one pound'. You take eight ounces of the 'true mercury' of the Bing-fire and briefly put it into the Elixial field.

At the downturned bow Yin is extending and Yang contracting; Yin is growing and Yang in decline, the Po advancing, the Hun in retreat and Yang is being transformed into Yin. At this moment, the 'true lead' is being produced and it must speedily be collected and taken.

The 'lead' stands for the water. The prenatal inner-world water of the kidneys is the Ren-water; the postnatal outer-world water of the kidneys is the Gui-water. But despite both waters appearing at the same time, the Ren-water alone of the prenatal inner world is the 'true lead'. Both waters amassed together 'weigh one pound'. You take eight ounces of the 'true lead' of the Ren-water and put it into the Elixial field to join up with the 'true mercury'.

As the quintessence of both 'bows' fuses into an Elixir, it is as if you open up a new heaven and earth. The eight ounces of 'true lead' fit together with the eight ounces of 'true mercury', and properly form one pound. The exact measurement of both is just the same as in the proper tallying of Yin and Yang necessary in the study of Change.

Master Shangyang says: The trigrams Dui and Gen each number eight; they flow from the Wu-soil and result in the Ji-soil. When the Hun- and Po-souls are 'in each other's arms', gold and wood are no longer set apart. Both bows are 'quietessentially joined' and the body of the trigrams Qian and Kun 'complete'.

For the method of Change to be unfailing, the 'two eights' must each form an integral part of one another and together form 'one pound'. The 'one pound' is the symbol of completeness. For this number to be reached you accumulate small amounts to arrive at something larger.

He concludes: One ounce is made up of 24 grains. Thus if 16 ounces make up 1 pound, 1 pound is made up of 384 grains. The ancients divided up the pound into grains in order to enable them to make it correspond to the number of lines in the hexagrams [64 × 6 = 384].

Li Chade says: The crescent-moon on her back lies in the position of the woman during intercourse. If the 'white tiger simmers at the nodal point' the 'true lead' must be taken to govern the true mercury. During their time together, the feminine passion, the 'other', the Dui-tiger, the lead, should govern the male, the 'self', the azure dragon, the mercury.

The text to Treading [Hexagram 10] says: You step on the tiger's tail, it does not bite the man! Blessings. This is to caution one against the dangers of depletion and debauchery. The last line says: Observe your own stepping, and record the omens. Turn back to the original – there is good fortune. If this is made the ultimate intent when the Yin steps on the Yang, then a favourable result is achieved for all!

29

GOLD REVERTS BACK TO ITS
NATURE

The constancy of material gold and its lack of reactivity illustrate our unalterable and original nature. But this chapter does not speak of any material gold dug out of the ground; it describes the gold born in a mysterious fashion from out of the great transformation wrought by Qian and Kun.

> When gold is put into a blazing fire
> It will stay unsullied and bright.
> From the very start of time
> The sun and moon never lost their light;
> So gold never fails in weight,
> Just as the sun- and moon-phases stay constant.
>
> Gold's origin obeys the moon's birth:
> At the new moon's light, at the mark of the sun,
> The gold turns and flees back to its mother,
> The old moon and the sun in each other's arms.
> Hidden away, then redoubled in strength,
> Well engulfed within a bottomless void.
> So gold retrieves its former nature
> And awesome in the cauldron is set alight!

This section takes the fundamental qualities of material gold as an illustration of the 'true lead' or 'true gold' which is the object of our cultivation when fashioning an inner Elixir. Although the gold lodges, as the 'true lead', within the central Yang line of Kan ☵, it really finds its origin within the sun as it first casts its light upon the moon.

On the very first day of the month, the single Yang begins to stir, as the moon catches the light of the sun. As 'Zhen ☳ arrives and

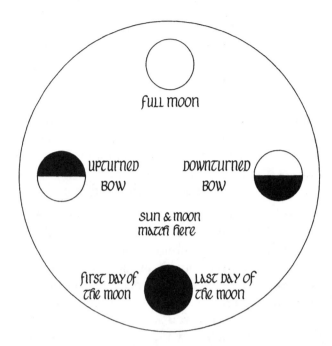

Fig. 34 The moon-phases

its token is received (Chapter 21)'; the old, darkened moon and mother's body, represented by Kun ☷, is touched by the brightly lit, golden sun and father, represented by Qian ☰. Then the first line of Qian becomes lodged within Kun to form Zhen ☳. In such a way 'gold's origin obeys the moon's birth'.

On the last day of the month, when the golden light of the moon is sunken and obscured in the northern skies, it is as if the spiritual light within the body were hidden away within the darkened 'cave of the energy'. This is the moment the medicinal ingredients for the Elixir are thrown into the cauldron. Very soon, as the Yin reaches its extreme point, the Yang returns and 'gold retrieves its former nature'. It is 'awesomely set alight' within the cauldron, just as the great medicine is born within the body.

Master Shangyang comments: Our Immortal here includes nothing at all superfluous. In this section, his method concerns the use of the gold. If good results are not achieved in fashioning this gold, you cannot form an Elixir. Thus it is described as a 'Golden' Elixir.

But this is not the gold found among the precious stones and minerals of this world. It is not a gold dug out from the soil and rocks, but a gold born from out of the creative activity of heaven and earth: it is the mystery of the inverted cycling five, which originates from the great transformation wrought by Qian and Kun within their 'darkened cavity'. This is what it actually represents.

He continues: To esteem the fundamental origin of things is the most favoured ability that man possesses. He needs to understand that this gold existed first within the 'makeshift chaos' [see Chapter 4]. It finds its origin in the moment just before the 'supreme pole' [*taiji*] is created, which splits apart the void into Yin and Yang.

Yuyan comments: Anything which is present in the common material world, which is put into fire, will spoil and become tarnished. Only true gold will not spoil.

In general, during the mutual production of the cycling five, when you reach gold [metal] you reach the ultimate. It is gold which is the most precious of them all. If you heat and fuse it, it turns into liquid [water]; if you strike it, it produces sparks [fire]; in its pliability it resembles wood; and in its colour it resembles soil [earth]. Water, fire, wood and soil – these four characters are all provided for by gold.

Thus true gold can pass through a hundred smeltings and still remain hard: it has never been known to lose its original substance or weight. From the very first splitting apart of heaven and earth, there have passed several hundred thousand years but the phases of the sun and moon have stayed just as constant and never lost their light!

30

ENTRY BY A SIDE ENTRANCE
WILL SEE NO RESULT

This chapter explains briefly how not to succeed in the cultivation of the Elixir. The people of this world 'love petty tricks' but the business is 'concise and uncomplicated'. To gain the Elixir you must 'subdue the inner energies'.

The people of this world love petty tricks,
Never examining the breadth and depth of the way;
They abandon the true Path to follow devious byways,
Wanting to hurry on but never getting through.

Like blind men not using a staff,
Or the deaf hearing the sounds of music,
They hunt under water for birds and rabbits,
And climb the hills in search of fish and dragons.
They plant wheat expecting to harvest millet,
Or turn a pair of compasses in order to draw a square –
If you waste your strength and weary your spirit,
By the end of your life you will see no result.
Should you wish to know the secret of inner cultivation,
The matter is concise and uncomplicated.

This section emphasizes the fact that relying on side entrances without making a direct approach to the Elixial method never yields any result. The more you want to hurry on, the less you are likely to see your way through. The matter is truly 'concise and uncomplicated'.

Master Shangyang says: The people of this world love petty tricks. Petty tricks are not involved on the true Path. If your imagination is mean and insignificant, you will never experience the supreme method. It is so supremely magnificent it envelops both heaven and earth, and is as deep and unfathomable as the oceans. But man obstinately will not hear of this. He prefers to suffer the poison put out by stupid teachers, and would rather be gripped by their words.

The true method seeks no reason for its instruction – while people on the side paths love to pick at different points and find contention between them. They abandon the true Path and follow deviating byways, swallowing down various medicines in order to 'lighten their bodies and rise above as Immortals'. They want to hurry on but never get through, and their vitality is wasted without it ever being used to nourish their nature.

This is just the same as 'blind men not using a staff' – they take any path and then consult endlessly about where it is going and where it leads. It is just the same as the 'deaf hearing sounds of music' or 'hunting under water for birds and rabbits'. Why do they not combine together things of the same kind?

If the cycling five are not turned on their heads and inverted, you are 'climbing the hills in search of fish and dragons'. If you sit like a dried-out old tree-stump, expecting to become an Immortal, you are 'planting wheat and expecting to harvest millet'! If you do not undertake to follow the true Path it is just like 'turning a pair of compasses in order to draw a square'! Similarly, just as these many activities waste your strength and intent, if you do not meet a teacher then 'by the end of your lives, you will see no result'.

If you should wish to know the 'secret of inner cultivation', you should know that the message given by the ancient Immortals is never complicated to understand.

The saying goes: To subdue the inner energies is not to submit to them, to make them submit you must subdue them. To submit to them does not bring everlasting life, to gain everlasting life you must subdue them.

These words contain within themselves the genuine secret, and they encourage the noblest and very best sentiments in man.

Yuyan comments: The great method of the Golden Elixir is completed through building up vitality and accumulating energy. This must not be halted, otherwise the whole process falls.

In the time taken to eat a meal the 'holy babe' is formed, in a hundred days the foundation is laid, in a single year the whole business is engaged, in three years the inner cultivation and nourishment has begun.

You yourself have to repeat the work over several seasons. There is no such thing as one day meeting your teacher and the next being able to ascend as an Immortal. So what can be done for the students who, time and time again, are misled by what they hear about such-and-such a method and such-and-such a way? If they never examine the 'breadth and depth of the way', they cannot pick out a true teacher from a devious one. They spend their time looking for quick results and only love the display of 'petty tricks'. If they understand 'the One' they never understand 'the two'. If they acquire a substance, they never acquire an understanding of its function. Their position is such that they only gain a partial view, and then think that they alone are capable of it. If this perpetuates itself they start to expound exalted and false doctrines, and calumniate the true Path. They act directly contrary to the proper principle of things and pick a belief in what they have never studied. Wild ideas encourage more wild ideas, and deception perpetuates deception. There are not a few people who act like this.

In the meantime, there may be a clever individual but he is not willing to submit himself to investigation. He only worms his way into the writings of the ancients, seeking and hoping for enlightenment. How is this different from a blind man not using a staff? The ignorant and blind will never penetrate the ultimate principle. Even if their innermost thoughts are perpetually tied to the alchemical books, how is this different from a deaf man saying he can hear the sounds of music?

He concludes: Wei Boyang [Xu Congshi] did write this book, although he did not want you to place undue value on what it said. Are you able then to do this?

31

THE GOLDEN ELIXIR ON A
KNIFE-POINT

This supreme chapter contains complete instructions for the Elixial method, but they are abstruse and brief. One needs a teacher in order to follow them, for the Elixir must be 'plucked out' of the cauldron in the nick of time. The gold is used as an 'embankment' or surround whilst the water is poured in and the firing begun. Finally the marvellous 'purple gold' is collected, 'luminous and shining' in the cauldron, and the restored Elixir is complete. Most illustrations are taken from outer alchemy.

> If you use the gold as the embankment,
> The water enters and flows unchecked.
> If the gold is reckoned at fifteen ounces,
> The amount of water is calculated with regard to it.
> In the firing decide on there being exact proportions,
> Five parts water are already too much.

> Two may be regarded as correct,
> The weight of the gold as it is at the start,
> Three may not be put in.
> Then two parts fire accompany them,
> So that these three take to each other,
> And become transformed in shape quite marvellously!

> Below there is the breath of the greater Yang,
> Subdued and steaming up instantly.
> First as a fluid, later congealing,
> To be known as the Yellow Carriage!

> As its time is about to be fulfilled,
> Its life is destroyed and shattered,
> Its body becomes like dried dirt or ashes,
> Appearing as dust in the window-light.

This section explains the first steps in the completion of the work of the Elixir. At the beginning we should concentrate on the mix of the gold and the water to see that the amount of liquid is not too great and the mixture too fluid. If the gold within the trigram Kan (manifest in the trigram Dui) is used as protection and 'embankment', the original water should not overflow or 'slop over' the side. Then afterwards, as the 'true water' within Li is built up, our inner vitality becomes self-contained and unlikely to be lost.

As the breath of the Great Yang fire is subdued, it warms the Kan-water so that it rises and travels upwards as steam. The 'mercurial sun', that 'unstable pearl', condenses and congeals, and the Yellow Carriage (an image of the mean) is formed. At this very moment the dry-as-dust Elixir is awaiting transformation by the fire – as described below.

The 'first change' referred to by Master Zhuxi is a transformation into inner vitality (*jing*); as it turns to 'dried dirt or ashes' it reaches the 'second change', a transformation of inner vitality into energy (*qi*).

The section is complicated and the traditional commentaries vary. There are also arguments as to textual irregularities, although the main tenor of the chapter is clear. I mostly follow Master Shangyang's views.

Master Shangyang comments: In this chapter our Immortal speaks of the firing process in detail. Here he actually describes us as being engaged in the firing, as actively gathering together the ingredients and transferring them into the cauldron. What you should primarily understand is that this text is put together in an orderly way and not carelessly. When it was compiled, this chapter was purposely made difficult. If the detail had not been included, how could later generations then engage the process?

According to the Elixial tradition, if you never encounter the practical teachings, you cannot understand the hidden parts of this text and its mysteries. You gaze at the chapter and it appears as dry and tasteless as chewed wax! Without knowing where to begin, you only suspect that it refers to something like the smelting of metals and minerals – which, in the end, brings no success whatsoever!

Truly we can sympathize with those who turn their backs on and resent the exaggerated style of these teachings. But now I will briefly explain them, in order to eliminate once and for all any further doubt.

To 'use gold as the embankment' is the supreme task of reparation undertaken by those who collaborate in the inner development of a 'nine times restored' Golden Elixir. You must understand that this gold is that which lies within the western-region Dui.

First we must provide a true heart – which is able to search earnestly for this Dui-gold. Set up an altar on some 'stamped-down ground', and constantly and especially be watchful. If the 'embankment' is solid and well built, you may await the gold to produce the water. Since it produces water, the amount of water similarly should be calculated and carefully understood. The essence lies in understanding the difference between the water of prenatal inner world and the water of the postnatal outer world. The water of the outer world is turbid and muddied, and cannot be used to develop a Elixir. If it is of the inner world, then also wait until it clears before you make use of it.

The old song goes: The river Jing is clear and the river Wei is muddied. This means the waters of the Jing ran clear but the waters of the Wei were muddied.

When cultivating an Elixir wait for the clear and free-running water, which will 'flow unchecked' past any obstacles, without disturbing or moving them. Thus the text says, 'The water enters and flows unchecked.' This is the clear water within which lies the true gold. There is a saying: The gold is produced with water clinging to it – the moment it runs clear!'

What is also essential is to understand the exact weighing out of the ingredients and the later use of them. Most often the Dui-gold will be estimated at fifteen ounces in weight – which relies upon the general principle of its weight being close to a single pound. Thus the text says, 'The gold is reckoned at fifteen ounces.' If the weight of the gold reaches fifteen ounces it is actually able to 'be produced with water clinging to it'.

What is meant by 'The amount of water is calculated with regard to it'? It does not say, 'The water is also reckoned at fifteen ounces', but it is essential to have the water and the gold in accord. If there are fifteen ounces of gold you certainly will be able to produce some water. Thus the text says 'The amount of water is calculated with regard to it.' Our Immortal reiterates that when engaged in the firing we must actually 'decide on there being exact proportions'.

If fifteen ounces of gold have already produced 'five parts' water, this amount of water is too great and it cannot be used. Thus it says, 'Five parts water are already too much.' If the Dui-gold has begun to produce water and you reach the moment when there are 'two parts', this is the correct amount and it can be used. Thus it says, 'Two may be regarded as correct.'

It is the 'two parts' water which must be estimated correctly along with the fifteen ounces of gold. Thus the reference is to 'the weight of the gold as it is at the start'. If the water has already reached 'three parts' it also is unfit to be used. Thus it says, 'Three may not be put in.' If the amounts of gold and water arrive at a moment when they are in exactly the correct proportion then quickly take 'two parts' fire and combine them all together. Thus the text says, 'Then two parts fire accompany them.'

Once the gold, water and fire are all together, the fire receives the inner energy of the gold, again using the water to regulate it in the formation of the restored Elixir. Then it can be 'transformed in shape, quite marvellously'!

When engaging in the task of the firing, it should never be done through force. Because of this the sages took the months which occur throughout the year to outline the idea of the gold; they measured the days which occur throughout the month and watched the tide of change. They chose the hours of the day to correspond to the lines of the hexagrams and settled the firing of the Elixir to the hour, through these 'tokens [*fu*]' of its progress. What is meant by the 'tokens'?

The wise saints and sages of old considered the smelting of a Golden Elixir to be a singly great affair. They calculated the timing of its separate divisions by setting up the 'clustering rule [*zuancu fa*]'. They took the seventy-two 'twenty-minute periods [*hou*]' as 'clustering' within a single day and the 360 lines [of the sixty hexagrams] as 'clustering' within a single month. Thus they took thirty-six tokens for the day and thirty-six tokens for the night – distributing them equally between the twelve double-hours. Therefore each double-hour corresponds to six twenty-minute periods which relate to the search for the Elixir – although you only use the time taken for two twenty-minute periods. Each double-hour corresponds to a single line in the two hexagrams for the day, which relate to the search for the Elixir – although you need not use even half a line. Each double-hour has three tokens which relate to the search for the Elixir – but you only use the rapid action of a single token. Thus the saying goes, 'A single token, and at once bursting through!'

When the Yellow Emperor described this in the scripture of the *Yin Shadow* he spoke of it similarly. The lines goes: Man knows the magical even though the magical is unknown! What appears not magical is actually magical!

This is it exactly. The inner cultivation of the Elixir of the Immortals uses just this instance of a single token, which contracts the true inner energy of the 360 days and turns it back to be taken within the foetus.

At this moment, in a second, you 'snatch the creative workings of heaven and earth' and reach through to the quintessential sun and moon. The hub of the earth, the form of the heart, the catch to the skies, they all lie within reach of your hand! The dragon and tiger join together as two inner bows of energy, and the gold and water are pounded together into a single true material. The tortoise and snake coil round each other within the Elixial furnace and the crow and rabbit follow their passage along the yellow highway. Black and white reflect each other, while the firm and yielding alternately arise. The jade furnace accumulates happiness, whilst purple flickering flames shine without; shimmering Mars guards the western heaven and the scarlet bird blazes up into an empty void. Hurriedly the water moves on to the gold, and the fire is directed upwards at the cauldron. As it is subdued it steams upward again, taking the inner energy of the greater Yang to fashion what is termed the 'Elixir of the Yellow Carriage'!

When you begin the work of smelting together the water and the gold, the 'embankment' and the timing are carefully calculated so as to arrive at the actual second the Elixir is wholly complete. This only takes the work of a single token. If the moment is drawn out its intrinsic nature is destroyed and the Elixir shattered – and once the Elixir has gone, any idea of lengthening our life has shattered as well. Thus the text says, 'As its time is about to be fulfilled, its life is destroyed and shattered.'

This single great affair of cultivating an inner Elixir is fundamentally concerned with lengthening our lives and promoting our true state. If we are a hair's breadth wrong, any idea of lengthening our life is shattered! Thus our Immortal instructs us to take the greatest care in the detail of the work. The 'dust in the window-light' stands for the very finest particles of Elixial substance.

Yuyan comments: 'Use gold as the embankment and the water will enter and flow unchecked'. This is using the upturned half-pound bow of gold to form a half-jewelled embankment outside, on the south-eastern corner of the furnace. Afterwards the downturned

Fig. 35 Water and gold

half-pound bow of water descends on the west to enter into the northern interior of the furnace whilst its power goes unhindered and unchecked, in its own fashion.

If 'the gold is reckoned at fifteen ounces', it means we have arrived at the fifteenth day from the first day. This is what is meant by the upturned half-pound bow of gold. If 'the amount of water is calculated with regard to it', it means we have arrived at the thirtieth day from the sixteenth day. This is what is meant by the downturned half-pound bow of water.

The Elixial method first uses mildness to ascend, then fierceness to come back down. If this were not so, it could not reach the depths of the world below. Thus the text says, 'In the firing decide on exact proportions, five parts water are already too much.' The gold and the water each make up half, joining together to form the 'two eights' which make up the single pound. One opens, the other closes, coming and going inexhaustably, as do the true Yin and Yang within my own body.

But the water needs in excess of its half-pound and the gold also cannot be less than its half-pound. Thus the text says, these 'two may be regarded as correct, the weight of the gold as it is at the start'.

He continues: At first the greater Yang is situated below, and the water and fire are in intimate union as two enshrouded universal energies, steaming up and producing fluid. Next the fire emerges out of the water, as the Yang gases are gradually extinguished and the fluid congeals into a solid mass within. This forces out the Golden Flower which is named the 'true lead' and as it reaches the moment to move it rises above, travelling and mounting upwards like the passage of a carriage along the Yellow Highway. This is termed the 'Yellow Carriage'.

Then, on the tenth day of the twelfth month, the skies have turned around until the days and months have exhausted their cycle. In terms of the Elixial method, there is also a heavenly cycle within the single body of man. He is in no way different from heaven and earth. If he can truly understand the kidney-energy born at this 'midnight-hour', he acquires the fire which heats it up, smelts it and condenses it into fluid, which then is recognized as the 'true lead'.

But if he wants to reform the 'true mercury' within the Li-palace, he really must not think of using a lead which is fluid. If it has body and substance, and it is muddied and unclear, how can it then be turned back against the direction of its flow and sent up above?

The work of the Holy Immortals in fashioning an Elixir involves no more than sending the fire – at the exact moment – down below. In this way they simply made use of the influence of its energy. Once the fire's strength has grown full its gases swirl and rise upwards, like the mist above rivers and hills. When they have climbed up into the 'mudpill palace' [brain] they are transformed into sweet rain [saliva] which falls down onto the 'double storeyed house' [throat]. Now this cannot happen with something which is solid and substantial.

The Elixial method is said to 'make clear what is muddied'. This is properly correct. What is clear floats up and rests above and so it appears as 'dust in the window-light'. What is muddied sinks and rests below and so 'its body becomes like dried dirt or ashes'.

Master Zhuxi comments: 'If you use the gold as the embankment, the water enters and flows unchecked . . . later congealing, to be known as the Yellow Carriage!' This describes the first change in the transformation of the Elixir.

'As its time is about to be fulfilled, its life is destroyed . . . appearing as dust in the window-light.' This describes the second change.

Then pound it down until it forms one mass,
And enter it in through the red-coloured gate;
Finally firmly block up any openings,
And attend until it reaches a firm conclusion.

A blazing fire extends upwards from below,
Night and day, its sound properly maintained;
At first a mild flame allows regulation,
In the end it becomes fierce, spreading out.

Now wait and watch with extra caution,
And examine the proper balance of the fire;
The whole cycle has twelve divisions,
And when the divisions end, a change will be seen.

Its breath is scattered, its life is cut short,
The body dies and the soul departs –
Then the colour turns to the deepest purple,
Luminous and shining, a restored Elixir is made!
Just the amount settling on a knife-point
Will prove to be quite efficacious ...

Now the actual formation of the Elixir is explained. As an inner Elixir it makes use of man's true fire, whilst the firing process passes through the twelve divisions of the hexagrams: Restored (☷☳ Hexagram 24), Approaching (☷☱ Hexagram 19), Opening (☷☰ Hexagram 11), Invigorating (☳☰ Hexagram 34), Eliminating (☱☰ Hexagram 43), Strengthening (☰☰ Hexagram 1), Encountering (☰☴ Hexagram 44), Retreating (☰☶ Hexagram 33) Closing (☰☷ Hexagram 12), Detaching (☶☷ Hexagram 20), Destroying (☶☷ Hexagram 23), Receiving (☷☷ Hexagram 2) (see Figure 6).

As the Yin departs the Yang arrives. As 'the divisions are used up, they abdicate, allowing Restored (Hexagram 24) to inherit – bringing forth the dragon (Chapter 22)'! This cycle occurs time and time again, 'in the end, retrieving again the beginning (Chapter 21)'.

At last the Yin ebbs, the body and soul depart, and only the purest Yang Elixir remains – being the colour of the 'deepest purple'. This is the restored Elixir, a tiny particle as small as a grain of dust shining in the window-light – if you take only the amount which settles on a knife-point it will prove extremely efficacious. This is the 'third change' referred to by Master Zhuxi. At this moment the inner energy is transformed into pure spirit (*shen*).

Master Shangyang comments: To 'pound it down' means to join Yin and Yang together in the smelting; to 'enter it in' means to keep it intact so it can be put in. The 'red-coloured gate' refers to the door of Qian. The Elixir follows through the door of Qian to return to its spiritual dwelling within. To 'firmly block any openings' means to close up the energies – the openings refer to all the openings into the body. And all this must reach a 'firm conclusion' without there being any mishap – as the 'blazing fire extends upwards from below'.

'Night and day, its sound is properly maintained' – meaning that now the Yang Elixir has begun to arrive, there is a trust developed. The first time you acquire this fire within Li, it circulates around you day and night, through every cell and atom of your body. If you can altogether accept your fate and correctly and most diligently guard it within, you enable its sound to become quieter and its manner more gentle. The inner energy becomes finely balanced, the pulses come to rest, and the inner Elixir begins to condense and form.

'At first a mild flame allows regulation', so at first you use a mild flame to develop the Elixir. But at both the very beginning and the end of the smelting, the flame is turned up fiercely. At the very beginning the flame is fierce to encourage self-discipline; while at the very end the flame is fierce to encourage its revival. Thus the 'Song of the Cauldron Vessel' [Chapter 35] says, 'fiercely at head and tail, mildly in between'. This is exactly correct.

You must 'wait and watch with extra caution' because you cannot do it all yourself. An old poem goes: If the work is not complete, you will be all at sixes and sevens! This is it exactly. 'Examine the proper balance of the fire' not to let it blind the eyes of men and all creatures. Zhang Boduan [in his *Awakening to Reality*] says: Adjust accordingly the firing to uphold Yin and Yang. This is exactly correct.

He concludes: This chapter provides a description of the actual work involved but its detail is slight and the meaning rather obscure. You must depend on the personal instruction of a teacher. How else can you follow the text and finish the task?

Yuyan comments: When first collecting the medicine you 'focus the mind and gather together the inner energies'. You regulate the breath at the nostrils evenly until you feel it respond.

Once the mind and the breath are entered in at the root of the body, close them up tightly or they will quickly disappear. If you let them loose they will be lost and bubble up. You need only cause them to be lengthened continuously and unbroken – like a silken thread which is never let loose. Then the mind eventually focuses itself and the breath eventually settles.

Master Zhuxi comments: 'Then pound it down until it forms one mass and enter it in through the red-coloured gate.' This describes the third change. You pound it down to form one mass. This should be to separate out something you have made.

The 'red-coloured gate' is the mouth. What is fluid congeals to be like 'dried dirt or ashes'. The reason must be obvious. It is ejected out, smelted and dealt with severely, then returned and popped back in. The 'blazing fire' means the 'greater Yang'. The sound of its 'breath' is properly maintained, as in the later chapter [Chapter 34] where it says, 'Ow! Ow! her screams tear into the heart, like those of a little child, longing for its mother.' This is it exactly.

32

THE TWO SOILS COMPLETE
THE WORK

This chapter explains the work of the Wu- and Ji-soils as fundamental to the whole method. If you wish to take in hand the
making of an Elixir, you must first understand the idea of the unity
of the soil. Then you can begin to make use of the gold and the
water in forming the medicine.

Midday and midnight number three together,
The Wu- and Ji-soils weigh in at five;
Once the three and the five are in agreement,
The eight minerals form a proper linking guide.

Breathing in, breathing out, they contain each other,
In each other's thoughts as husband and wife.
The yellow soil is father of all metals,
That 'unstable pearl', the child of water.

Water takes the soil as its devil,
The soil holds back the water so it cannot rise;
The scarlet bird is the vital fire,
She maintains balance through success and failure.

Fire is extinguished as water replenishes,
Altogether dying back to the generous soil;
These three natures joined as one,
At root sharing a common ancestry.

This section explains how the two activities of water and fire need
to coalesce along with the element soil (earth). The mystery in the
functioning of the soil lies in its ability to enable all three elements
– water, fire and soil – to converge together into one. Midnight's

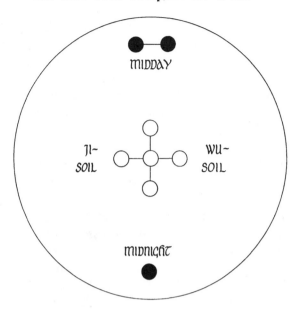

Fig. 36 Wu- and Ji-soils

water is one, midday's fire is two, and added together they form three. The Wu- and Ji-soils already each number five. The water and the fire cannot attain agreement themselves. They need to adopt the solidity of soil in order to join together – just as the forging of minerals over a fire needs an earthenware pot (fashioned out of soil). In the pot they can enter into congress, as husband and wife, and give birth to a true 'babe'.

   In the cycling of the five elements, soil produces metals (and gold) as it assumes the paternity of a father; and wood (the 'unstable pearl') relies on water, just as a child relies on its mother. Water dreads soil, which holds it back, absorbs it and prevents it escaping away; and fire dreads water, which cools it and prevents it blazing up. If the water does not escape and the fire does not blaze up, it is because both together adopt the moderate nature of the soil. As their three natures, water, fire and soil, converge, so husband and wife, father and son, and mother and child, reveal their common ancestry.

Master Shangyang comments: Midnight lies in the northern region, the proper position of the trigram Kan, and its number is one; midday lies to the south, the proper position of the trigram Li, and its number is two.

Within Kan there is a soil named Wu, its number is five; within Li there is a soil named Ji, its number also five. The Wu-soil is the sole gateway into Kan, which controls 'the true single energy of the prenatal inner world [*xiantian zhenyi zhi qi*]'. The Ji-soil is the door directly into Li, wherein there accumulates 'the ultimate reality of the mercury of this postnatal outer world [*houtian zhizhen zhi hong*]'.

If you are seeking the inner-world energy you must reach through to the Wu-soil, then you will acquire it. If you are making use of the outer-world mercury you must subdue it through the Ji-soil, then you can pacify it.

Once midnight and midday are happily in agreement, the Wu- and Ji-soils are already joined. As the essential mystery of the two fives [Wu and Ji] is touched upon they are united, and condense and flow together. The Wu then assumes the Ji and they become of one kind in the cauldron. The two soil characters bind together to form the character for 'knife-point' [because of their shapes].

The eight minerals are represented in Kun. Qian and Kun are father and mother to all minerals and stones. If Kun were not involved you could not say there was any flexibility within the 'proper linking guide'. Thus midday and midnight 'breathe in and breathe out', the Wu and Ji 'contain each other', and the lead and mercury bind together, truly becoming as husband and wife.

He continues: The gateway into Kan is termed the Wu-soil and the central line in Kan is called the Dui-gold. The gold is born from out of the water of Great Oneness [*taiyi*]. Once the told is born from the water, it is the Wu-soil which then controls it. These are 'the three natures joined as one'.

Wood's nature is shown in the Ji-soil and the door into Li is termed the Ji-soil. The Wu-soil, gold and water, these three, join with wood's nature in the Ji-soil. The wood very slowly takes command of them and they are totally changed into a supreme Elixir. Thus it says that 'at root' they share 'a common ancestry'.

Yuyan comments: The midnight-water is one; the midday-fire is two. The numbers of midday and midnight are joined together to form three. Soil's number is five, so the central region of Wu and Ji 'weighs in' at five. The three and five unite together and so form eight. Thus the text mentions the 'eight minerals'.

'Once the three and the five are in agreement' refers to these three, water, fire and soil, joined together. Moreover soil subdues water, and water subdues fire.

But how does this bring about their 'agreement'? The earth stands as go-between for the water and the fire – it mediates between them and arranges a marriage. The fire and the water join as husband and wife, and thus comes the 'agreement'.

How do the eight minerals form 'a proper linking guide'? When water, fire and soil join together as one, they form 'a proper linking guide' to the course of action, which is displayed where every eye can see it!

He continues: As the Yang rises up and the Yin comes down, they form the inbreath and outbreath of heaven and earth. The breath comes from within – therefore it lasts a long time. If man's breath can imitate this breath of heaven and earth in coming from within, it may also last a long time in the same manner.

The *Golden Elixir Compendium* collection says: Breathe out from the heart and lungs, breathe in to the kidneys and liver. Breathe out joined to the root of the sky, breathe in joined to the root of the earth. Breathe out and the dragon moans, the clouds billow and build up; breathe in and the tiger screams and gusts of wind arise. Breathe in and breathe out, and the wind and clouds drip golden juices!

Here the one single energy is secreted spontaneously in the breath without involving the breathing of the mouth and nose. The saying goes: Just begin in the place where the real breath passes in and out, and you set free the mild-mannered maiden to trip daintily back and forth. If someone can 'humble his heart and focus his mind [*xuxin ningshen*]; he may 'reflect back his brightness to light up within [*huiguang neizhao*] – at the position where the real breath passes in and passes out. If he follows its rise and fall, accepting its spontaneous nature and preserving it, then in a short while the breath 'contains itself'. It becomes immovable and still – whilst within this minuteness the inbreath and outbreath knot together just as husband and wife.

Where is 'the position where the real breath passes in and out'? The poem goes: In front, it faces the wheel of the navel. Behind, it faces the kidneys. Centrally it stands as one single, true Golden Cauldron. This is the place where the true breath passes in and out. The *Yellow Courtyard* classic says: Behind there is a secret door, in front lies the gate to the living. The dawning sun, the dying moon are both preserved within this breath.

If the human imagination cannot realize this state then neither can it find the breath. The *Zhuangzi* classic [Chapter 6] says: The

breath of the realized person rises from his heels, the breath of the
common person rises from his throat.

Now when the breath is in the throat it comes abruptly, it is
short and hurried and very shallow. When the breath is joined to
the heels it is extended and prolonged, and much deeper. When
your inner cultivation attains this state, involving the deeper
breath, then your life rests in yourself and it has nothing to do with
any fascination with the foundries!

> Sesame may sustain your years,
> But the restored Elixir may not be taken by mouth.
> As gold by nature never spoils or decays,
> It is the most treasured of all ten thousand things!

> Adepts with their secret of inner cultivation,
> Extended their lives over a long while,
> But it was through the soil as it ranges over every season
> That they guarded their limits as set by square and
>   compasses.

> As gold-dust it enters the five organs,
> Scattering like mist or windborne rain;
> Its fragrance wafts to all four limbs,
> And the face turns back glossy and young.

> White hair changes back to dark,
> Fallen teeth reappear in their former places,
> Old men restore their male vigour,
> And old women regain their shapely youth;
> Changing to escape the toil of this world,
> Then they may be named – 'realized people'!

This section especially explains the marvellous effects which result
from consuming an inner Elixir. But it is through the rigid boundaries set by the soil on the activities of the wood, fire, minerals
(gold, metals) and water, that the work proves effective.

As the Elixir enters the body, renovating and reforming within,
we may be truly termed realized people. Compare Chapter 12,
which states:

> Those wise saints and sages of old cherished the mystery and treasured
> the truth ... they moistened their skin and flesh, and softened and

strengthened their tendons and bones. All sickness cast out and eliminated, their health was constantly preserved; so that, accumulating over a long time, it transformed their bodies until they became Immortals.

Master Shangyang says: This chapter explains that if you wish to engage in developing an inner Elixir, you must first harmonize the two soils, Wu and Ji. Then you can pluck the gold from out of the water, and complete the formation of the Elixir.

Yuyan comments: Spring, summer, autumn and winter all describe the 'ranging' of the soil. Thus the text says, 'It was through the soil as it ranges over every season.' Soil can absorb water and put out fire; as it protects water, the water does not leak out; as it protects fire, fire does not blaze up. Now through the guarding of the Kun-soil you gather the medicine, and through the guarding of Qian you circulate the fire. Thus the text says, 'They guarded their limits, as set by square and compasses.'

He concludes: The gold-dust rises from the cauldron, it penetrates the two kidneys, and is guided upwards by the spine through the heart to enter the 'sea of marrow [brain]'. It scatters into the open lungs, across the liver, through the spleen, and returns back to the Elixial field [lower belly].

As it rises above, it resembles 'mists' rising through the empyrean; as it gusts through, it resembles a sudden shower of 'windborne rain'; as it dashes above, it resembles the first remembrance of dreams upon awakening; as it swells out, it is like the boon of recovering from a long illness. The mind all becomes one, like the interchanged feelings of husband and wife, and the bones and flesh soften and fuse together, giving the comfort one feels after bathing. All these are true-to-life experiences, not metaphor.

The book *Returning to Life* says: If you do not understand what is meant by this energy, its natural after-effects will themselves make it real. In general if you have never felt it, you will never understand it!

33

WATER AND FIRE, INNER
NATURES AND FEELINGS

This final chapter describes the kernel of the alchemy. The cycling five comprise only 'gold, wood, water, fire and earth'. Take 'silver, mercury, lead, sand and earth' and you have joined Yin and Yang, and the Golden Elixir is made! The alchemy is as concise and uncomplicated as this.

The practice of this art of the cycling five
Is comparatively concise and uncomplicated;
The raising of water soon intimidates fire,
Extinguishing its shining light.

The sun and moon eclipse one another
At regular intervals of the month.
As the water fills up Kan, encroaching on the Yang,
So the fire fades away in Li, darkening the day;
Yin and Yang drink and devour each other,
In natural affection on the path.
Through their reputation you settle their feelings,
Through their characters their natures are fully expressed;
And as gold reverts to its original inner nature,
So it may be declared a 'restored Elixir'.

This chapter points to the inner cultivation which takes place through natural law – it does not happen through the sedulous pursuit of perfection. This all depends upon the rule of the cycling five elements, not upon empty intellectualization.

As water (Kan) douses fire (Li), so the moon eclipses the sun; this indicates a natural means of control, inherent in their very natures. The inner cultivation of an Elixir uses this natural means of control, whereby fire and water intrinsically possess the ability to overcome each other's deficiencies.

Once Yin and Yang are identified by name within the body, their 'characters' are made clear and their 'natures' fully expressed. Owing to their interpenetration, the 'gold reverts to its original inner nature' – in the nebulosity surrounding the origin of all matter, in the 'palace of True Oneness', at the source of the one single energy of the prenatal inner world, whereupon it truly may be declared a restored Elixir.

In human terms, this depicts the restraining of the inner fire (or desire) of the body and the attainment of spiritual immortality as a reparation for one's worldly life. This is the everlasting life in which, very importantly, one's worldly and material existence is also enshrined as gold.

Master Shangyang comments: Gold [metal] and water have the same 'reputation' and the text mentions their 'feelings'; wood and fire have the same 'character' and the text mentions their 'natures'. 'Feelings' may be said to dwell in the north-west, whilst 'natures' command the south-east. The south is named the 'self' and the north is named the 'other'. The 'feelings' of the gold and water are outwardly naturally expressed to subjugate wood and fire; the 'natures' of the wood and fire inwardly return to coalesce as a Golden Elixir. This is what is meant by 'gold reverting to its original inner nature, so it may be declared a "restored Elixir"'. These two lines give the very essence of the *Can Tong Qi*.

Yuyan comments: The *Book of Change* [Great Appendix I.9] says: Heaven is one, the earth two. Heaven is three, the earth four. Heaven is fire, the earth six. Heaven is seven, the earth eight. Heaven is nine, the earth ten. These are the 'generated' and 'completed' numbers of the cycling five elements as they interact together. There is a saying: Of all the numbers in heaven and earth, there are no more than five and they contain no more than five [see Figure 16].

Generally speaking five is the number of the soil [earth], and it is positioned centrally. It joins to the north with the one of water and so six is complete [5+1]; it joins to the south with the two of fire and so seven is complete [5+2]. It joins to the east with the three of wood and so eight is complete [5+3]; it joins to the west with four of metal and so nine is complete [5+4]. Nine is the very last number. The numbers of the world progress towards nine and then halt. In terms of the nine numbers, as five dwells in the middle of one, two, three, four, six, seven, eight and nine, it truly is the number of the mean.

The numbers originally had no ten. In order for the earth to 'complete the number ten' it must mean the one of the north, the two of the south, the three of the east and the four of the west all gathering in the central region, at the hub, to make the number ten [1+2+3+4=10].

Therefore if you take the central region of the five [soil] and distribute it among the four directions, the numbers six, seven, eight and nine are complete – and so then through relying on the soil [5], water [1], fire [2], wood [3] and metal [4] all become complete. If you take the one, two, three and four of the four directions and return them to the central region to complete the ten, then water, fire, wood and metal all 'return to their source, and travel back to their original nature [*fanben huanyuan*]'; they join together at the central soil. A mystery indeed!

The book *Awakening to Reality* says: The two materials' whole cause lies in them as children begetting their mother. The cycling five's total meaning is contained in them entering the middle realm.

The poem entitled 'The Jewelled Brooch of the Muddied Source' says: Once the four posts are identified, then turn them on their

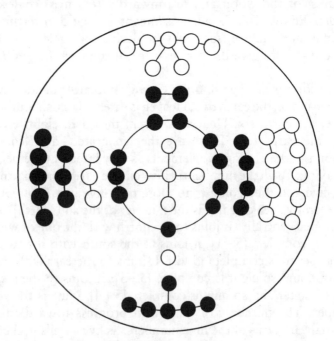

Fig. 37 The numbers

heads! The cycling five arise as one, so return them to their one source! Both these illustrate the same meaning.

As for the interacting numbers of the cycling five elements, although a three-foot child could chant them through and understand them, how many of those who are truly searching for their meaning can understand their positioning? And if they do not understand their positioning, how can they gain an understanding of their true function? Indeed the true Path is essentially recondite and hidden, and the workings of heaven truly profound! If you apprehend them, they are so simple and easy. If you pass them by, they are so complicated and difficult!

He continues: As Yin and Yang intersect, they reach the point of mutual consumption. This is the way with all the myriad created things in the world.

Wei Boyang [Xu Congshi] partook of the intricate fashion in which the sun and moon eat into each other, in order to illustrate the mysterious Elixial method. He also brings up the idea of the mutual subjugation of water and fire so that, through the joining together of them, he makes it possible for us to consider the whole process in detail. Despite the fact that ordinarily the sun and moon eat into each other only at the 'interval of the new moon' [see Chapter 4], the inner cultivation of the Golden Elixir is a way for each one of us to rob from heaven and earth and to steal this process of creation!

Can you ever allow yourself to be neglectful in your search for the so-called 'interval of the new moon'?

Master Zhuxi comments: The above explains the reason why the name 'restored Elixir' is applied in the text. It is because the fire is doused and the gold returned.

I dare not speak falsely,
But copy from the writings of the sages:
The ancient records brought to our notice the dragon and
  tiger,
The Yellow Emperor esteemed the Golden Flower,
Huai Nan smelted the 'autumnal stone',
Wang Yang cherished the 'yellow sprout'.
These wise ones were able to maintain the work
While those unfilial did not share in it.

From olden times this method has been one,
Comparisons, discussions, they are all scheming;
Learned pupils exert your own strength,
And remain in deep contemplation and thought.
The ultimate knowledge here is extremely obvious
And so clear, it could never be imposed upon you!

This final section adduces historical illustrations which have inspired this writing. There is a strict warning not to become involved in empty comparisons and discussion on the alchemical matters. Simply through your own involvement with the internal fashioning of an Elixir may you stumble across its making – and 'snatch the workings of heaven and earth', find the 'catch to all creation' and finally form yourself into a realized person.

Master Shangyang comments: Our Immortal has gained the true intent of the sages. He again took hold of the ancient writings of the Dragon and Tiger classic and followed their method of inward cultivation, which resulted in the formation of an Elixir. Then he wrote this book in order to instruct us later generations.

Thus he lists, in order, the Elixir made by the Yellow Emperor, called the 'Golden Flower'; the Elixir made by the Prince Huai Nan termed the 'autumnal stone'; and the Elixir made by Wang Yang, named the 'yellow sprout'. There are any number of made Elixirs, each one identified by a unique name, but they are all the same 'restored Elixir'; they are all the one single energy of the prenatal inner-world and all the same kind of thing.

Later generations have heard of the Golden Flower and suspect it to be a metal; they have heard of the 'yellow sprout', and suspect it to be a mineral; and they have heard of the 'autumnal stone', and suspect it to be formed out of the chemical distillation of urine. What knowledge have they of the wise saints and sages of old, who set up these individual terms when they cultivated their Elixirs? How can they depart from Yin and Yang and set off on this other path?

The true Path is only that of the sages. It means being able to complete the work diligently. From olden times to the present there has only been this one true Path and that is all.

He concludes: You later generations, exert your own strength in 'deep contemplation' and search out some instructions from a teacher. Then you will understand this writing. Its meaning will be laid bare and made obvious; quite truthfully 'it could never be imposed upon you'.

The three sections of the *Can Tong Qi* [which translates literally as 'Combining Similars Together'] are all essentially practical and not meant to be confusing. The work may be somewhat mystical in nature, but it is never necessary for it to be prolonged. 'Can' ['combining'] refers to combining along with the essential creative power of heaven and earth; 'tong' ['similars'] refers to depending on the practicality of similars acting together; and 'qi' ['together'] refers to the joining of this creative power and this interaction of similars in the work.

Yuyan comments: As you, my children, gain the One, so all affairs reach completion. Great indeed is the One! It is the origin of all the thousands of classics and writings, the ancestor of all tens of thousands of changes and transformations! Believe me! Under all heaven there are not two paths. The sages were never in two minds over anything. All the phrases in the tens of thousands of alchemical scrolls come back to one single same thing. the Golden Elixir. It is this which is our true foundation!

He continues: What Wei Boyang [Xu Congshi] meant was this. If you, my 'learned pupils', are able, now and again, to spend time with and savour these writings, then one day the heart will guide the mind into union and you will recognize once and for all the significance of its real knowledge. As a result it will become extremely obvious and so clear that not a particle of dust will cling to it or obscure it.

Alas! He has guided our scholars' hearts but they have stayed tightly closed. They are not able to trust or have sympathy with his ideas. If they do not chant over and maintain his writings, how will they ever remain in deep contemplation and thought?

ADDENDUM

34

A MODEL OF SUCCESSFUL ACHIEVEMENT

This chapter and the next were written by disciples following in the same alchemical tradition. They continue the emphasis on natural change and transformation, and use imagery both from the natural world and from outer alchemy to illustrate this 'subtle art'. They emphasize the use of similars or 'things of the same kind', all in order to effect the transformation of an Elixir.

As a model nothing ranks higher than heaven and earth,
Their dark pool may be fathomed at 10,000 miles.
When the Herdboy star diverges from his yearly route,
The people all startle and are afraid.

If the gnomon of the sun-dial is erratic,
Then nine years we suffer misfortune and blame.
The Sovereign-on-High looks on as witness,
And kings themselves withdraw back to reform.

The key to this all is variation and change,
A demise of energy follows on a hurried pace –
Just as the Yangtse in flood is eventually exhausted,
Its great waters flowing onwards to the sea.

The cock and hen of heaven and earth
Flit back and forth 'twixt midnight and midday;
Early dawn and afternoon, the ancestral Yin and Yang
Exit and enter in, finally returning to the start.
This all follows the Dipper, swaying back and forth,
Holding to the measure to decide the year.

This section compares the inner cultivation of an Elixir to the transformation which takes place in heaven and earth. Throughout the world, nothing oversteps the boundaries of the transformations which occur between heaven and earth. Portents of the sun, the stars and the planets are directly linked to affairs down here on earth; and affairs down here on earth also reveal this rule of 'variation and change'.

The resonance within heaven and earth also matches with the inner cultivation of an Elixir. The medicinal ingredients of the 'sun and moon', the 'cock and hen', 'water and fire', flit back and forth; the ancestral Yin and Yang (early dawn, afternoon) enter and retreat; and out of our deep comprehension of this whole process we manage the fashioning of an immortal Elixir.

Master Shangyang comments: The doctrine of the sages, in its greatness, envelopes heaven and earth; in its minuteness, it enters into every small particle of matter. Tradition holds that it ultimately encompasses all and yet that it is also something entirely abstruse and obscure.

Being extremely grand and all-encompassing at its limits, it is also the doctrine of the 'unvarying mean [*zhongyong*]'. The doctrine of the 'unvarying mean' is a secret hidden in every item of the natural world – truly it cannot be displayed in writing, but only passed on by word of mouth. Is there any alternative then to the sages? They have produced all sorts of examples which have been presented for later generations.

When the Yellow Emperor first questioned his minister Qibo, Qibo replied: If the vitality within is insufficient then replenish it with the flavour of food. If the body is failing then replenish it through the inner energies [from the *Yellow Emperor's Book of Medicine*]. In just these two lines the Golden Elixir is entirely manifest. Additionally King Wen added to Fu Xi's *Book of Change* the line, 'to the south-west gaining friends' [Hexagram 2, Receptive], which also manifests the idea of achieving 'replenishment through the inner energies [*buqi*]'.

Confucius also stated that 'similar sounds resonate together, similar energies divine each other [the *Analects*]', which points to a type of 'replenishment through inner energies'. And Laozi mentioned the 'gateway to the Dark Female [*Daode Jing* Chapter 6]' which he named the 'foundation of heaven and earth'. Again this can be explained as the gateway to achieving 'replenishment through inner energies'.

The *Can Tong Qi* continually gives examples of this idea through its instruction in the 'medicinal ingredients', the 'cauldron and furnace', the 'graduations of the firing times', the 'gold and inner energies assisting each other [see Chapter 10]', and the 'truth in man which lies at the very depths [see Chapter 25]'. These do much to explain further the close relationship illustrated in the models and examples of this last chapter. The transmission of the sages is managed entirely as one process, therefore the golden fluid, nine times restored and supreme Elixir is nothing other than a replenishment through this one single energy.

Yuyan comments: The Dipper dwells in the centre of the sky, just as the heart dwells in the centre of the body. The sky takes the Dipper as its mechanism, whilst man takes the heart as his mechanism.

During the Elixial method, the heart circulates the fire around the body according to differing graduations of temperature. This is just the same as the Dipper circulating the stars around the sky according to the differing hours of the night. The book *Kingfisher Flashing in the Void* says: You catch hold of this subtle mechanism of the heavens! During the night you wake and glimpse its hour-hand!

Zhu Yuanyu says: The Elixial method is modelled on the heavens; it wholly relies on the wheel which revolves around the single core of the sky. This single core of the sky, located at its extreme northern tip, is sturdy and immovable, and is only revealed by the turning handle of stars shown in the constellation of the Dipper. The turning handle of the Dipper is shown in the passage of midnight and midday, which represent the 'flitting back and forth' of water and fire; it is shown in the progress of early dawn and afternoon, which represent the joining in tandem of gold and wood. The 'swaying back and forth' of the Dipper is the doorway to understanding all this confusion.

Above simmers the cooking-pot,
While a blazing fire is built up below.
The white tiger leads out in glory,
And the green secretions keep in pace.

The scarlet bird soars into play,
Flapping about in brilliant colouring.
Then tangled up as a net is thrown,
Wearied with the struggle she cannot rise.

Ow! Ow! her screams tear into the heart,
Like those of a little child longing for its mother.
Set to boil, head-over-heels she goes,
Her feathers snapped off and broken.

Quarter of an hour by the water-clock,
And there appear clustered fish-scales, bristles beginning,
A hundred-and-one colours, flickering patterns,
Turning, changing, constantly.

The cauldron suddenly boils up fiercely,
Bubbling up repeatedly, without stopping;
Until after many times it wearies,
And there appear dogs' teeth set against each other.

Shaped like midwinter icicles,
Like a rough-cut gem, they send out
Precipitous peaks in a jagged confusion,
Piled up and pressed up on each other.
Now Yin and Yang make the perfect match,
Lying calm and dispassionate in each other's grasp.

In this section the imagery of outer alchemy is richly employed. After the Elixir has been formed, it must be transformed through heat. The white tiger is the gold (metal); the green secretions come from the dragon (wood). The struggle comes as the scarlet bird (the 'mercury', or fire) is tangled up in the net (of 'lead', or water). By being turned head-over-heels, the fire is inverted beneath the bubbling water while the water covers over the raging fire. This is the interpenetration of Yin and Yang, the overcoming of the outer-world deficiencies created in both water and fire. Eventually a precious substance crystallizes – 'Yin and Yang make the perfect match' – and through neither trying nor not trying, through their being 'neither forgotten nor aided', the Golden Elixir is born.

Master Shangyang comments: The 'cooking pot' forms the gateway into the dark; the 'swaying back and forth' of the Dipper is the doorway into all this confusion. The 'white tiger' is something made of gold; the 'scarlet bird' is the essence of fire. The 'thrown net' represents the idea of getting on with the work; the 'setting to boil' refers to the management of the heating. The 'cauldron boiling up fiercely' illustrates the inner energy becoming full. 'Until, after many times, it wearies' represents the medicine becoming whole. The 'rough-cut gem' represents the Elixir when first found. Its edges are in 'jagged confusion ... pressed up on each other', whilst they unite their strengths together as Yin and Yang.

Yuyan comments: In general, when the true breath is prolonged without interruption, Yin and Yang make a match together. If you 'humble the heart and focus the mind [*xuxin nengshen*]', it becomes utterly one without any unruly thoughts, and Yin and Yang naturally protect each other.

The green dragon dwells in Scorpio, its number six,
Spring flowers bloom, and Zhen's in the east at dawn;
The white tiger rests in the Pleiades, its number seven,
There are autumn ears of wheat, and Dui to the west at dusk;

The scarlet bird's in the constellation Hydra, its number two,
And the true Yang is in the south at midday.
These three arrive at court together –
Close companions all of one family.

Originally they were separate as the 'two materials',
Until finally they became the 'three fives'.
The 'three fives' also united as 'the perilous One',
The whole assembly comes back together.
They are ordered as prescribed above,
So by a count of days you may pick a time to begin.

First white then later yellow,
Black passes through red within.
Through its reputation known as 'the number one cauldron'
It contains something to eat the size of a grain of millet!

The one single energy of the prenatal inner world originates simply in these two materials: water and fire. As water and fire interact they produce four images: the green dragon (Scorpio, six, spring, flowers, the trigram Zhen, east, dawn); the white tiger (Pleiades, seven, autumn, ears of wheat, the trigram Dui, west, dusk); the scarlet bird (Hydra, two, the true Yang, south, midday); the dark warrior (the One); and also five elements (wood, metal, earth, fire and water).

The four images and the five elements form the 'three fives': water (1) and gold (4) form 'five'; fire (2) and wood (3) form 'five';

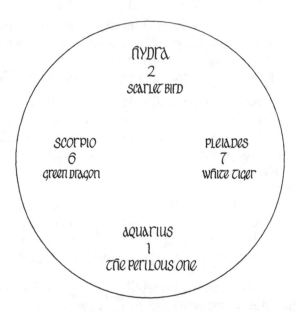

Fig. 38 Numbers and constellations

and the soil alone is the last 'five'. These 'three fives' join together as 'the One'. They all join in the position of the 'dark warrior' water.

What is white (metal, gold) becomes yellow (earth, soil); from black (nothing) it becomes red (something). But it grows no larger than a single red grain of millet!

Master Shangyang comments: The 'green dragon dwells in Scorpio' as, at engagement of the work, you gain understanding; the 'white tiger rests in the Pleiades' as, at the gaining of the medicine you thrust it again into the furnace. When the 'scarlet bird's in the constellation Hydra', the mind is already one with the inner energies. The 'two materials' are the lead and the mercury. The 'three fives' means the cycling five clustering together. The 'One' means the water of Kan.

'First white then later yellow' results because the 'white' is the gold, while the 'yellow' describes the form of the earth. The 'black passing through red within' results because the fire appears 'red' while the lead is 'black'.

The 'cycling five' are nothing but Yin and Yang. They join their reputations in 'the number one cauldron' which 'contains something to eat the size of a grain of millet'. This is comparable to

the saying: In the very beginning of things, there was a single
suspended jewelled pearl – the size of a grain of millet.

It is something quite naturally occurring,
There is nothing pretended in its method:
As the gases of mountain and marsh interfuse,
So rising clouds turn to rain.
As when mud dries it finally becomes dust,
And fire extinguished burns down to earth,

Just as plant-dyes will turn a cloth yellow,
Or indigo finish it off with a bluish tinge,
As cooked skin and hides turn to glue,
And yeast ferments to make wine,
So things of the same kind make the work easier,
The wrong materials make it difficult to achieve skill.

This section continues the emphasis on the following natural
methods and natural law. There is nothing weird, fashionable or
uncanny in the Elixial art. It is only using 'things of the same kind'
to facilitate the creation of an inner Yang Elixir of everlasting life.
Compare the passage, 'If you want to perform the method of inner
cultivation, it is best to use things of the same kind (Chapter 27).'

Yuyan comments: The supreme method of the Golden Elixir was
mostly regarded by the ancient Immortals as something 'naturally
occurring'. Now if this thing is 'naturally occurring', how can it be
measured and given voice to? If it really is delivered only 'naturally',
what use is a teacher?

But this reasoning is all wrong. The method of the supreme
Elixir is 'very simple and easy'. Its divine workings are merely
subtle in function – there is nothing artificial in the way they are
made. Because there is no reason for the intrusion of thought it is
described as 'naturally occurring'.

However something is necessary, and that is to withdraw the
sight and turn back the hearing, sinking the mind deep within.
Then each inbreath and outbreath is lengthened and drawn out
continuously, neither quickly nor slowly, without any interruption. After a while, the mind returns into the breath, and the
breath and the mind become one, knotted together to form the
'babe'. Such a process is not delivered naturally.

The *Golden Jade Dragon* and *Tiger* classic says: The essence of something which is naturally occurring, is that first it is cared for and then later neglected.

Thus first you take care that the mind enters into the 'cave of the breath [*qixue*]'; and then later, as they merge together, you forget their existence. When you act in this way the mind focuses itself, the energy gathers itself, and the breathing settles itself. This is not the method of quietening the heart until it becomes 'as pure as dry sticks and dead ashes'. This is because if you quieten the heart until it becomes 'as pure as dry sticks and dead ashes' you may be able to become a Daoist monk but you will never cultivate within yourself a true Elixir!

The book *Pointing Into the Dark* says: Achievements which naturally occur are the natural gone wrong! Views which occur naturally are not natural!

Now this is just what is meant here. As when, at the solstice, the energy changes over, or when a key is pushed down and a pipe sounds out; so in the midst of this naturally occurring process, there also occurs the necessity for a secret care to be taken with the decoction made, by advancing the fire. The book on *Awakening to Reality* states:

> That it begins in activity, some people find it difficult to realize.
> But when it comes to non-action, they all understand!
> They only see non-action as something refined and mysterious.
> Can they not understand that it has a basis in activity?

My scholars, if you do not yet understand the activity of the Elixial method and search for the natural occurrence of non-action, how is this different to neither ploughing nor weeding but sitting and waiting for your pots to be filled with grain at the harvest?

Zhu Yuanyu says: This section describes the reason why the work of fashioning the Elixir can produce results – it merely lies in these two words – 'naturally occurring [*ziran*, 'self-nature', 'spontaneous']; and the mystery of what is meant by 'naturally occurring' merely lies in these two words – 'similar things [*donglei*]'. Take only those things as your true ingredients which do in fact share similar qualities and you cause a sympathetic effect to occur 'quite naturally' between them. This must, once and for all, be understood.

This alone is the method of the 'subtle art':
Watch closely – and do not be led astray by the words.
Its transmission has been through 10,000 generations,

So clear and able to be tested!
Brilliant as the stars thronging the Milky Way,
Shining as the waters hastening to the Court of the Sea!
Your thoughts must follow the mandate of experience,
Again and again look on what is here, above and below;
Everything is included, everything in detail,
And after ten-thousand attempts the light may be gazed
   upon!

Then the brilliance of his spirit may perhaps inform man,
And his own soul suddenly compose its own awakening.
As he searches for a clue and feels for the thread,
In the end it will lead to the open doorway.
The natural method is open to everyone –
It is a constant transmission to the wise!

This section is a final summation of the whole chapter and of the whole work. In Chapter 19 'Qian and Kun are described as the door and gateway to change'. Now, in this last chapter, we are shown a clue, which will 'lead to the open doorway'.

The natural resonance of similars together and the subtle principle of mutual antagonisms and sympathies, has been tried and tested countless times. Wei Boyang has laid out clearly the whole matter in his work, and it can also be studied further in the work of his pupil Xu Congshi and in these last two additional chapters. The details here are laid bare and should be deeply pondered upon. All in all, the way of heaven befriends nobody – except that it is a constant transmission to the virtuous and wise!

Yuyan comments: In the world of men there are many side tracks and petty tricks played upon us, why stop at only 3600 different schools? Yet it is only 'One Gate' which leads to the heavenly jewelled, great canopy, the transfigured and immortal golden fluid, the nine times refined and greatly restored Elixir. This is the 'subtle art' which is that of 'clarity and quietist non-action [*qinjing wuwei*]'. It is a method which is so 'very simple and easy'. Any husband or wife can manage and practise it, and he or she will be able to transcend this common world and enter into sagehood.

Therefore portents in the sky should be taken seriously and never lightly received by the wrong sort of people. If the collected scholars of this world do not feel a sense of pre-ordained unity [the

One], they will never find it easy to come across the meaning of this work.

He concludes: The natural method has no preference for anyone – it is the constant companion of the good man. But unless you can be this person, the method is merely vain practice. Can you deny a difference exists between the happiness or misfortune which are transmitted down by the wise? Alas indeed! The ways of this common world are not in line with ancient practices and the ordinary people sink further and further into decline. Even the good on their own cannot achieve them, they can only gain sight of them. To gain sight of them and then constantly to keep them in view. This is what is demanded!

35

THE MYSTERIOUS USE OF THE
CAULDRON VESSEL

In this, the last chapter of the text, two or three brief poems and sayings are brought together. Beginning with simple numerology, the selections end with the ascent of an Immortal into the sky seated upon a flying crane. These legendary tales and poems are legion in the Daoist corpus; contain further implicit instructions for the firing of the Elixir.

> The rim by 'three fives', sharing in the 'one inch';
> The mouth 'four by eight', 'two inches' the lip.
> The length, 'one foot and two inches', you adjust the
> thick and thin.

The metre of this whole chapter (pairs of three-character lines) is different from the others and it most likely has a different authorship. The style is cryptic and difficult, suggesting a forced composition. The commentators are in very little agreement as to much of the symbolism.

The 'three fives' are wood and fire (2+3), water and metal (gold) (1+4), and the earth (5): each unit comprises five. These numbers derive from the *River Diagram* (see Figure 15). Three fives make fifteen, which is the moon when full. This is the 'one inch', an image of the single Golden Elixir.

The book on *Awakening to Reality* says:

> The Three Fives as One, yet each has a separate character,
> Throughout all time those that understood this fact are truly few.
> The east, three, the south, two, they make up five;
> The north, one, the west, four, together the same.
> The Wu- and Ji-soils themselves, in their own position produce five;
> Three families gazing upon each other to fashion a little child.
> The little child is the One, containing the true inner energy;
> When you realize this, you can enter into the workings of sagehood!

'Four', 'eight' and 'two' make up fourteen. Again this points towards the number of days for which the Yang fills the moon. On the fourteenth day the moon is 'almost full'. The *Book of Change* says: 'The moon almost full. If the true person goes on an expedition, misfortune (Top Line, Hexagram 9, Cultivation of the Small)'. The idea is to halt before the Yang topples at its extremity.

'One foot and two inches' makes up twelve inches in all (one Chinese foot is ten inches). The 'twelve inches' are the twelve months of the year, in which the energy is adjusted 'thick and thin' – neither weak nor overabundant.

Master Shangyang comments: The people of this world do not understand our Immortal's subtle discrimination here. He has concealed subtlety within subtlety, and put meaning beyond meaning!

Three days past in the belly, sitting until a warmth
    descends,
The Yin situated above, the Yang situated below.
Work them fiercely at head and tail, gently in between,
Seventy at the start, thirty at the end –
While for 260, you balance them together.

On the third day, the 'trigram Zhen arrives' (see Chapters 4 and 21), which brings the warmth of the Yang. The belly of the cauldron and the belly of the human body are the same: both find sympathies in the trigram Kun, which is penetrated by the first Yang line of Qian. The Yang line is below, lying beneath the Yin.

The flame used in firing the Elixir is worked 'fiercely' at the beginning and end, and 'gently' in between. 'Seventy', 'thirty' and '260' make up the 360 days of the single year. As the process begins and ends, it acts in a more violent manner; during the intervening growth and decline, it acts gently. This is the epitome of organic life depicting the natural activity of birth, growth, maturity, decline and finally death.

Master Shangyang comments: The Yin is the water within the vessel; the Yang is the fire within the cauldron. Water above and fire below make up water and fire 'already overcoming' each other's deficiencies [Hexagram 63, Already Overcome]. When the Yin is above and the Yang is below, the whole world is at peace [Hexagram 11, Peace].

Zhang Boduan in his book *Awakening to Reality* says: I forgive

*the other for being host, I myself am the guest. The meaning is the
same here.*

He continues: 'Seventy at the start' – because to collect yourself
together at the beginning is extremely difficult. 'Thirty at the end'
because it describes the time for gentle support when similarly you
must take care.'

He concludes: The people of this world all see the words 'seventy'
and 'thirty', and consider them to mean three parts gentle and
seven parts fierce. Can they not understand that one dare not
disclose directly the secrets of the alchemical classics? If they can
totally comprehend the instant token which enables us to attain
the actual moment to claim the Elixir, at that single moment they
can gently fuse both it and themselves into one!

Yuyan comments: The 'head and tail' are the time of the dark and
new moon. The 'in between' is the full moon. The time of the dark
and new moon is the time the Yin is at its extremity and the Yang
is born; then use a fierce flame. When the moon is full then the
Yang is at its extremity and the Yin is born; then use a gentle
flame. However what is meant by the dark, the new or full moons
is actually all metaphor. They really are a lot more than merely
clever thoughts put down onto paper!

**The clear flame of the Yin, the yellow shoot from lead:
Both 'sevens' combined to support and shelter man.**

The 'clear flame' is the true Yin mercury within the trigram Li
(fire); and fire (2) and soil (5) form one seven. The 'yellow shoot' is
the true Yang lead within the trigram Kan. 'Both sevens' refer to
the Yang-fire and Yin-fire which combine to fashion the inner
Elixir which 'supports and shelters man'.

Yuyan comments: From midnight up to just before midday is the
period of the Yang-flame; from midday up to just before midnight
is the period of the Yin-flame. The time of dusk is situated in the
west. The west belongs to gold [metal, white, clear]. Thus it
mentions, 'the clear flame of the Yin'.
    The book *Awakening to Reality* says: The moon-toad's glory
shining in the western skies, at the end of the day. This is the same
thing.
    The lead is born from the soil, and the silver is born from the

lead. The silver is smelted and brought out from the lead; it is formed into a 'yellow shoot', which is commonly called the 'true lead'. There is the saying: When smelting the lead one should look for the colour yellow.

'Both sevens' refer to the seven constellations of the dark green dragon of the east and the seven constellations of the white tiger of the west. They exist also in man. Man positions them within the 'central region' of the soil. 'Both sevens combine to support and shelter man', meaning the tiger encircles the dragon and the dragon embraces the tiger. They cluster and gather together in their central territory.

> With sufficient to regulate the brain, settled in tranquil darkness,
> You rest the child within, quietly cared for.
> Then up, off and abroad, without straying from the gate,
> Succeeding gradually to greatness, your temperament unadulterated,
> Returning to the One, to the root, to the source.
> Good-loving, respectful, like ruler and minister,
> You reach the 'circulation of the One' through bitter toil.
> Protect it closely without being deluded,
> You may journey far but you return to the Mystery.

> If you succeed, you join with Qian and Kun,
> And on a moistened knife-point, purify the Hun-soul and the Po.
> You achieve immortality and dwell in the Pixie Village.
> Those who enjoy the method will seek out its origin,
> And watch the 'cycling five' to settle the minutest share.
> The thought behind them, I need not express,
> It is concealed in close keeping and neither can it be written.

These final two sections consist of a eulogy on the eventual completion of the Elixir and our ascent into the skies. The 'child rested within' is the kidney energy of the trigram Kan, referred to as 'the children' in Chapter 15. It suggests the playfulness and vigour of our vitality, lying stored up within the lower belly.

This energy rises up to nourish the mental faculties and produce a clear spiritual enlightenment. The 'gate' is the 'gate of life', described on the lower lumbar spine. The 'circulation of the One' is the infusion of the Yang energy out of this gate and through the whole person. During this time the Yin and Yang, Qian and Kun, Hun- and Po-souls unite and the immortality of the spirit is made real.

Master Shangyang comments: This section superficially describes the scholar who acquires the medicine. He attends to it without being idle or remiss, and does not neglect it even for a short while. Then, by being charged with extreme diligence, every phrase of this writing becomes completely clear and understood and need not be further commented upon. The Elixir has already been made, the little child has gradually grown big. By being unhindered during his nine seasons, he has already achieved his upward growth!

Yuyan comments: The little child is resting within the womb. He acquires the special care and attention of the Kun-mother, who nourishes and feeds him. So then he is 'quietly cared for'.

The gate is the 'gateway of the Dark Female'. 'Then up, off and abroad' refers to the movement of our breathing, in and out. Moving in and out, it never strays away from the 'gateway of the Dark Female'. So then the Yin and Yang inner energies are sufficient for you to enter into a spiritual life. Walking, standing, sitting, lying – continuously this breath is cared for. Day after day it gradually focuses and condenses, and once the 'holy babe's' energy is focused, the form of the little child appears and one's temperament becomes further unadulterated and mature.

The method of the supreme Elixir merely means one carries in one's arms the primal energies of all life – it is just to protect the One, this is all. At his beginning man rests in the Yin and the Yang and the cycling five; at his end he returns to the dark chaos where there is 'no ultimate pole [*wuji*, the "limitless"]'. This is what is meant by 'returning to the One, to the root, to the source.'

Harness the white crane and yoke up the scaly dragon,
You roam the Great Void to visit the Fairy Ruler.
Now noted in the divine scheme of things, you are a
'truly realized' person!

Now, you roam the void, and call on 'His Majesty', the supreme Fairy Ruler, to take your place in the divine scheme of things as a realized person.

Master Shangyang comments: Everyone and everybody is able to realize this great achievement. The power to realize it is great enough within them all. Do not say it is difficult and then cast it aside. Do not say it is unimportant and refuse to take it on.

Laozi, Zhang Boduan and Pengzi [the Chinese Methuselah] were also human beings just like you. They did not descend down from the heavens to end up here below. Shakyamuni [the Buddha] and Bodhidharma [who brought Buddhism to China] were also human beings just like you. They did not arrive on earth through breaking forth from below.

They had determined hearts and were intrepid and daring; and the business for every one of them was easily complete. A strong-minded individual, who cultivates the Elixir within himself, 'exerts his own strength, in deep contemplation and thought'.

Yuyan comments: After the 'holy babe' is complete and the task finished, you attune the mind to enable it to escape from the body's husk. Perhaps you clamber onto the back of a white crane, or else ride off on a fiery dragon. You transcend the boundaries of this world's troubles – passing through and beyond to the furthest regions of the sky. Now you wander off hopefully and happily, your years one with the age of the sky and can be termed a 'truly realized' person!

TERMS USED IN THIS BOOK

The red bird, green dragon, white tiger, black tortoise and snake, etc. are the active spirits of the elements; the trigrams show their more 'metaphysical' aspect – thus Qian and Kun, Kan and Li act as guiding emblems to the unseen. It is the actual process of forming the Elixir which grants one benefits.

Chinese internal alchemy and laboratory science paralleled each other in meditative practice and identical terms were often used for separate activities. Ambiguity was not always discouraged – indeed it was sometimes necessary to impress on the reader the multi-faceted nature of the Dao and the grand scale of its subject.

We have to intuit the activity of the 'firing times' directly within both our own bodies and the universe. Then along with the sages we can to some extent 'enter into' the infinite.

Wang Bing, the third-century *Yi Jing* scholar, said:

> Therefore he who clings to words does not get the imagery, and he who clings to imagery does not get the ideas. The imagery is intended for the ideas, but, if clung to, is no longer the imagery. The words are intended for the imagery, but if clung to, are no longer the words.
>
> (*Fung*, Vol.II, p.184)

Cycling Five (Five Elements). Wood, fire, soil, metal (gold), water.

Dynasties

Zhou	1066–221 BC	
Qin	221–207 BC, first unification	
Han	207 BC – 220 AD	
Three Kingdoms	221–65	
Six Dynasties	265–581	
Sui	581–618	
Tang	618–907	
Five Dynasties	907–60	
Northern Song	960–1127	
Southern Song	1127–1279	influx of
Liao (Qitan)	916–1125	northern tribes
Jin (Tartar)	1115–1234	culminating in
Yuan (Mongol)	1271–1368	Mongol invasion

Ming	1368–1644
Qing (Manchu)	1644–1911
Republic	1911–49
People's Republic	1949–

Earthly Branches, Twelve. Midnight (*zi*), after-midnight (*chou*), early dawn (*yin*), dawn (*mao*), early morning (*chen*), mid-morning (*si*), midday (*wu*), just after midday (*wei*), afternoon (*shen*), dusk (*you*), evening (*su*), just before midnight (*hai*).

Heavenly Stems, Ten. Jia-wood, Yi-wood, Bing-fire, Ding-fire, Wu-soil, Ji-soil, Geng-metal, Xin-metal, Ren-water Gui-water. Also, according to the system of the cycling five, the ten Heavenly Stems accord with directions of the compass: Jia and Yi, east; Bing and Ding, south; Wu and Ji, central; Geng and Xin west; and Ren and Gui, north.

Method of the Inherited Stems. The method of the Inherited Stems shows how the eight trigrams are matched to the ten Heavenly Stems. Zhen matches Geng-metal (west), Dui matches Ding-fire (south), Qian matches Jia-wood (east) and Ren-water, Sun matches Xin-metal (west), Gen matches Bing-fire (south) and Kun matches Yi-wood (east) and Gui-water; while Kan and Li match with the Wu and Ji soils centrally (see Figure 25). These serve to explain the manufacture of the Elixial medicine and the timing of its firing.

Trigrams, Eight
Qian ☰, heaven, father.
Kun ☷, earth, mother.
Zhen ☳, thunder, eldest son.
Sun ☴, wind, wood, eldest daughter.
Kan ☵, water, moon, middle son.
Li ☲, fire, sun, middle daughter.
Gen ☶, mountain, youngest son.
Dui ☱, marsh, lake, youngest daughter.

Qian and Kun signify the cauldron and furnace. Kan and Li signify the medicines within. Zhen, Dui, Qian, Sun, Gen and Kun signify the timing of the firing.

Yin-Yang. The theory of Yin-Yang holds that every phenomenon in the universe is made up of two forces, Yin and Yang, at once in conflict and interdependent.

TRANSLATION AND HISTORY OF
THE TEXT

The Translation

I have used three main sources. The first is the definitive text, the *Zhongjiao Guwen Can Tong Qi, A Reprinting of the Ancient Guwen Can Tong Qi*, with the original Yang Shen 1546 preface. This was produced in 1839 by Zhu Ama. This is the famous *guwen* text, first reconstructed by Du Yicheng, which incorporates the Master Shangyang (the 'Master who Honours the Yang') commentary. It was later edited by the Ming scholar Yao Ruxun. I have incorporated some of Yuyan's textual corrections.

Also of inestimable value for the Chinese commentaries has been the compiled edition of Zhuxi's *Examining Differences in the Zhouyi Can Tong Qi* (1197), Yuyan's *Expounding on the Zhouyi Can Tong Qi* (1284), and Master Shangyang's *Commentary and Explanation of the Zhouyi Can Tong Qi* (1330), published in China by the Tianjin Guji (Ancient Books) Publishing House in 1988.

Lastly I have made use of the excellent notes within the *Zhongguo Qigong Si Da Jingdian* or *The Four Greatest Classics of Chinese Qigong*, (Zhejiang Guji Publishing House, 1988) which follows Peng Xiao's pioneering AD 947 text and commentary.

The *Zhou Yi Can Tong Qi Hui Kan* (1990), has been the main source for the following history. It lists sixty-nine editions from the Eastern Han up to the present day and I reproduce all the titles. The dynasty is shown where known. A glance shows that work was progressively directed towards authenticity of transmission, the *guwen* ('ancient text') idea, etc. Many texts (marked *) have been lost through the vicissitudes of time and the massive book-burnings which regularly took place; in such cases the book is only known through a mention in a catalogue or list. Indeed seventeen texts were lost between Peng Xiao (AD 947) and Zhuxi (AD 1197).

A Complete Bibliography of the Text

1. *Yinyang Tongliu Can Tong Qi* (*A Summary Sketch of the Yinyang as Outlined in the Zhouyi Can Tong Qi*), Eastern Han, attributed to Xu Congshi, under various titles.
2. *Can Tong Qi Zhu* (*A Commentary on the Can Tong Qi*), Three Kingdoms, attributed to Yu Fan, under various titles.
3. *Yin Chenzi Can Tong Qi* (*True Ruler Yin's Zhouyi Can Tong Qi*), falsely attributed to Yin Changsheng (first century AD), probably Tang, anon, under various titles. This and the next two texts are the earliest surviving.
4. *Jinbi Wuxiang Lei Can Tong Qi* (*The Precious Jaden Treatise on the Five Mutual Similars and Can Tong Qi*), anon. Also falsely attributed to Yin Changsheng, probably Tang.
5. *Zhouyi Can Tong Qi Zhu* (*The Zhouyi Can Tong Qi with Commentary*), Tang, anon, preserved in the *Dao Zang* where it is attributed to Rong Zihao.
6. *Zhouyi Can Tong Qi Fenzhang Dong Zhenyi* (*The Zhouyi Can Tong Qi Divided in Separate Chapters in Order to Explain its True Meaning*), Five Dynasties, dated AD 947, Peng Xiao, seven differing copies preserved. This is the renowned Peng Xiao edition.
7. *Can Tong Qi Taiyi Zhitu* (*Recorded Diagrams of the Supreme Changes Preserved in the Can Tong Qi*), Chang Chu.
8. *Can Tong Qi Taiyi Zhitu* (*Recorded Diagrams of the Supreme Changes Preserved in the Can Tong Qi*), another text with the same name, Chong Yuanzi.
9. *Can Tong Qi Taiyi Danshu* (*Alchemical Writings Describing the Supreme Changes Recorded in the Can Tong Qi*), anon.
10. *Can Tong Qi Taiyi Shier Qi Xiulian Dadan Tu* (*A Diagram Depicting the Twenty-Four Energies used in Forging the Great Elixir According to the Supreme Changes of the Can Tong Qi*), anon.
11. *Can Tong Qi Jie* (*Solving the Problems in the Can Tong Qi*), Zi Yang (Zhang Boduan), probably forged.
12. *Can Tong Qi Jie* (*Solving the Problems in the Can Tong Qi*), Song, Zhang Sui.
13. *Dayi Tu Zhi Can Tong Qi* (*Diagrams of the Great Changes Recorded in the Can Tong Qi*), anon.
14. *Can Tong Qi Shoujian Tu* (*A Hand-held Mirror Showing A Picture of the Can Tong Qi*), anon.
15. *Can Tong Qi Huandan Hejue* (*The Secret Art of Firing the Returned Elixir of the Can Tong Qi*), anon.
16. *Can Tong Qi Texing Dan*, (*The Unique Alchemical Activity Involved in the Can Tong Qi*), anon.
17. *Zhouyi Can Tong Qi* (*The Zhouyi Can Tong Qi*), with a commentary by Master Bao Su ('Embrace Simplicity').

18. *Zhouyi Can Tong Qi, (The Zhouyi Can Tong Qi)*, Zhai Zhengong.
19. *Can Tong Qi Jinbi Qiandong Jue (The Hidden Deep Mysteries of the Golden Jaden Spectacle of the Can Tong Qi)*, anon.
20. *Can Tong Qi Taidan Zixu Heshu (The Serial Ordering of the Firing Calculations Involved in the Supreme Alchemy of the Can Tong Qi)*, anon.
21. *Can Tong Qi Jinshi Lun (A Discussion of the Ultimate Medicine made of Precious Minerals Described in the Can Tong Qi)*, anon.
22. *Can Tong Qi He Jindan Xingzhuang Shiliu Biantong Zhenjue (The True Secret Rhyme of the Sixteen Suitabilities Concerning the Can Tong Qi and the Practice of the Golden Elixir)*, anon.
23. *Can Tong Qi Zhouhou Fang (A Plan for Keeping the Can Tong Qi Up Your Sleeve)*, anon.
24. *Zhouyi Can Tong Qi Kaoyi (Examining Differences in the Zhouyi Can Tong Qi)*, dated 1197, Song, by the Neo-Confucian Zhuxi. Partly translated in this present edition.
25. *Zhouyi Can Tong Qi (The Zhouyi Can Tong Qi)*, Song, Chu Yong.
26. *Zhouyi Can Tong Qi Jie (The Zhouyi Can Tong Qi Explained)*, dated 1234, Song, Chen Xianwei. Partly used in this translation.
27. *Can Tong Qi Bian (The Can Tong Qi Debated)*, Song, Tian Qunshi.
28. *Can Tong Qi Wuxiang Lei Biyao (The Secrets of the Can Tong Qi and the Five Mutual Similars)*, Song, Lu Tianji.
29. *Can Tong Qi Xinjian (The Core of the Can Tong Qi)*, Zheng Yuanzhi.
30. *Zhouyi Menhu Can Tong Qi (The Can Tong Qi, Door and Gateway into the Zhouyi)*, anon.
31. *Can Tong Qi Zhu (A Commentary on the Can Tong Qi)*, Yuan, by the Daoist Master Bao Zhen ('Preserving the Truth').
32. *Zhouyi Can Tong Qi Fahui (Expounding on the Zhouyi Can Tong Qi)*, dated 1284, Yuan, Yuyan; and *Zhouyi Can Tong Qi Shiyi (Clearing up Doubts Within the Zhouyi Can Tong Qi)*, also by Yuyan, same date, both preserved. Partly translated here. Yuyan first saw the division into four-word and five-word lines. The most accessible, popular and influential of all commentaries.
33. *Zhouyi Can Tong Qi Zhujie (A Commentary and Explanation of the Zhouyi Can Tong Qi)*, dated 1330, Yuan, Chen Zhixu, (Master Shangyang). A very popular commentary. A large part translated here.
34. *Zhouyi Can Tong Qi Zhu (A Commentary upon the Zhouyi Can Tong Qi)*, anon.
35. *Can Tong Qi Jingwen (The Classic Text of the Can Tong Qi)*, c.1515, Ming, Du Yicheng. The renown text of Du Yicheng and main source for the reordering of the text which Yang Shen falsely claimed to have 'been discovered in a rock chamber'. The first work on the *Can Tong Qi* to be published during the Ming dynasty, Du

Yicheng's work ushered in a whole new age of *Can Tong Qi* scholarship.

36. **Zhouyi Can Tong Qi Wuming Zi Zhu (An Anonymous Master's Contribution to the Zhouyi Can Tong Qi)*, anon.

37. **Can Tong Qi Zhinan (A Pointer towards Clarity in the Can Tong Qi)*, Wang Youzi.

38. *Can Tong Qi Shuliu (A Brief Scan of the Can Tong Qi)*, dated 1564, Ming, Wang Wenlu. A good brief text.

39. **Dingzhu Can Tong Qi Jingzhuan (Settling the Can Tong Qi Classical Tradition)*, Ming, Shang Tingshi.

40. *Guzhu Can Tong Qi Fenshi (A Clear Explanation of the Ancient Commentaries on the Can Tong Qi)*, Ming, Xu Wei. This was the first *guwen* text to appear which survived any length of time. Xu Wei reordered Du Yicheng's work and attached Master Shangyang's commentary. Preserved in a later edition by Yao Ruxun which formed the basis for the definitive 1839 edition.

41. *Zhouyi Can Tong Qi Ceshu (A Survey of the Zhouyi Can Tong Qi)*, dated 1569, Ming, Lu Xixing.

42. *Can Tong Qi Kouyi (The Oral Interpretation of the Can Tong Qi)*, dated 1573, Ming, Lu Xixing.

43. *Can Tong Qi Buzhu (A Restored Commentary to the Can Tong Qi)*, anon.

44. *Guwen Can Tong Qi Jiyie (Collated Explanations of the Ancient Text of the Can Tong Qi)*, Ming, Jiang Yibiao.

45. *Zhouyi Can Tong Qi Zhujie (An Explanation of the Commentaries to the Zhouyi Can Tong Qi)*, Ming, Zhang Wei.

46. *Gujin Can Tong Qi Jie (Explanations of the Can Tong Qi, Old and New)*, Ming, Shen Yaozhong.

47. *Zhouyi Can Tong Qi Jiejian (An Explanation with Notes of the Zhouyi Can Tong Qi)*, Ming, Zhang Wenlong (explanation) and Zhu Changchun (notes).

48. *Guwen Can Tong Qi (The Ancient Text of the Can Tong Qi)*, Ming, Peng Haogu.

49. *Jiaozhu Guwen Can Tong Qi (A Revised Commentary to the Ancient Text of the Can Tong Qi)*, Ming, Wang Jiachun.

50. *Can Tong Qi Zhu (A Commentary Upon the Can Tong Qi)*, Ming, Chen Jinmo.

51. *Can Tong Qi Changyou, (The Can Tong Qi and its Mysteries Expounded)*, dated 1669, Qing, Zhu Yuanyu. An excellent edition. Zhu Yuanyu also wrote a companion volume, on the *Wu Zhen Bian* (The *Awakening to Reality Scripture*). I have used his commentary several times.

52. *Can Tong Qi Zhu (A Commentary upon the Can Tong Qi)*, Qing, Li Guangdi.

53. *Can Tong Qi Zhu (A Commentary upon the Can Tong Qi)*, Qing,

Chen Zhaocheng. He tried to explain it as being strictly about the *Yi Jing*.

54. *Zhouyi Can Tong Qi Maiwang* (*Gazing upon the Life-pulse of the Zhouyi Can Tong Qi*), Qing, Tao Susi.

55. *Guben Zhouyi Can Tong Qi Jizhu* (*An Ancient Edition of the Zhouyi Can Tong Qi with Collated Commentaries*), Qing, Qiu Zhaobie.

56. *Guben Can Tong Qi* (*An Ancient Edition of the Can Tong Qi*), Qing, by the 'Old Fellow Eminent Highway'.

57. *Du Can Tong Qi* (*A Study of the Can Tong Qi*), Qing, Zhu Fu.

58. *Gu Can Tong Qi Jizhu* (*Collated Commentaries on the Ancient Can Tong Qi*), Qing, Liu Wulong.

59. *Guwen Zhouyi Can Tong Qi Zhu* (*The Ancient Text of the Zhouyi Can Tong Qi with Commentary*), dated 1732, Qing, Yuan Renlin.

60. *Can Tong Qi Zhu* (*A Commentary on the Can Tong Qi*), Wang Yuanjing.

61. *Zhouyi Can Tong Qi Zhengyi* (*The True Import of the Zhouyi Can Tong Qi*), dated 1788, Qing, Dong Dening.

62. *Can Tong Qi* (*The Can Tong Qi*), Qing, Jiang Zhongzhen.

63. *Yushi Can Tong Qi Fahui Wuyan Zhu Zhailu* (*The Five-word Texts with Their Commentaries Extracted from Yuyan's Can Tong Qi*), Qing, Ji Dakui. An interesting idea. Only the 'five-word line' verses are taken out of the Yuyan edition, thus completing Yuyan's intention in the briefest way possible.

64. *Zhouyi Can Tong Qi Jiyun* (*The Collected Rhymes of the Zhouyi Can Tong Qi*), Qing, Ji Dakui.

65. *Can Tong Qi Zhizhi* (*The Plain Intent of the Can Tong Qi*), Qing, Liu Yiming.

66. *Zhouyi Can Tong Qi Zhushi* (*Explanations and Commentaries upon the Zhouyi Can Tong Qi*), Qing, Li Shixu.

67. *Zhongjiao Guwen Can Tong Qi* (*A Reprinting of the Ancient Text of the Can Tong Qi*), dated 1839, Qing, compiled by Zhu Ama. The definitive text.

68. *Zhouyi Can Tong Qi Fenzhang Zhujie* (*An Explanation with Commentary of the Zhouyi Can Tong Qi in Separate Chapters*), dated 1840, Qing, arranged by Chuan Jinquan.

69. *Can Tong Qi Fenjie Bijie* (*Untying the Secrets of the Separate Chapters of the Can Tong Qi*), dated 1879, Qing, Lu Huilian.

Authorship and the Early Text

During the early Tang period (618–907), as recorded for instance in the *Tang Dynastic Bibliography*, the generally accepted view was that Wei Boyang wrote the *Can Tong Qi*.

However gradually a broader tradition began to emerge. The *Dao Zang* (Daoist Canon) contains an anonymous Tang preface to the Yin Changsheng edition, (see No. 3 above), which says: 'Now I have heard it said that the *Can Tong Qi* originated from the ancient first volume of the *Dragon and Tiger Book*, originally produced by the adept Xu [Xu Congshi].'

There are also at least four possible sources for the text which have been identified as existing between the Tang and the later Five Dynasties (907–60). Three authors are mentioned among these books, Wei Boyang, Xu Congshi and Chunyu Shutong, although the sources do not agree as to the order of transmission between them. Thus the idea of a single author is probably disputable.

With the coming of Peng Xiao (No. 6), the first self-confessed editor of the text, another important stage is reached. Peng Xiao clearly states in his introduction, that 'Wei Boyang wrote the *Can Tong Qi*'; the age has now long past when the accuracy of this statement could be determined. Actually the weight of the evidence points to the text being an amalgam of writings, in line with other Han texts – the *Huangdi Neijing* (*Yellow Emperor's Book of Medicine*) and *Zhuangzi*, to name but two.

If we look at the form of the work itself, one fact becomes immediately obvious. The composition of the work is in verses of unequal length, but all the verses are made up of four-character or five-character lines (there are a few of irregular length). This in itself would suggest a work containing a number of styles – perhaps the work of master and pupil, the one distancing himself from the other through a different approach.

It was the brilliant young mind of the recluse, teacher and Daoist scholar Yuyan which first spotted this. His *Expounding on the Zhouyi Can Tong Qi* (No. 32), written when he was twenty-six, is a stunning *tour de force* of Daoist writing. I have translated only the clearest expository part of his commentary; many of his quotes from rare Daoist books (now lost) have had to be left untranslated. His view of the *Can Tong Qi*, one which is avowedly quasi-physiological, is always penetrating and informed.

He says in the postface to his commentary:

> Suddenly one night, when I was sitting quiet and still, it was as if I heard a voice speaking to me, saying 'Wei Boyang wrote the *Can Tong Qi*, Xu Congshi followed on his commentary, and then briefly there were compiled the various random other texts. Thus there are the dissimilar four-word, five-word and other irregular writings.' When I awoke I was in quite a state and looked carefully into this idea.

Now the first half of the work contains the trigrams Qian, Kun, Kan, Li, and the hexagrams Innocence and Sprouting Forth, and the second half also contains the trigrams Qian, Kun, Kan, Li, and the hexagrams Innocence and Sprouting Forth; the first half of the work refers to the numbers 7, 8, 9 and 6, and the second half refers to the numbers 7, 8, 9 and 6 ... therefore my humble view is that there were at least a few people who each wrote a chapter of the work. It must have happened just like this.

Therefore if the work itself and its commentaries are all mixed up, we do not know which is the work and which are the commentaries. I venture to say that the four-word, five-word, and random texts should each be divided as to their own kind, making three texts in all. It may be then that if the text and commentary can be properly untangled later scholars will be able to really investigate them. However my own work is now finished and I cannot change it about again.

Yuyan's writing shows a clear and uncluttered grasp of the text's essentials. His quietism epitomizes his meditative stance.

Later Clarification of the Text

Following the bibliographical history above, it is clear that the fascination this book has had for the Chinese mind cannot be overstressed. The best of all the Yuan commentaries after Yuyan must surely be those of Master Shangyang (No. 33), patriarch of the Northern School of Daoism and properly titled Chen Zhixu; he is said to have 'embraced the Dao' about his fortieth year. His commentary (preface dated AD 1330) exists under varying titles, in many editions, from the early Ming (a 1484 edition is the earliest survivor) up to the present day. His approach is decidedly that of an internal alchemist, whereby one is urged to purify and purge oneself, tempering the 'fire of desire', in order to create the presence of a divine Immortal. Celibacy was certainly practised by his school. His is the main commentary I append to the text.

The next significant event in the development of the work occurred during the early 1500s. Sometime before 1522, the Daoist Du Yichang (No. 35) reordered the text as had been suggested by Yuyan (see above). He rearranged it, separating it into three sections: an original set of eighteen chapters attributed to Wei Boyang (in four-word lines), a later set of fifteen chapters attributed to the disciple Xu Congshi (in five-word lines) and an addendum of later writings in irregular style.

Copies of Du Yichang's work are extremely rare. It was referred to in several later prefaces but even they never caught the public eye. It took another edition for his work to become popular. Yang Shen's 'ancient text' edition (dated 1546), with all its romance of the 'discovery of an old copy unearthed from a rock-chamber in distant southern China', was the vehicle through which the 'ancient text' reached the world. But Yang Shen had covered his sources, stealing Du's work and inventing a tale to make the work credible. Yang Shen is well known as forger of other Confucian textual 'discoveries' – he was no doubt making capital out of the fashionable 'back to the Han' movement which gripped sixteenth-century China.

Many people adhered to Yang Shen's views, and during the two or three ensuing centuries, several editions of the work were produced. The name *guwen* ('ancient text') use to identify any subsequent editions means they used Yang Shen's (or rather Du Yichang's) ordering. However none of these editions which appeared during the late Ming properly credited Du Yichang with originating the work.

Someone who did stress Du's involvement was the Ming scholar Xu Wei who styled himself the 'Green Cane' Daoist. It is probably to him that we also owe the later popularity of Master Shangyang's commentary. Xu Wei was a leading poet, artist, writer, painter and musician of the times, who also led an active public life. He states in the preface to his *A Clear Explanation of the Ancient Commentaries on the Can Tong Qi* (No. 40) how he considered that Du had perhaps been too severe in separating out the four-word and five-word stanzas, not paying enough attention to the sung rhythm and sound of the work when spoken out loud. Therefore he again divided up the text, making slight adjustments where he deemed them necessary; and at the same time he attached to it Chen Zhixu's (Master Shangyang) commentary. There was a 1570 edition of this work by Xu Wei, but the best known is the Wanli (1573–1620) edition prepared by Yao Ruxun. This was the edition used as a basis for my 1839 reprinting.

The late Ming and Qing dynasties continued to produce editions of the work. Most markedly the tradition split into two: one following the *guwen* idea and the other following the earlier view of an original 'untouched' version. One of the greatest 'untouched' editions is Zhu Yuanyu's 1669 Kangxi edition, *The Can Tong Qi and its Mysteries Expounded* (No.51), which set standards which have never been equalled. He adopted the tripartite division of the text but rejected any kind of *guwen* multiple-author tradition.

I quote several passages from his work in the commentaries. Other notable editions during the following two centuries were Ji Dakui's *A Printing of the Five-word Commentaries from Yuyan's Explanation of the Can Tong Qi* (No.63) and Chen Zhaocheng's *Commentary on the Can Tong Qi* (No.53). Chen Zhaocheng made studies of all the available commentaries and concluded that its ideas were originally based upon the principles of the *Zhou Yi*, which later become fixed and 'deified' into the principles of regulation and government. His views influenced later commentators.

In bringing this discussion to a close, we at last come upon the edition used in this first translation. It originated from the School of African and Oriental Studies library and its entitled *A Reprinting of the Ancient Guwen Can Tong Qi* (No.67). The text contains Yang Shen's 1546 preface and also a preface to the reprinting of this 'ancient work' in 1839. The editor Ma Yizhen comments:

> Where something was missing it has been added, where there were errors they have been corrected, and anything that was confused has been reassessed and put back into place. Again, as for many characters or phrases about which I felt unsure, I have further searched extensively through many editions and examined each in my heart to see which was correct ... as for the use of commentaries upon the text, there is always the matter of 'analysing that before you have fully understood it', so I have taken Master Shangyang's original commentary material and, for better or worse, gone along with with his revision.

Master Shangyang's commentaries are enormously helpful and this reprinting of the text is clear, as well as containing the best of the commentaries. I have adhered strictly to this 1839 reprinting for my translation; adding also Yuyan's commentary and part of Master Zhuxi's – both well representative of the Song and Yuan. Deviations from the 1839 text are mostly where I have been swayed by Yuyan, and in these rare cases this has been noted.

I have used perhaps a third of Master Shangyang's work, but not even a tenth of Yuyan's. Zhu Yuyuan's splendid flowing Qing edition has also been followed. I have also translated Master Shangyang's useful chapter headings and appended them to each chapter. Thus the forty-odd chapters of the book consist of eighteen from the Master Wei Boyang, fifteen from Xu Congshi and two supplementary ones.

All errors and mistakes are of course my own and I invite correction.

ADDITIONAL SELECT BIBLIOGRAPHY

In Chinese

Lu Guangrong. *Zhongguo Qigong Cidian* (*A Dictionary of Chinese Qigong*). People's Health Publishing House, 1989.
Qi Gong (*Qi Gong Journal*), Zhejiang Science and Technology Publishing House, China. Especially 1985(1), pp.35ff; 1984(6), pp.273ff; 1986(2), pp.77ff.
Cui Xifan. *Ruyao Jing* (*Entering the Mirror of the Medicine*), Wu Tai, *c.*940. Commentary by Master Hun Ran ('Truly Confused' Master). TT/132 (Weiger).
Xiao Tingjin. *Jindan Da Cheng* (*Golden Elixir Compendium*), Song, *c.*1250, TT/260 (Weiger).
Zhang Boduan. *Jindan Sibai Zi* (*Four-Hundred Word Essay on the Golden Elixir*), Song, *c.*1065.
Zhang Boduan. *Wuzhen Bian* (*Essay on Awakening to Reality*), Song, 1075, TT/138 & TT/260 (Weiger). Also contemporary versions in *Qi Gong Journal*, 1986.

In English

Chou Yi Ts'an Tung Ch'i (*The Kinship of the Three According to the Book of Changes*), trans. Zhou Shiyi. MSS. in the Needham Research Institute, Robinson College, Cambridge.
Chuang Tzu, trans. Gia-fu Feng and Jane English. Wildwood House, London, 1974. Also trans. H. A. Giles. Reprinted George Allen and Unwin, London 1961 (originally published 1889). Also trans. B. Watson. Columbia University Press 1968.
Fung Yu-lan (*A History of Chinese Philosophy*), trans. Derk Bodde. Princeton University Press, 1953.
Gia-fu Feng. Tian Xian Zheng Li (*The Truth about Fairies*), unpublished draft.
Lao Tzu. *Tao-te Ching*, trans. Gia-fu Feng and Jane English, Wildwood House, London, 1972. Also trans. Arthur Waley. George, Allen and Unwin, 1977.

Needham, J. *Science and Civilisation in China*, Cambridge University Press, various dates.

Sung, Z. D. *The Text of the Yi King*, Shanghai, 1935.

Ware, J. R. *Alchemy, Medicine and Religion in China of* AD.320, (The Pao Po Tzu, or N'ei P'ien of Ko Hung/Ge Hong), MIT Press, 1966.

Wilhelm, R. *The Secret of the Golden Flower*, RKP, London, 1962.

Wu, Lu Ch'iang & Davies, T. L. 'An Ancient Chinese Treatise on Alchemy Entitled the Ts'an T'ung Ch'i, written by Wei Po-yang', *Isis*:55 (1932), pp.210–89.

INDEX

292   *The Secret of Everlasting Life*

Ren-water 101, 169, 182, 226–7
Resting 161
Restored (Renewal) 58, 60, 66, 67, 68,
  156, 161, 178, 181, 183, 189, 192,
  241
Restoring the Original Mind 206
Restraint 161
Retreat *see* Withdrawing
Returning to Life 89, 106, 206, 249
Returning to Marriage 161
Returning to the Source 219
reward 35
righteousness 34, 35, 37
ruler 31–2, 33, 35, 72, 73, 76, 103

Sacrificial Cauldron 161
Sagittarius 53
sand 80–1, 86, 126, 131–2, 133,
  217–18, 250
Saturn 72
Scorpio 263–4
self-development 110–11
sesame 248
Separation 161
Shadowy Tally see Yin Shadow
Shaking 161
Shakyamuni 274
shoot, yellow 117–18, 124, 133, 253–4,
  272
Silver 80, 126, 133, 250, 271–2
sincerity 39
sixes 156, 167–9
small circuit of the heavens *see* lesser
  circuit of the sky
Small Cultivation 157, 161
Small Excesses 161
snake 14, 30, 36, 82, 90–1, 92, 133,
  140, 238
soil (*see also* earth) 15, 30, 47, 48, 80,
  87, 104–5, 119, 126–7, 131, 196,
  230, 244–7, 248–9, 264, 271–2
Solitary Isle 107
'Song of the Cauldron Vessel' 242
'Song on Smashing Superstition' 215–16
'Song on the Great Path' 130
'Song on the Great Pathway to the
  Marvellous Source' 124
solstices 38–9
south 80, 82, 126, 129, 134, 136, 138,
  140, 151, 158, 168, 181, 182, 184,
  190, 251, 252, 263
south-east 251
Southern Flower 219
Sovereign-on-High 259
spirit (*shen*) 109, 111, 148, 225–6, 242
spleen 73, 104, 131–2
spring 35, 36, 40, 47, 163, 249
Spring and Autumn Annals 176
Sprouting Forth 34, 35, 36, 160, 161–2,
  163, 164, 173

Stagnation (Closing, Decay, Decline) 62,
  63, 65, 157, 161, 181, 241
Stimulation *see* Influence
stone, autumnal 253–4
Strengthening *see* Creative
stuffs, three yellow 221
Su Qin 91
summer 35, 36, 38, 40, 47, 163, 249
sun 14, 21, 27, 28, 30, 45, 46, 50, 51,
  53, 56, 66, 68, 75–6, 85–7, 98, 104,
  109, 133, 156, 157–8, 163–4,
  170–4, 179, 181, 183, 184–5, 196,
  199, 201, 219, 223–5, 228–30, 235,
  252, 253, 260
Sun 20–1, 27, 28, 44, 46, 55, 56, 63,
  155, 157, 160, 169, 181–2, 183–4,
  185, 188, 190, 191, 196
Supporting (*ren*) Vessel 41–2, 69
supreme pole 16–19, 44, 95, 103, 141,
  156, 166, 177, 230

teacher, finding 143–4, 254
Tearing Apart (Destroying) 62, 63, 65,
  156, 157, 161, 181, 241
Three Families 126, 132
thunder 27, 28, 196
tiger 14, 21, 28, 36, 73, 80, 82, 123,
  127, 128, 131–2, 136–7, 140, 175,
  238, 247, 272
white 47, 130, 133, 134, 138, 223–5,
  261–2, 263–4
tigress, white 81
tortoise 14, 30, 36, 82, 90–1, 92, 133,
  140, 238
'Tranquillity Within' 206
Transformation 161
Treading 157, 161, 227
trigrams (*see also individual trigrams*) 27,
  56, 57, 96, 149, 182, 190
True Scripture of the Dark Truth 113

understanding 35
Unerring 161
Unvarying Mean 77

Valley Spirit 32
Venus 72, 127–8, 129
vitality, inner (*jing*) 28–9, 71, 105,
  109–11, 117–18, 123, 131, 133,
  148, 225, 235

Wang Liangqi 215–16
Wang Yang 253–4
Waiting 36, 161
warrior, dark 47, 134
water 15, 21, 27, 28, 30, 34, 45, 47, 69,
  72, 75, 79, 81–3, 84, 85–6, 87, 91,
  94, 97, 98, 99–101, 104–5, 106,
  107, 119, 120, 125, 126–7, 128,
  131–2, 134, 135, 137, 145, 151,